Information Sources
in Patents

A series under the General Editorship of
Ia C. McIlwaine,
M. W. Hill and
Nancy J. Williamson

Other titles:

Information Sources for the Press and Broadcast Media
    edited by Sarah Adair
Information Sources in Architecture and Construction (Second edition)
    edited by Valerie J. Nurcombe
Information Sources in Art, Art History and Design
    edited by Simon Ford
Information Sources in Development Studies
    edited by Sheila Allcock
Information Sources in Finance and Banking
    by Ray Lester
Information Sources in Grey Literature (Fourth edition)
    by C. P. Auger
Information Sources in Law (Second edition)
    edited by Jules Winterton and Elizabeth M. Moys
Information Sources in Music
    edited by Lewis Foreman
Information Sources in Official Publications
    edited by Valerie J. Nurcombe
Information Sources in Polymers and Plastics
    edited by R.T. Adkins
Information Sources in the Earth Sciences (Second edition)
    edited by David N. Wood, Joan E. Hardy and Anthony P. Harvey
Information Sources in the Life Sciences (Fourth edition)
    edited by H.V. Wyatt
Information Sources in the Social Sciences
    edited by David Fisher, Sandra P. Price and Terry Hanstock
Information Sources in Women's Studies and Feminism
    edited by Hope A. Olson
Information Sources in Engineering, Fourth edition
    edited by Roderick A. MacLeod and Jim Corlett

Stephen R. Adams

Information Sources in
Patents

2nd completely new edition

K · G · Saur München 2006

Bibliographic information published by Die Deutsche Bibliothek

Die Deutsche Bibliothek lists this publication in the Deutsche Nationalbibliografie;
detailed bibliographic data is available in the internet at http://dnb.ddb.de.

Printed on acid-free paper

© 2006 K. G. Saur Verlag GmbH, München

Typesetting by Florence Production Ltd., Stoodleigh, Devon, Great Britain.

Printed and bound by Strauss GmbH, Mörlenbach, Germany.

ISBN-10: 3-598-24443-6 · ISBN-13: 978-3-598-24443-8

For Kitty Silva,
Sri Lanka, 26 December 2004

Contents

List of Figures and Tables

FIGURES

TABLES

Series Editor's Foreword

In the first years of the 21st century, there is a popular belief that the Internet gives us easy world-wide access to all the information anyone can reasonably need. Experience, especially by those researching topics in depth, proves otherwise. It is ironic that, despite all the technical advances in information handling that have been made and the masses of information that assail us on every side, it remains as difficult as ever to ensure that one has what one wants when one needs it.

Of course the computer and the Internet have made a huge difference to our information gathering habits, especially in the hands of those who, through experience, have gained skill in their use, an ability to contain the amount of information within manageable limits and discrimination in assessing the reliability and adequacy of the resources accessed. No one nowadays would be without the Internet but it is only one among several sources each of which has its value according to the searcher's needs. In all cases, the speed and effectiveness of a search can be greatly enhanced by the advice of those who are experts in the techniques and in the subject field involved.

The aim of each volume of this K. G. Saur series of *Guides to Information Sources* is simple. It is to reduce the time which needs to be spent on patient searching; to recommend the best starting point and sources most likely to yield the desired information. To do this we bring you the knowledge and experience of specialist practitioners in the field. Each author regularly uses the information sources and services described and any tricks of the trade that the author has learnt are passed on.

Like all subject and sector guides, the sources discussed have had to be selected. The criteria for selection will be given by the individual editors and will differ from subject to subject. However, the overall objective is constant: that of providing a way into a subject to those new to the field and to identify major new or possibly unexplored sources to those who already have some acquaintance with it.

Nowadays two major problems face those who are embarking upon research or who are in charge of wide-ranging collections of information. One is the increasingly specialised knowledge of the user and concomitant ignorance of other potentially useful disciplines. The second is the trend towards cross-disciplinary studies. This has led to a great mixing of academic programmes – and a number of imprecisely defined fields of study. The editors are only too aware of the difficulties such hybrid subject fields raise for those requiring information and Guides for these sectors are being established as well as those for the traditional "hard disciplines". In addition to commissioning new titles, constant attention is given to the production of updated editions for subject fields which are fast moving and subject to rapid development.

The Internet now gives access to many new sources (and to some, but not all, of the old ones) and being discipline-free can be particularly attractive to those working in new fields. At the same time it gives access to an overwhelming mass of information, some of it well organized and easy to interrogate, much incoherent and ill-organized. On top of this there is the great output of new information from the media, advertising, meetings and conferences, regulatory bodies, letters, reports, office memoranda, magazines, junk mail, electronic mail, fax, bulletin boards and so on and so on. Inevitably it all tends to make one very reluctant to add to the load by seeking out books and journals. Yet they, and the other traditional types of printed material, remain for many purposes the most reliable sources of information. Quality encyclopaedias are excellent for an overview of a topic but there are also many other time saving reviews and digests of information. One still needs to look things up in databooks, to consult the full text of patent specifications, standards and reports, both official and commercial, and to study maps and atlases. Increasingly these are available on CD-ROM as well as in print and choice depends on one's circumstances. Some archives are becoming available electronically but the vast majority are still in paper form. Many institutions are making some at least of their expertise available on websites but contact with individuals there is often still necessary for in depth studies. It is also worth remembering that consulting a reference book frequently produces a more rapid result than consulting an online source.

Fortunately, in these times when the amount being published is increasing rapidly, it is rarely necessary to consult everything that has been published on the topic of one's interest. Usually much proves to be irrelevant or repetitive. Some publications (including in that term websites and e-journals) prove to be sadly lacking in important detail and present broad generalizations flimsily bridged with arches of waffle. Many publications contain errors. In such cases the need to check against other publications, first making sure that they are not simply derivative, adds greatly to the time of a search. In an academic field there is normally a "pecking order" of journals, the better ones generally having a "peer review" system which self-published articles on the web do not (though there are moves to introduce a peer review process to some web-published journals). Research workers soon learn – it is part of their training – which sources in their field of study to use and rely on, which journals, co-workers and directories are trustworthy and to what extent. However, when searching outside their own field of expertise and for other people, lay researchers and information workers alike, serious problems have to be overcome. This makes the need for evaluative guides, such as those in this series, even more essential. The series attempts to achieve evaluation in two ways: first through a careful selection of sources, so that only those which are considered worthy are included, and second through the comments which are provided on those sources.

Guides to the literature and other sources of information have a long and distinguished history. Some of them retain their value for many years as all or part of their content is still relevant but not repeated in later works. Where appropriate these are included in the sources referred to in this series along with the wealth of new sources which make new Guides and new editions essential.

Michael W. Hill
Ia C. McIlwaine

Preface

Since the first edition of this book, edited by Peter Auger and published in 1992, a complete revolution has taken place in the dissemination of patent information. Technical developments – most notably the internet – have caused great changes in the information industry, including the patent sector. Perhaps the largest influence has been upon the nature of the databases emerging from different suppliers, which in turn affects our choice of the "right" database for a particular patent search. In writing a book which purports to be a "Guide to Information Sources" in the subject, I therefore feel duty-bound to give some space to considering how the current range of products has developed over time, and to provide some background on how patent publications come to be at all, rather than merely provide a shopping list of alternative search files.

A fundamental point to recognise is that patent offices are required to publish information, as an integral part of the patenting process. The commitment to provide such data to the public was foreseen by the framers of the 1883 Paris Convention, who included Article 12, which states that:

> 12(1) Each country of the Union undertakes to establish a special industrial property service and a central office for the communication to the public of patents, utility models, industrial designs and trademarks. [*i.e. to establish a patent office*]
>
> 12(2) This service shall publish an official periodical journal. It shall publish regularly:
>
> (a) the names of the proprietors of patents granted, with a brief designation of the inventions patented; [*i.e. to produce some form of gazette*]

Despite the clear requirements of Article 12, there was – and still is – considerable variation in the degree of enthusiasm and commitment with which countries complied with this aspect of their operations. Some of the larger, well-established offices, such as the United States, the United Kingdom, Germany and France, have a history of producing regular documentation; others have a less-impressive record. For many patent offices, however, generating this information is seen as essentially a spin-off product from the primary function of the office, namely to examine and grant patents. Few patent offices believed that the development of sophisticated retrieval tools should be part of their function.

During the 1950's to 1970's, the commercial information sector took the lead in developing patent information into a more 'industry-friendly' tool. The raw 'first-level' data from the patent offices were obtained by pioneer information companies such as Derwent Publications in the UK and Information For Industry (IFI) in the US, and re-issued as 'value-added' products, such as printed bulletins or batch-searchable (later online, inter-active) electronic files. The patent offices were happy to co-operate with this, as it provided a means of getting their information out to a wider audience than the small numbers of industrial users who could reach their public search rooms. Through to the early 1990's, the patent offices gener-ally saw no mandate – or opportunity – to enhance their role by becoming direct suppliers to the end user.

With the advent of the internet, the established chain of distribution (patent office-database producer-host-user) has begun to break down. Many patent offices are using the internet to supply their first-level data directly to the user. Some database producers have either begun to buy into the host industry, or to sell their products on a web-based platform, circum-venting the hosts completely. As a consequence, users are being exposed to patent information products from multiple suppliers, with varying degrees of refinement. The same basic data set may now be available through many routes, resulting in a proliferation of products and services.

Efficient searching depends upon both the data quality and the plat-form used to search it, and free internet sites offering first-level data from the major patent offices cannot deliver to every type of user, nor for every type of search requirement. Research-based industries rely upon good patent searching for their commercial survival, and are prepared to pay for access to premium tools if they provide the necessary degree of insurance against accidental duplication of research or – worse – infringement of others' rights. Despite the growth in browser-based systems, these users largely continue to rely upon the established value-added data sources, with sophisticated command languages, developed prior to the internet.

It is clear that the information sector has not seen the end of devel-opment in browser-based tools, and they will certainly have a role to play in the future of patent information systems. However, it will always remain true that the choice of 'best database' for a patent search will be influenced by a complex combination of the information need (data source), the tech-nical requirements (search engine) and the available budget (free or fee). It is the hope of the author that this work will help with the decision-making process, irrespective of whether the user is a beginner or more experienced searcher.

I would like to give my sincere acknowledgement to the many friends and colleagues in the industry, who through useful discussions – both electronic and verbal – have contributed to the shape and substance of this book. There are too many to name individually, but many are co-workers in one or more of the various user groups in the UK, Europe and the United States. I hope that I have done justice in capturing your expertise for the benefit of all.

SRA

Part 1: Patent processes and documentation

Principles of patenting

▶ **LEGAL PROCESSES**

The English word 'patent' is derived from a Latin phrase *litterae patentes*, meaning 'open letter'. For centuries, a 'letters patent' was a circular communication from the State (be it monarchy or republic) to its subjects or citizens, to announce the conferring of certain privileges upon an individual. Typically, the opening sentences might address the letter "to all to whom these presents come". Letters patent are still issued in the United Kingdom by the College of Arms when a grant of arms is made to a new peer. Other uses are for the creation of a public office (e.g. Queen Victoria issued Letters Patent when creating the post of Governor-General of Australia), on the creation of a new public body, the transfer of land rights or in the commissioning an individual to a certain task, in which case the letters patent could be seen as a form of passport or warrant of authority.

Letters patent were also issued in order to confer a State monopoly right over a trade or craft. During the 14th and 15th centuries in England, the Crown used the grant of monopoly rights to control trade in cloth and the manufacture of glass. This procedure was open to abuse, and the creation of future monopolies was banned by the Statute of Monopolies in 1623. However, this statute specifically excluded Letters Patent for "the sole working or making of any manner of new manufactures" issued to their inventors – in other words, modern-day patents for inventions. By the mid-19th century, the most common usage of a letters patent was for exactly this purpose, to confer rights in a new invention for a limited period, and consequently the layman's understanding of the word 'patent' has come to be limited to a patent for invention.

The retrieval and use of early patents is a fascinating field in its own right, and one which calls for distinct information skills. On the development of patents, readers are referred to the introductory chapter of Liebesny's classic book[1] or the more recent work by Grubb[2]. A good source for setting patents in the wider context of the whole of intellectual property is the 1997 publication by the World Intellectual Property Organization (WIPO) in Geneva, particularly the section on the history and evolution of intellectual property[3]. This is now out of print, and the successor publication[4] unfortunately contains less of this background material.

From the point of view of the information specialist, rather than the attorney, the prime importance of patents is not the legal rights to work an invention which they confer upon the patent holder, but the volume of technical information which is laid open to the public as a result of the granting procedure for the patent. The British Library in London holds stocks in excess of fifty million patent documents, capturing the progress of technology from the 17th century to the present day, in many countries around the world. The bulk of this present book will be devoted to the use of modern-day patent documents (say, from around 1950 to the present), but that is not to say that the older material is useless. Students of the history of technology can gain great insight from the examination of original patents for invention from the Industrial Revolution onwards. An comprehensive overview of the English system and its social context is provided by McLeod[5]. Retrieval of older documents presents distinct challenges, for which the reader is referred to the work by van Dulken[6] for British patents, or the briefer outline chapter by Comfort[7] in relation to the United States. Further afield, background information on some historical patent series for a range of countries can be found in the survey by Rimmer[8], at the beginning of each country chapter.

Defining a patent

There are many definitions of a patent. One possible definition (from reference 2, p.1) is that a patent is:

- a grant of exclusive rights
- by the state
- for a limited time

in respect of a new and useful invention.

Each of those three aspects has a bearing upon our perception of patents and how we can use them as information tools.

In respect to *"a grant of exclusive rights"*, this implies that a patent is not 'for the taking'. The popular press often refers to patents as being 'registered', as if one merely has to turn up at some Dickensian establishment and submit your application to a large rubber-stamp, in order to walk away as a satisfied patent-holder. The word 'grant' carries with it the implication that certain fixed criteria need to be satisfied in order for the application to be allowed. Failure to satisfy these criteria will result in the patent being refused, irrespective of how good (or how expensive!) the research behind the patent application has been. In the information context we should never overlook the legal implications of the documents which we are using – many published patent applications are destined never to emerge as granted patents.

The second aspect is that a patent is *"by the state"*. This implies that patents are not universal. There has never been a single global patent system, granted by a central authority and having effect in all the territories of the world. There are a very few regional patent systems, which grant on behalf of a limited number of countries, but these are the exception rather than the rule. In general, if an inventor wants to protect their invention by patent, they must apply in each and every country individually, complying with local filing requirements and having their case examined under local laws. One consequence of this is that the same invention may be allowed patent protection in one country but refused it in another. In countries for which no protection is sought, no protection is obtained.

The final aspect of our definition is that a patent is *"for a limited time"*. Again, the popular media image of patents sometimes portrays them as tools with which multi-national companies can dominate trade in a particular invention in perpetuity. The fact is that all patents eventually expire. The most common term of a modern patent is 20 years, counted from the date of filing the application. In addition to expiry at the end of this period, a substantial proportion of granted patents never reach their 20th birthday, but die earlier. If the owner finds that their invention is less of a commercial success than they hoped, they can choose to allow the case to lapse when the next round of renewal fees becomes due. Once a patent expires or lapses, any third party can enter this previously protected market space, and start to operate the invention, without being liable to the erstwhile patent holder for any royalty or other licence.

The consequences of our three-part definition are multiple. For the information user, it is clear that we need to pay close attention to the various dates associated with a patent, its status (e.g. How far is it along the process towards grant? or, Is it still in force?) and its geographical limits. If a database fails to address these issues, it will be of less use in certain types of patent searching than one which does. We will see the implications of this in later chapters of this book.

The concept of priority

Before discussing the historical and current processes used in examining patents, it is necessary to introduce a very important idea, namely that of 'priority'.

The legal concept of priority was first created by the International Convention for the Protection of Industrial Property, signed in Paris in 1883 and commonly referred to as the "Paris Convention"[9]. Signatory states are referred to as belonging to the 'Paris Union' or simply as 'Union countries'. In Article 4 of this document, it is stated that:

> A (1) Any person who has duly filed an application for a patent. . . . in one of the countries of the Union. . . . shall enjoy, for the purpose of filing in the other countries, a right of priority. . . .
>   C (1) The periods of priority referred to above shall be twelve months for patents. . . .

The essential result of this Article is that a patent applicant is allowed a period of 12 months from their first filing (which usually takes place in their home country) in which to lodge corresponding applications for the same invention in other countries. Provided they file within this deadline, their corresponding applications will be treated as if they were filed on the first date, which is thus referred to as the 'priority date'. This reciprocal treatment by other Union countries means that an company or individual inventor may make multiple applications for patent protection of the same invention in many countries around the world, and be assured that they will be given equal treatment when examined – in effect, their applications are treated as they were all filed simultaneously. By September 2004, there were 168 countries in the Paris Union, giving a very wide applicability to this right of priority.

The existence of the right of priority has a fundamental effect upon the activities of the patent information specialist. Firstly, it affects which part of the literature has to be searched, for each of the major search types discussed in Chapter 8 onwards. Secondly, the priority details – reproduced on the front page of modern patent documents – are used in the compiling of databases of patent documents, and need to be understood if the output from a search is to make sense. The priority details are used by database producers as the common key to link individual national publications relating to the same invention into a so-called 'patent family'. The construction of patent families is discussed in later in this chapter.

The historical examination process for patents

It is often remarked that the process of granting a patent is a 'bargain' or 'contract' between the patentee and the national patenting authority. The national authority (usually but not invariably a government department) issues a statement – in the form of the grant certificate – which establishes a *prima facie* right of the patent holder to prevent other people making, selling, using or importing the defined invention without their prior permission. Clearly, third parties cannot be expected to avoid infringement if they do not know what they have to avoid. Hence, the reverse side of the bargain is for the patentee to allow the full details of their invention (in the form of a descriptive document, the patent specification) to be made available to the public.

For many years, the publication of details of the invention only occurred once – at the point when the patent was about to be granted or had just been granted. To initiate the process of examination, the applicant was required to pay certain statutory fees to the patenting authority (for simplicity, I will use the term 'patent office' hereafter, although it may not occur in the actual title of the organisation concerned). In return for these so-called examination fees, the patent office would complete the legal steps required to ensure that the application complied with their national patentability requirements. These steps varied enormously, from a simple check to ensure that the pages were correct in layout and that certain bibliographic details were complete, through to a rigorous examination of the entire contents of the application, line-by-line. After examination had been completed, the patent was granted and the specification published.

The problem with this approach is that all the steps in the procedure – and all the fees which the applicant must pay – have to be completed before any document sees the light of day. In the course of many years, patent offices started to take longer to complete the examination stage and backlogs started to develop.

The worst backlogs were experienced in those countries which required a particularly strict examination process. During a typical examination, the patent office seeks to establish whether the invention complies with a number of legally defined criteria of patentability. These would generally include:

(a)   Novelty
(b)   Inventive step
(c)   Industrial applicability
(d)   Non-excluded material

The simplest criteria to satisfy are usually (c) and (d) – it is generally fairly straightforward for the applicant to show that their invention has some usefulness in industry, and does not fall into one of the classes of non-patentable material, such as being a literary or artistic work (which is covered by copyright and hence excluded from the patent law), or a set of rules for playing a game. The classes of excluded material can be modified from time to time; for example, the Patents Act 1977 in the United Kingdom has been amended since it first passed, in order to bring certain micro-biological inventions within the scope of permitted patentable subject-matter.

The harder parts of the examination process come in establishing (a) and (b). Criterion (a), novelty, is on the face of it fairly easy to establish – either the invention is new or it is not. However, different countries have historically had different definitions of novelty. In some places, an application may be regarded as new if its subject matter has not be published in earlier patents from the same country within the previous 50 years; that is, there is a limitation both in terms of the type of publication consulted and in the time-scale concerned. At the other extreme, a definition of so-called 'universal novelty' is increasingly being used, which requires that no publication of any sort (including non-print media and verbal disclosures) may occur anywhere in the world prior to the filing date of the invention. Clearly, this sort of definition of novelty places a much greater burden on the patent office, as there will be a much larger volume of literature to screen in order to establish novelty.

The size of this literature (the prior publications or, as it is often called, the 'prior art') is affected by the right of the priority. This is because the filing date of a patent application is an intrinsic part of the definition of novelty. To illustrate, consider the United Kingdom Patents Act 1977, at section 2(1)–(2):

> 2(1) An invention shall be taken to be new if it does not form part of the state of the art.
> 2(2) The state of the art in the case of an invention shall be taken to comprise all matter (whether a product, a process, information about either, or anything else) which has at any time *before the priority date of that invention* been made available to the public (whether in the United Kingdom or elsewhere) by written or oral description, by use or in any other way. [*my emphasis*]

In other words, the priority date becomes a cut-off point in defining which literature should be considered against our application. Anything published *after* that date will not, on its own, damage the chances of obtaining a patent, whereas a careless disclosure by the inventor, or a competitor's publication, occurring *before* the priority date may indeed jeopardise the application on the grounds of lack of novelty. This is not a unique British situation – corresponding laws exist in many other countries.

Possibly the hardest criterion to satisfy is (b), that of inventive step (or, as it referred to in some countries, non-obviousness). The essential task for the patent office during examination is to answer the question, "Is this application a trivial extension of what is already known, or does it have inventive merit?". In practice, this process may involve taking several pieces of prior knowledge and trying to prove whether or not they point unambiguously to the invention. This can be the cause of much argument between applicant and examiner before grant, and between patent holder and third parties after the grant.

Given the above criteria for patentability, and its application during a sequential examination process, it was perhaps inevitable that most patent offices around the world were facing a manpower crisis by the early 1960's. As each application had to be rigorously compared with an extensive set of previous publications (the 'prior art') and argued for inventive step, it could take many years for an application to be granted. During this period, the applicant was uncertain whether they could take steps to commercialise their invention, and third parties were generally in ignorance of pending cases. This could have the costly result of a third party making extensive preparations to operate an invention, only to be faced at the last minute with a granted patent and the threat of litigation. Clearly, the patent office's processes had to be reviewed, and the revised system of deferred examination was created.

The development of deferred examination and early publication

The factors leading up to the development of the deferred examination process have been reviewed elsewhere ([10] and references therein). Briefly, the first country to adopt the system was the Netherlands, effective from 1964, followed shortly afterwards by West Germany in 1968 and Japan in 1970. During the 1970's, it became the method of choice for most patent offices as they revised their patent laws.

The characteristic of deferred examination was the separation of the expensive procedure of substantive examination from the relatively cheaper steps of establishing a search report against the prior art. This built in extra 'thinking time' for the applicant, between receiving the search report and having to pay the substantive examination fees. The hope was that this would result in a higher percentage of voluntarily withdrawn cases, leaving the patent offices to concentrate on the 'real' inventions. In return for this flexibility, most deferred examination laws required that an application was published whilst it was still pending (sometimes referred to as being 'laid OPI' or Open to Public Inspection). As a result, the main feature of the system for the information specialist is that each "patent" is published twice – once as an unexamined application and a second time (if granted) as the final patent itself.

One complication, when compared with the traditional system of only publishing after grant, was the effect upon bibliographic control. With single publication – such as happened in the United States from 1836 until 2001 – documents could be identified with a simple running series of publication numbers. Under the new regime, incorporating early publication, it was necessary to devise a system which allowed the user to distinguish between multiple stages of processing – usually two documents, the early published unexamined case and the later granted patent. Some countries did this by using a distinct number series for each set of documents, whilst others introduced a system of alphanumeric suffixes to the publication number. These suffixes were picked up by the database producers and have gradually become formalised into the present-day system of Kind-of-Document (KD) codes, which will be discussed in more detail in later chapters, for each country.

Under deferred examination, the same processes of examination against patentability criteria are used as for the historical one-stage system, so delays in pendency still occur. However, the information specialist – and industry in general – is no longer penalised by the lack of information coming out of the patent office. The early publication of pending applications, typically around 18 months after the earliest filing date, serves to warn industry that a case has been filed. This information helps them to keep track of developments in their field of technology, and to become aware of competing applications which might impinge upon their activities, and which could be an infringement threat if they are granted. As a result of the deferred examination system, patents have, over the last 50 years, become a hugely important tool for commercial current awareness. They are used by scientists and technologists, lawyers, marketing and financial experts and others to monitor, evaluate and guide research and development activities all over the world.

A typical sequence in modern patent examination

By following one invention, we can start to see the range of processing activities which take place across different patent offices during pendency. In Figure 1, the columns indicate activity carried out by a single patent office, and the vertical axis represents time, increasing from top to bottom of the page.

A number of points can be taken from this Figure.

Firstly, it is clear that each member of the family receives its unique national filing application number, in a wide variety of formats. For example, the European Patent Office (EPO) number has a decimal and check-digit at the end, whereas the US number has an additional series code 08 at the beginning.

Secondly, we can see that although the case started life in the Netherlands, there is no Dutch publication as such. It is important to realise that there is no absolute reason why a patent family should include a publication from the country of origin. Often, a 'home' filing may be used simply to establish a priority, and then allowed to lapse in favour of the applications in other countries, where protection is sought, or under a regional system which incorporates the home country. In this case, the Dutch application was cited as priority under the Paris Convention, to create a so-called "Convention filing" under the European Patent Office system. Since the EPO includes the Netherlands amongst its members, the emerging granted European Patent provides protection within the Netherlands by this route.

Thirdly, we see that although the EPO unexamined case was published promptly around the 18-month mark after priority, the Japanese member

Figure 1: Example time line for processing a patent family

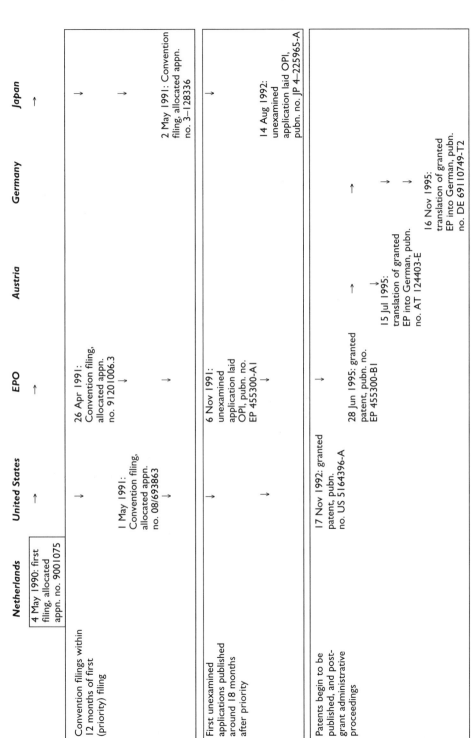

was substantially delayed, and did not publish until some 9 months later, or 27 months from priority. This is somewhat unusual, and in this case was due to a large backlog of cases during a Japanese Patent Office (JPO) automation project. The guideline of "18 months after priority" for the unexamined publication is not fixed in law, and can be subject to this degree of variation.

Finally, we note an example of the use of KD codes, with the European patent. The unexamined case is numbered EP 455300-A, and it retains this through to the later grant stage, but with the suffix changed to a –B. Some authorities retain the number across stages, others use a new number – in which case the KD code becomes vital to determine the nature of the document. We also see that after the grant of the EP-B, some countries republish translations of the document in their local language, and these enter the bibliographic record in their own right (in this case, for Germany and Austria). More detail on this will be discussed in Chapter 2.

▶ PATENTS AS INFORMATION TOOLS

Language of publication

One of the issues surrounding the use of patents as information tools is that of language. As noted above, in our definition of a patent, these documents are territorial and political – they only have effect in a specified country. As such, they are published in the national language of the country granting the patent. This can be a hindrance to effective communication, especially considering the large numbers of patent applications published in Asian anguages such as Japanese, Chinese or Korean, which are effectively lost to most Western researchers. Although English is accepted as the primary language of communication in science and technology, any suggestion that all patents be published in English is fraught with political difficulties.

Unlike other scientific and literature, where the bulk of the expected user community usually has some knowledge of technical English, patent documents have multiple roles, and consequently multiple readerships. The same published patent document has to stand as both

- a statement of the technical nature of the invention, which requires the use of technically precise language, and
- a legally binding description of the precise nature of the trading monopoly which the patentee can exert.

This dual role means that all the parties – legal, technical, industrial and commercial – which may be affected by the scope of a patent need to be able to access its contents in an efficient manner. For many, that means that it should be available in their national language.

Despite the fact that translation into national languages is an expensive process, it therefore has an important function. If the government of a country is granting to a private enterprise the means with which to control a defined sector of industry within that country, then it is only reasonable that the citizens of that country (or at least its affected industrialists and the courts) are granted the corresponding means quickly and effectively to understand the legal extent of that control. This can only really be achieved if the claims of a patent document are readily available in the national language. The arguments concerning how to implement this dissemination without inordinate cost have been central to the discussion in Europe concerning the Community Patent for many years.

The issue of communicating patent contents to their user community has traditionally been solved – in part – by commercial information providers, who have undertaken the systematic collection of multi-lingual patents and created abstracts of each in a common language – usually English. In recent years, particularly since the advent of the Internet as a search tool, there has been a greater emphasis on so-called 'first-level' data released by the patent offices, in their national language. This has brought a great advantage in terms of the speed of availability of the data, but at the expense of searching convenience. In order to take advantage of the full range of first-level data sources, the searcher must be multi-lingual. There is now a move to utilise machine translation technology, in an attempt to create full text databases in English from a multiplicity of original document types. For the moment, however, the searcher should be aware that multiple publication languages are the norm. In the event that a patent is challenged in the courts, it will certainly be the national language version which will be in dispute. At Table 1, there are some examples of patent publishing authorities which allow the use of more than one language in their publications. Some countries use a multi-lingual gazette, whilst in others, both gazette and specifications can appear in more than one language.

There has been a trend in recent years for more patent offices to issue official English-language abstracts of its patent publications, in addition to adopting English as a second language for issuance of basic bibliographic data through the national Gazette. However, the bulk on national patent applications still issue in the national language of the country concerned.

Patents as accessible documents

Irrespective of the 'human' language involved, all patent publications to a great extent are published in 'patentese', a peculiar mixture of technical and legal terminology. The business of learning to interpret the text of a patent (and particularly the claims, which will be discussed below) is really outside of the scope of this book. The role of the information specialist is

Table 1: Multi-lingual patent publishing authorities

Country / authority of publication	Publication languages
Australia	May be any one of the PCT languages (see below) at the first publication stage; English at the grant stage
Belgium	French, Dutch, German
Canada	English, French
Cuba	Spanish, English, Russian (Gazette)
Egypt	English, Arabic (Gazette)
European Patent Office	English, German, French
Finland	Finnish, Swedish
Israel	English, Hebrew
Korea (South)	Korean, English (Gazette)
Kyrgyzstan	Kyrgyz, Russian (Gazette)
Luxembourg	French, German
Macedonia	Macedonian, English (Gazette)
Moldova	Romanian, Russian
PCT	English, French, German, Japanese, Russian, Spanish, Chinese
South Africa	English, Afrikaans
Switzerland	German, French, Italian
Uzbekistan	Uzbek, Russian (Gazette)

to locate the documents – they should then work in close co-operation with a qualified patent agent or attorney in order to understand the implications of the documents for the particular commercial decision facing the user. However, it is helpful if the information specialist can get at least a basic understanding of the legal principles involved. Various introductory texts in the legal field can help, for example the book by Philips[11] and the previously cited work by Grubb[2]. There is also a useful booklet produced by the American Chemical Society, which provides an inventor's-eye view of the US patent system and discusses some important concepts specific to the American law[12]. A similar approach is taken by Amernick[13], again considering only the US situation.

Despite many efforts over the years, it is still sadly true that patents are regarded as 'difficult' documents, and frequently ignored by small businesses. The most recent evidence for this is contained in a large-scale survey by the European Patent Office[14], which underlined many of the lessons of an earlier report[15], but there are other examples in the literature of the extent of use (or non-use) of patent documents in industry and academia (see, for example, the papers by Hall et al.[16], Schofield[17] and earlier work by Stephenson[18]). The advent of the internet has certainly boosted the accessibility of patents, in terms of getting them onto people's desks, but there still remains a basic problem with information literacy. The processes for locating the *right* documents out of the many millions 'available', and using them in practical situations, are still far from routine.

Patent families

As discussed earlier in this chapter, the concept of the patent family arises from the use of priority details when compiling a patent database with multiple country coverage. If a number of patent applications are filed to protect the same invention in different parts of the world, the corresponding published patent applications and granted patents will clearly contain a technically equivalent text, albeit in the national language of the publishing authority. For example, if an invention originates in the United Kingdom but protection is applied for in Japan, the United States, France and Germany as well, it is conceivable that the database producer will be faced with at least 5 different documents in four different languages, effectively disclosing the same technical details.

Rather than create new records and abstracts for each document in this cluster, various database producers – such as the Derwent WPI file, INPADOC, Chemical Abstracts and the free EPO esp@cenet ® service – have devised a mechanism for identifying the duplicates and grouping them together. In this way, the database producer will only have to go to the effort of indexing each invention once. Later documents with corresponding subject matter can be added to the cluster – the so-called patent family – without further comment. This is not only cost-effective for the producer, but also saves time for the searcher, who will not have to de-duplicate their search results manually.

The main criterion for grouping technically equivalent patent documents into a family is the priority details. Since all applications which claim the same priority under the Paris Convention are – by definition under Article 4 – relating to the 'same invention', the database producer is able to group together all documents citing such priority into a family cluster. At its simplest, a patent family can be defined as "all patent documents which have priority details in common." However, it should be emphasised that the process is not as precise as might appear, for two reasons:

   a)   The definition of a family is not defined by law, but by each
        database producer for their own convenience. It is therefore
        quite possible that the family structure produced by one
        database will vary from the structure in another, due to
        differing rules of application. For many families, there will be
        very similar results; the main cause of variation is where one or
        more cases in the family claims multiple priorities. Some rules
        will put these members into a second distinct family, whilst
        others will group all cases into a single large family.

b)   The use of priority data to group family members does not preclude the possibility that the legal rights pertaining to any given member may vary from the others. This happens when, for example, the claims of one case may be cut down under the local examination requirements more than the claims in a corresponding case. The changes in subject matter created by examination do not get reflected in the priority data, which is the grouping criterion. Consequently, whilst it is reasonable to assume that the technical disclosure in all family members will be substantially the same, the same assumption should not be made concerning the enforceable rights for each family member.

The formation of a patent family can be seen in Figure 2. Each of the published documents indicated by the heavy boxes is a patent application or granted patent which claims priority under the Paris Convention from the initial filing in the United States, indicated by the light box at top left. This priority filing is not itself laid open until it emerges as either a US patent or another case claiming priority from it. Each member of the family can be linked with its parent by means of the cross-references on the front page, using INID field code series 30 (for more on INID codes, see the section on Bibliographic Standards later in this chapter). When patent database producers receive the corresponding published documents (or more commonly, the electronic data-feed from patent offices, which includes the front-page data), they are able to link together the family members and treat them as if they were identical documents for indexing purposes.

Some database producers use the concept of 'basic' and 'equivalent' to assist in defining the patent family. The first appearance of an invention described in a patent document – irrespective of the country from which it comes – is treated as a 'basic', and usually fully abstracted and indexed according to the producer's policy. Any later-published documents which claim the same priority as the basic are termed 'equivalents', and added to the same family with minimal added value indexing applied. This means that indexing effort can be concentrated on new documents, and that other members of the family can be retrieved as if they were fully indexed, by virtue of being put into the same database record.

It is important to note in this context that the basic is not necessarily published by the same country that originated the invention. For example, under the old US patent law when US cases were slow to publish, many database records list an EP or German family member as the basic, since it was the first to appear in the public domain, and the later published US family member is classed as an equivalent.

It is equally important to remember that there is no guarantee that a family member will ever appear which corresponds to the country of priority filing. This is particularly true in cases which are filed in one of the

Figure 2: The formation of a patent family

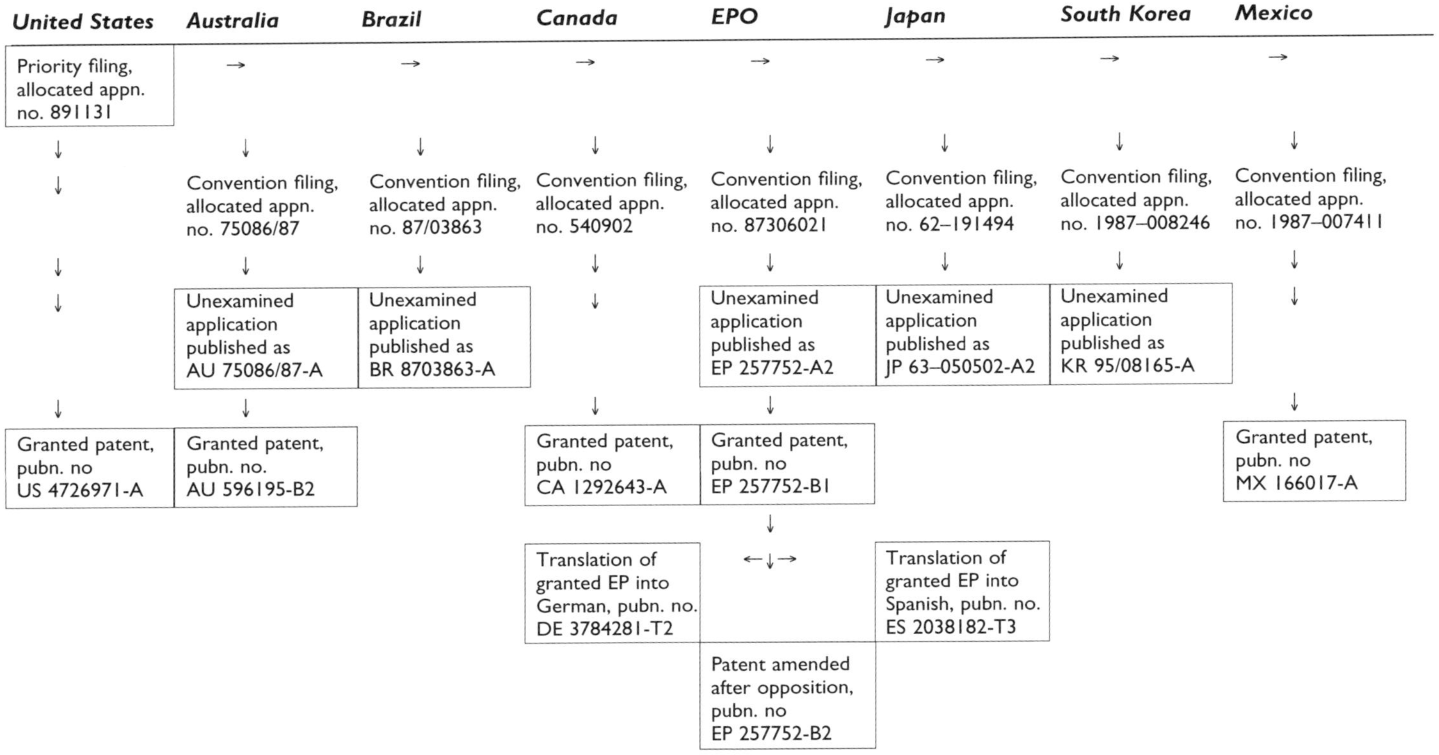

United States	Australia	Brazil	Canada	EPO	Japan	South Korea	Mexico
Priority filing, allocated appn. no. 891131	Convention filing, allocated appn. no. 75086/87	Convention filing, allocated appn. no. 87/03863	Convention filing, allocated appn. no. 540902	Convention filing, allocated appn. no. 87306021	Convention filing, allocated appn. no. 62-191494	Convention filing, allocated appn. no. 1987-008246	Convention filing, allocated appn. no. 1987-007411
	Unexamined application published as AU 75086/87-A	Unexamined application published as BR 8703863-A		Unexamined application published as EP 257752-A2	Unexamined application published as JP 63-050502-A2	Unexamined application published as KR 95/08165-A	
Granted patent, pubn. no US 4726971-A	Granted patent, pubn. no. AU 596195-B2		Granted patent, pubn. no CA 1292643-A	Granted patent, pubn. no EP 257752-B1			Granted patent, pubn. no MX 166017-A
			Translation of granted EP into German, pubn. no. DE 3784281-T2		Translation of granted EP into Spanish, pubn. no. ES 2038182-T3		
				Patent amended after opposition, pubn. no EP 257752-B2			

member states of the EPO. Applicants in these countries will often file a national priority case (for example, in the United Kingdom) and use this to file a corresponding EPO case within the Convention year. The parent national case can then be safely abandoned, and patent protection in that country obtained by means of a designation on the corresponding EP patent. In our example, no national (GB-A) publication will ever appear corresponding to the original filed priority document.

As indicated above, different database producers use distinct sets of rules for creating families. It is important when searching that the appropriate documentation is consulted to ensure that the searcher is thoroughly familiar with the implications of the rules for the database in use. Few comparative studies of any detail have been published, although conference papers such as the one by Austin[19] have compiled some useful examples. Some useful examples are provided in the WIPO Handbook on Industrial Property Information and Documentation[20], which recognises and defines five types of family (simple, complex, extended, national and artificial). However, this does not include all the variations from different database producers, and should be supplemented by consulting the Knowledge Base on the website of the PIUG. This can be found by using the Knowledge Base link off the home page <http://www.piug.org>, or the direct URL <http://www.piug.org/patfam.html>.

► BIBLIOGRAPHIC STANDARDS AND THE FORM OF A PATENT DOCUMENT

One of the advantages of working with patent documents is the extent to which their citation and physical form is controlled by well-established standards. Since the late 1970's, patent documents from all over the world have become increasingly fitted to a common format, which makes it easier to use the original documents, and easier for database producers to compile them into a common record format.

The major technical standards relating to patent documents are promulgated by the World Intellectual Property Organization (WIPO), based in Geneva. Initially produced on paper, many are now available on the WIPO website, in the section on the Standing Committee on Information Technologies (SCIT). The list of standards available is at <http://www.wipo.int/scit/en/standards/standards.htm>, and it is also possible to find the working documents relating to their revision, in the section devoted to the work of the Standards and Documentation Working Group (SDWG). The entire set of standards is available in CD-ROM format[21], as PDF files.

The most significant bibliographic standards are shown in Table 2. Of the standards in this Table, at least one (ST.3) was under consideration for revision at the 2004 meeting of the SDWG.

Table 2: Key WIPO standards for bibliographic control of patents

Standard number	Latest revision	Title
ST. 1	Sep. 2001	Recommendation concerning the minimum data elements required to uniquely identify a patent document.
ST.3	Feb. 2004	Two-letter codes for the representation of states, other entities and organizations.
ST. 6	Apr. 2003	Numbering of published patent documents.
ST. 9	Feb. 2004	Bibliographic data on and relating to patents and SPCs.
ST. 13	Nov. 1997	Numbering of applications for patents, SPCs, designs and layout-designs of IC.
ST. 16	Jun. 2001	Standard code for the identification of different kinds of patent documents.
ST. 50	Nov. 1998	Corrections, alterations and supplements relating to patent information.

The ST.3 standard for two-letter country codes is based upon the international standard ISO 3166, with some additions for non-state authorities. The most-commonly occurring national codes, plus the active regional codes, appear in Table 3 – refer to the main standard for the full listing. Users should note that a number of codes have changed as a result of

Table 3: Some commonly occurring national and regional codes

Code	Country / regional publishing authority
AP	African Regional Industrial Property Organisation [English-speaking Africa]
CA	Canada
CN	China
DE	Germany
EA	Eurasian Patent Office [some former Soviet Union states]
EP	European Patent Office
FR	France
GB	United Kingdom
GC	Patent Office of the Cooperation Council for the Arab States of the Gulf
IT	Italy
JP	Japan
KR	South Korea
OA	Organisation Africaine de la Propriété Industrielle [French-speaking Africa]
RU	Russian Federation
US	United States
WO	Patent Co-operation Treaty

political developments in recent decades – see the corresponding chapters or sections on individual countries in this book, or the appendix to the main standard, for details. Refer to Table 5 for the codes for individual members of the European Patent Office.

Appendix 1 to standard ST. 9 is a particularly important introduction for users new to patent information. It defines a set of field tags, called INID codes, which are used on the front pages of patent documents to define certain key data elements. The INID codes (Internationally agreed Numbers for the Identification of bibliographic Data) appear in brackets or a ring on the printed front page, in Roman numerals, and can be extremely helpful to locate the significant data item when a user is unfamiliar with the language of the document. Many of the codes have corresponding machine-readable tags in SGML, which are used to speed up the loading of electronic records by commercial patent database producers. The full listing of INID codes is in ST.9, but some key ones are noted in Table 4.

Moving beyond the front page, most modern patent documents also adhere to a common sequence of elements. Not all elements will be present in every case, but a typical sequence will be:

- the '**front page**' data, which may spread over two or more physical pages, comprising the data defined by INID code
- the detailed description (**disclosure**) of the invention, which may be sub-divided into sections such as
  - technical **preamble**, describing the need for the invention and earlier attempts to meet that need
  - **description**, giving general guidelines on how the invention is made and used
  - **examples**, consisting of more detailed, step-by-step implementation of the invention (in the case of a chemical patent, this is typically a set of synthetic methods)
  - efficacy **data** (for pharmaceutical and agrochemical patents, including drug trial or glasshouse trial results)
- **claims**, providing a precise definition of those invention aspects for which the applicant is seeking legal protection
- a set of **drawings**, particularly important for mechanical inventions
- a **search report**, in the case of an unexamined patent application, consisting of the retrieved literature which, in the opinion of the examiner, constitute the most likely obstacles to patentability for the application.

Patent documents from the United States vary from this format, by moving the drawings section to the front, immediately after the front page data. Their granted patents also have a listing of 'references cited' as part of the front page data, which is sometimes mistakenly referred to as a 'search

Table 4: Some important INID codes

Code number	Shortened definition
(Series 10)	*(Identification of the publication)*
11	Number of the patent, SPC or patent document
12	Kind of publication (plain language)
13	Kind of publication (using Kind-of-Document code from ST.16)
19	Country code (ST.3), or other identification, of the publishing office or organization
(Series 20)	*(Local filing details)*
21	Number(s) assigned to the application(s)
22	Date(s) of filing the application(s)
(Series 30)	*(Priority details)*
31	Priority application number(s)
32	Priority application date(s)
33	Country in which priority application was filed
(Series 40)	*(Publication dates)*
41	Date of making available to the public an unexamined patent document (view or copy on request)
42	Date of making available to the public an examined patent document (view or copy on request)
43	Date of making available to the public an unexamined patent document (printed specification)
44	Date of making available to the public an examined patent document (printed specification)
45	Date of publication by printing of a granted patent
(Series 50)	*(Technical information)*
51	International Patent Classification
52	Domestic or national classification
54	Title of the invention
57	Abstract or claim
58	Field of search
(Series 70)	*(Identification of parties)*
71	Name of applicant
72	Name of inventor
73	Name of grantee
75	Name of inventor who is also applicant
(Series 80)	*(Data relating to international conventions)*
81	Designated states according to the PCT
84	Designated states under regional patent conventions

report'. As will be discussed in the chapter on the United States (Chapter 3), differences in the legal process here mean that this is not an exactly equivalent data element.

▶ SPECIAL DOCUMENT TYPES

With the proliferation of databases available, it is important to be aware that not all sources contain the same data, even if they superficially cover the same country from the same starting date. Patents are just one part of a spectrum of intellectual property rights, each generating its own national registers and databases. A given source may contain all the patent and patent-like documents produced by that country, or only a selection, and accordingly indicate a different answer to a given query. Three areas need to be considered; alternative forms of IP rights, patent amendments & corrections and patent-related protection mechanisms.

Alternative forms of intellectual property (IP) rights

In most countries of the world, the same authority (IP office) will be responsible for issuing a range of different IP rights. Historically, these were quite distinct and searches tended to be confined to a single right. However, in recent years some of the boundaries around each set of rights have become a little more blurred, at least from the information retrieval point of view.

In the case of designs, the protection is focussed upon the aesthetic aspects of the appearance of a product. It is therefore quite feasible for a given product to be protected both by patent (for the technical innovation) and by registration of the design. For example, in the pharmaceutical industry, a marketed drug may contain a patented active ingredient and also have design protection for the size, shape or colour of the pill itself. The message for the searcher is to be aware that, even if a search for patent protection on a product returns a negative answer, that product may still have some enforceable rights behind it, and it would be extremely unwise to undertake copying the product until all avenues have been investigated.

In the same way, trade marks are words or graphic devices which distinguish a given product (or, in the case of a service mark in some jurisdictions, a service) from those offered by competing companies in the same sector. The use of a trade mark guarantees that certain goods and services originate from a recognised supplier, and infringement of the mark occurs if the same or a similar mark is used without permission by another supplier, in such a way as to create confusion in the mind of the consumer. When originally created, trade marks were derived from the medieval guild marks, and were limited in application to words (real or invented) and designs (logos). In recent years, trade marks have been granted for designs of vehicles, certain shapes, colours, sounds and even smells. As with registered designs, this has had the result that a given invention may attract multiple intellectual property rights, any or all of which may have been applied for by the inventor. If the invention being researched has any substantial element to it which could be protected by alternative IP rights, it is a wise precaution to search the corresponding databases as well as the obvious patent sources.

A detailed discussion of the search sources for registered designs and trade marks is beyond the scope of this book. However, readers are advised to start by contacting the appropriate national patent office, who will be able to advise on their web-based sources, as a starting point for more detailed searching. A good directory listing is available at the British Library website; under Collections, consult the section on "Patents, trade marks and designs", which provides a series of links on the subject of trade marks at <http://www.bl.uk/collections/patents/tmlinks.html> and for designs at <http://www.bl.uk/collections/patents/deslinks.html>

In addition to designs and trade marks, some other countries in the world have special IP rights for such areas as plant varieties, software or semi-conductor topographies (the design of chip masks for semi-conductors). Depending upon the jurisdiction of the searcher, it is helpful to be aware of which alternate protection routes are available, since industries may employ a mixture of IP rights around the same product. For example, some advocates of open-source software tend to use copyright as their principal protection mechanism, whilst other companies will use the conventional patent system.

Patent amendments and corrections

Patent documents and databases containing them are generated by a process which includes a long chain of human activity. As such, they are not immune from errors. The European Patent Office, which operates some of the largest bibliographic databases in the field, estimate that they make up to 1,000,000 corrections per year to the data flowing into their database production centres, from over 70 countries. However, not all producers are this painstaking in their approach, with the consequence that the same search conducted over several databases may well produce different results, simply because of errors in the source data. Clearly, this is not a desirable situation, and by the mid-1990's, major industry users were lobbying for the introduction of a more rigorous method of handling corrections. This was finally agreed in 1998 with the introduction of WIPO Standard ST.50 "Guidelines for issuing corrections, alterations and supplements relating to patent information." This provides a framework for patent offices to announce amendments at any stage in the public processing of a patent application, on any media. For example, if a patent office issues an announcement both in its paper gazette and on a CD-ROM product, it is possible that the first will be correct but the second may get corrupted in the production process. The ST.50 guidelines allow the patent office to issue medium-specific correction notices.

The types of notification which ST.50 addresses fall mainly into the class of bibliographical amendments. The information specialist also needs to be aware of legal amendments – that is, when a document progresses from one version to the next by virtue of the normal patent office procedure.

Bibliographical amendments

A bibliographical amendment may be required as a result of a simple recording error, such as a mistake in the name of an inventor on the front page, or a transposition of two digits in an application or priority number. At the time of writing, the European Patent Office, the United States Patent and Trademark Office (USPTO) and the WIPO are operating all or parts of ST.50, to issue corrections which enter the formal bibliographic record. Details of the operation and the special KD codes used are dealt with in Chapters 2, 3, and 5, respectively.

Legal amendments

A legal amendment may come in one of two forms. In a few cases, progression from one stage of the legal procedure to the next is implicit in the issue of a new document. For example, the grant of a European Patent is formally notified by the issue of a notice in the European Patent Bulletin, but this is accompanied by the simultaneous publication of the specification, bearing the EP-B code. Hence, simply by monitoring the publication of a document series, the user is operating a *de facto* monitoring of a change in legal status.

However, a substantial majority of legal amendments are issued not in the form of documents, but as notices in the appropriate patent office's official journal (often referred to as a 'Gazette', even if that word does not appear in the title). These notices of change in status may include, for example, a re-assignment to a third party (either through sale of the patent, or as a result of company merger, acquisition or demerger activity), the notice of payment of renewal fees, indications of certain legal proceedings involving the patent, term extensions and so on. Although such Gazette notices often fall into recognised chapters within the Gazette, they are not accompanied by a new document issue. The principal sources for tracking such changes are either the Gazette itself (in paper or electronic form), or a specialist register or database. Individual registers are increasingly becoming available via the internet, using data supplied by the national patent office and often mounted on a patent office server. The only database which collates and publishes legal status changes for a range of countries is the INPADOC file produced by the European Patent Office; it currently has some legal status information for approximately 45 countries.

Patent-related protection mechanisms

This book is devoted to the information aspects of patents, but the information specialist should be aware of a number of other 'patent-like' intellectual property rights. They may be found during searches within patent databases, or sometimes as special sub-sets or document types. The two most important variations on the conventional patent are the utility model and the supplementary protection certificate (SPC).

Utility models

The utility model is used as a parallel protection mechanism in a number of countries. It is not possible to protect the same invention simultaneously by both utility model and patent, so if an applicant reaches the situation where both have been granted, they must make a choice of which to maintain, and withdraw the other.

The characteristics of a utility model are that it is granted for a shorter period than a conventional patent (typically between 6 and 10 years, instead of 20 for the patent), and the examination process is less rigorous than that for a patent. In some countries, utility models are not examined at all unless challenged by a third party; in others, they may be examined against the novelty criteria, but not against inventive step. Utility model protection is usually not available for all the classes of patentable subject matter – a typical exclusion is that utility models may not be available for chemical compounds or processes of manufacturing them.

The background to the utility model system is often based upon the desire to promote the concept of intellectual property rights to small industries. These companies may be producing products which represent a small, but nonetheless useful, advance on known technology, and for which there is a time-limited demand in the marketplace. For such products, the procedure of obtaining full patent protection may not be cost-effective; the product may be out-of-date by the time the patent is granted. The utility model, with a lower hurdle to cross, is granted relatively quickly (months rather than years), and provides a simple mechanism for such products to have a reduced level of protection.

Utility model protection is an attractive option for mechanical products, and indeed in past years it has been part of some utility model laws that the applicant has had to supply a three-dimensional model of their product as part of the application process. Given the limited range of products which benefit, and the limited term of the protection, it is not surprising that the system is commonly used by inventors from within the country granting the protection. Two of the best-established utility model systems are in Germany and Japan, and in both countries, a substantial proportion of the applicants are local inventors.

Utility models appear under a variety of names, and the corresponding documentation in a variety of formats. The archetypal German Gebrauchsmuster (Gbm) and Japanese utility models (Kokai jitsuyo shin'an koho) have a distinct document numbering series and use the kind-of-document code U. In Ireland, the same system is known as a 'short-term patent', whilst in France, they are 'certificats d'utilité' and in Australia there is the 'innovation patent', which replaced the earlier 'petty patent'. Taiwan presents an interesting approach, in that its patents and utility models are published in successive contiguously numbered blocks each week, with only the kind-of-document suffix to distinguish them.

Few of the commercial databases have bothered to include utility models in their coverage, at least until recent years. However, they still form part of the state of the art, and should be considered for inclusion in a search whenever the subject matter is appropriate. The searcher may have to make their best efforts based upon free-of-charge web-based services from the originating patent office, or arrange for a visit to the patent office in question to obtain access to in-house indexes.

Supplementary Protection Certificates

Despite the discussion in earlier sections which emphasised that all patents eventually expire after a fixed term, it is a long-established practice in many countries to make provision for extension of the term of a patent under particular circumstances. For example, one of James Watt's early patents on "a new method of lessening the consumption of steam and fuel in fire engines" (today, we would call it a steam engine), was granted on 5th January 1769. It would normally have had a term of 14 years, expiring in 1783. However, by 1774, Watt had a new commercial partner, Matthew Boulton, who was concerned about the relatively short period of life left in this seminal patent, and also had experience of lobbying in Parliament. By early 1775, a petition for a special Act of Parliament had been submitted, as this was the only process available at the time for a patent term extension. After much debate, on 22nd May 1775, the Act was passed allowing a 25 year extension, giving an expiry date of 1800. Furthermore, the same Act extended the effect of the patent into Scotland. The importance of this extension can be seen from the fact that it was not until the late 1790's that Watt was in a position to commence infringement action against some of the Cornish mine owners who had copied his engine. The settlement eventually netted several million pounds in today's terms.

Today, the pharmaceutical industry is probably the most sensitive on the issue of patent term. This is for two reasons. Firstly, drugs are relatively easy to copy, and new manufacturers will be waiting to enter the market as soon as the patent on a successful drug expires. This means that the inventing company can see their profit margin eroded very rapidly after patent expiry, as new (generic) forms begin to be sold. Hence, they need to be able to make as much profit as possible whilst the patent is in force; this income has to support both the cost of marketing the successful drug and the research costs invested in the many candidate drugs which have failed. As a consequence, the longer that an inventing company can hold off generic competition, the greater its chances of being able to make a financial return over the lifetime of the drug.

The second reason which affects the pharmaceutical industry is that they are effectively prohibited by law from utilising the full life of their patents. In most sectors, once a patent has been obtained, the holder can go to market, secure in the knowledge that they will be able to warn off competitors. However, in the pharmaceutical sector, there may be a gap of several years between the grant of the patent on a drug and the date when it is launched on the market. This period is taken up by a strict regime of government testing, to prove safety and efficacy. Until these tests are completed and a Marketing Authorisation (MA) awarded, the product cannot be sold. This means that a granted patent effectively sits idle on the shelf for several years, until the MA is available. A typical timescale may be that the patent is granted 4–6 years after initial discovery, but the MA is not granted until a further 5 years, leaving as little as 9 years during which the drug can be sold under patent protection.

In order to address these issues, various national governments and the European Union have devised schemes to extend the protection for a marketed drug beyond the original expiry date of the patent. Different countries have adopted distinct mechanisms, but all are based upon a formula designed to restore part or all of the lost exclusivity period.

There are essentially two mechanisms being used to obtain term extension. The first is to extend the term of the original patent – this is the approach used in the US and Japan. The alternative approach, used in the European Union, is to create an entirely new legal instrument, which only enters into force upon patent expiry. This new instrument is usually referred to as a Supplementary Protection Certificate, or SPC.

The US introduced comprehensive provisions for term extension in 1984 (often called the Hatch/Waxman Act), followed by Japan in 1988. The European Union has two provisions, dating from 1992 and 1996 respectively. Unfortunately for the information specialist, the introduction of these provisions was not straightforward – both France and Italy implemented national SPC legislation before the EC Regulations entered into force, so some products may be extended under these laws rather than the wider EU system.

At the time of writing, only Canada (from amongst the G8 countries reviewed in detail in later chapters) does not have provision for pharmaceutical patent term extension. In addition, the EU states recognise an equivalent scheme covering agrochemicals, which also face a regime of marketing authorisation.

The information aspects of term extension will be discussed in more detail in the country chapters, and also in the context of legal status searches in Chapter 10.

► **REFERENCES**

1. "Mainly on patents; the use of industrial property and its literature." F. Liebesny (ed.) London: Butterworths, 1972. ISBN 0–408–70368–7.

2. "Patents for chemicals, pharmaceuticals and biotechnology: fundamentals of global law, practice and strategy". P.W. Grubb. Oxford: Clarendon Press, 1999. ISBN 0–19–876520–7. New (fourth) edition due November 2004, ISBN 0–19–927378–2.

3. "Intellectual Property Reading Material". WIPO Publication No. 476(E). Geneva: WIPO, 1997. ISBN 92–805–0629–3.

4. "WIPO Intellectual Property Handbook: Policy, Law and Use" WIPO Publication No. 489(E). Geneva: WIPO, 2001. ISBN 92–805–1004–8. or via <http://www. wipo.int/about-ip/en/iprm/index.htm>

5. "Inventing the Industrial Revolution: the English patent system 1660–1800". C. McLeod. Cambridge: Cambridge University Press, 1988. ISBN 0–521–30104–1 (hbk.). Reprinted 2002, pbk, ISBN 0–521–89399–2.

6. "British Patents of Invention, 1617–1977: a guide for researchers." S. van Dulken. London: British Library: 1999. ISBN 0–7123–0817–2.

7. "Finding Grandpa's Patent: using patent information for historical or genealogical research." J. Comfort, pp. 39–56 :in "Patent and Trademark Information: uses and perspectives." V. Baldwin (ed.) New York: Haworth Press, 2004. ISBN 0–7890–0425–9.

8. "International Guide to Official Industrial Property Publications." B. Rimmer; S. van Dulken (3rd revised edition). London: British Library, 1992. ISBN 0–7123–0791–5.

9. "Paris Convention for the Protection of Industrial Property 1883". Official English text. WIPO Publication 201(E). Geneva: WIPO, 1979, reprinted 1996. ISBN 92–805–0291–3.

10. "A comparison of early publication practices in the United States and Europe". S. Adams, World Patent Information 25(2), 117–122 (2003).

11. "Introduction to Intellectual Property Law". J. Phillips; A. Firth. London: Butterworths, 1995. ISBN 0–406–04515–1.

12. "What every chemist should know about patents." L-N. McLeland (ed.), ACS Joint Board-Council Committee on Patents and Related Matters. Washington DC: American Chemical Society, 2002 (3rd edition).

13. "Patent law for the nonlawyer: a guide for the engineer, technologist and manager." B.A. Amernick. New York: Van Nostrand Reinhold, / London: Chapman and Hall, 1991. ISBN 0–442–00177–0.

14. "Usage profiles of patent information among current and potential users; report on the main results of the survey commissioned by the European Patent Office". R. Doornbos; R. Gras; J. Toth. Amsterdam: Motivaction Research & Strategy, 2003. Available from the EPO at <http://www.european-patent-office.org/news/info/survey2003/epo_user_survey.pdf>.

15. "Utilisation of patent protection in Europe; representative survey carried out on behalf of the European Patent Office, Munich." Published as volume 3 in the EPOScript series (ISSN 1021–9390). Munich: European Patent Office, 1994.

16. "Barriers to the use of patent information in UK small and medium-sized enterprises. Part 1: Questionnaire survey." M. Hall ; C. Oppenheim ; M. Sheen. Journal of Information Science **25**(5), 335–350 (1999) and "Barriers to the use of patent information in UK small and medium-sized enterprises. Part 2(1): Results of in-depth interviews." ." M. Hall ; C. Oppenheim ; M. Sheen. Journal of Information Science **26**(2), 87–99 (2000).

17. "Patent information usage by chemists in universities." H. Schofield :in Proc. Chemical Information Conference, Nimes, 21–23 October 1996, pp.111–120. H. Collier (ed). Calne: Infonortics Ltd, 1996.

18. "The use of patent information in industry". J. Stephenson. World Patent Information, **4**(4), 164–171 (1982).

19. "Patent families and where to find them." R. Austin. Proc. PIUG Annual Conference, 22–27 May 2004, Baltimore, MD, USA, 2004

20. "Glossary of terms concerning industrial property information and documentation." Appendix III to Part 10, of the WIPO Handbook on Industrial Property Information and Documentation.". WIPO Publication No. CD208. Geneva: WIPO, 2003. ISBN 92–805–0352–9.

21. "WIPO Standards, Recommendations and Guidelines concerning industrial property information and documentation. Part 3 of the "WIPO Handbook on Industrial Property Information and Documentation.". WIPO Publication No. CD208. Geneva: WIPO, 2003. ISBN 92–805–0352–9.

2 The European Patent system

The European Patent system is the best known example of a regional patent system, in which a central body takes on the function of examining and granting patents on behalf of its member states. As such, it breaks the 'one country, one patent' rule and has important implications for the searcher.

Regional patent systems are not a totally modern phenomenon. In the United Kingdom, prior to 1852, there were separate systems granting patents in England (which included Wales), Scotland and Ireland. During the 1950's, the four Scandinavian countries (Denmark, Norway, Sweden and Finland) tried to set up a Nordic patent system, and got as far as passing identical legislation with a view to facilitating this process. However, the principal regional patent system in the modern era is the European Patent Office (EPO), founded on a diplomatic Convention signed in Munich on 5th October 1973, the European Patent Convention (EPC). Technically, this Convention brought into existence the European Patent *Organisation,* which comprises two organs, the European Patent *Office* and the Administrative Council. The latter supervises the work of the Office and sets general policy directions.

The main European Patent Office website can be found at <www.european-patent-office.org>, which provides links to much of the documentation and databases produced by the EPO.

▶ HISTORY AND DEVELOPMENT

The EPO started operation in 1978, and is now recognised as one of the most influential patent offices in the world, alongside the US and Japanese offices. Table 5 shows the membership as of 1st July 2005, in chronological order of their joining. Candidates for membership over the next year include Malta and Norway.

Table 5: Membership of the European Patent Organisation

Country name	ST.3 Country Code	Date of entry into force	Membership status
Belgium	BE	07-Oct-1977	Member
France	FR	07-Oct-1977	Member
Germany	DE	07-Oct-1977	Member
Luxembourg	LU	07-Oct-1977	Member
Netherlands	NL	07-Oct-1977	Member
Switzerland	CH	07-Oct-1977	Member
United Kingdom	GB	07-Oct-1977	Member
Sweden	SE	01-May-1978	Member
Italy	IT	01-Dec-1978	Member
Austria	AT	01-May-1979	Member
Liechtenstein	LI	01-Apr-1980	Member
Greece	GR	01-Oct-1986	Member
Spain	ES	01-Oct-1986	Member
Denmark	DK	01-Jan-1990	Member
Monaco	MC	01-Dec-1991	Member
Ireland	IE	01-Aug-1992	Member
Portugal	PT	01-Sep-1992	Member
Albania	AL	01-Feb-1996	Extension state
Finland	FI	01-Mar-1996	Member
Macedonia	MK	01-Nov-1997	Extension state
Cyprus	CY	01-Apr-1998	Member
Turkey	TR	01-Nov-2000	Member
Bulgaria	BG	01-Jul-2002	Member
Czech Republic	CZ	01-Jul-2002	Member
Estonia	EE	01-Jul-2002	Member
Slovakia	SK	01-Jul-2002	Member
Slovenia	SI	01-Dec-2002	Member (extension state 1 Mar 1994 – 30 Nov 2002)
Hungary	HU	01-Jan-2003	Member
Romania	RO	01-Mar-2003	Member (extension state 15 Oct 1996 – 28 Feb 2003)
Poland	PL	01-Mar-2004	Member
Croatia	HR	01-Apr-2004	Extension state
Iceland	IS	01-Nov-2004	Member
Serbia & Montenegro	YU	01-Nov-2004	Extension state
Bosnia & Herzegovina	BA	01-Dec-2004	Extension state
Lithuania	LT	01-Dec-2004	Member (extension state 5 Jul 1994 – 30 Nov 2004)
Latvia	LV	01-Jul-2005	Member (extension state 1 May 1995 – 30 Jun 2005)

Member states and extension states

It is clear from Table 5 that many member states of the EPO are also members of the European Union (EU), although Switzerland and Turkey are prominent exceptions. The relationship between the EPO and the EU institutions does not require that the membership of the two bodies is identical, and it is important thus to realise that a European Patent is not equivalent to 'an EU patent'. In legal terms, the European Patent Convention is part of the *acquis communautaire*, meaning that a country which commits to joining the EU is obligated in due course to ratify the EPC and hence become a full member of the EPO. However, the reverse does not apply – joining the EPO pre-supposes no commitment to joining the EU. In 1973, all the member states of the EU (then the EEC) signed the Munich Convention, but over the following decades, the membership of the two institutions has not followed in step as originally planned.

When a country becomes a member of the EPO, it undertakes to accept the patents examined and granted by that body as being valid on its territory without further restriction. The member state does not abolish its own office, but continues to grant national patents and to accord the European Patents an equal status with them. As a consequence, inventions in EPO member states may be protected in theory by one of two equivalent routes – a national patent or a European Patent. However, an application for a European Patent does not necessarily result in a patent in all member states. The applicant has the option to select (or 'designate') those member states in which they wish to obtain protection; this list can vary from one to all 30, and anywhere in between. In order to establish whether an invention has been protected in an EPO member state, it is necessary to determine firstly whether a European Patent for the invention has been granted and secondly whether that patent has designated the member state of interest.

A number of smaller East European states have opted for status as extension states, rather than full members. An extension state has entered into a bilateral agreement with the EPO, to recognise granted European Patents as being valid on its territory. There may be differences in the documentation issued by extension states, compared with full members (for example, they may issue a national patent document with a special number series or KD code to represent the converted European Patent). Extension states do not have voting rights on the Administrative Council, and in some cases this status has been a transition to full membership in due course (e.g. for Slovenia and Romania).

▶ EP PATENT DOCUMENTS – CENTRALISED AND NATIONALISED PROCEDURES

The operation of the European Patent system is a mixture of activities, some carried out at the EPO offices and some at the national level. Typically, the national level stages are at the very beginning and the end, with the EPO taking responsibility for the main process of examining and granting.

At the point of initial application, the EPO can be considered as if it is a single 'mega-country' for claiming their priority rights under the Paris Convention. Hence, an applicant in (e.g.) the United States to make a single application to the EPO, claiming a US priority date, in order to initiate the process of obtaining a European Patent. Each of the member states of the EPO can act, via their national patent office, as the receiving point for an application to the EPO. Specific ranges of application numbers are allocated to each office or group of offices, enabling a user to determine where and how an application was filed, simply from the format of the EPO application number. The most recent listing was published in 2001[1].

Formal examination and search report

In order to proceed through the official stages, the applicant must provide a translation of their application into one of the three official languages of the EPO (English, French or German). This language is then used as the language of proceedings throughout the granting stages. Further translations into other European languages can thus be deferred, with significant cost savings for the applicant at this stage. A brief examination for formal completeness of the document is carried out shortly after application, and provided that the necessary fees are paid and formalities completed in time, a search report will be prepared. The application is published unexamined around 18 months from the priority date.

Unexamined publication

Unexamined applications are published regularly on Wednesday of each week – during 2004, average production was some 1,200 documents. A further 1,100 sets of bibliographic data are also issued, covering the PCT documents entering the regional phase at the EPO without republication of the specification.

At the time of publication, the application is given a new number with the appropriate ST.3 country code 'EP' prefix, and one of two possible KD suffixes. If the search report is available at the time of publication of the specification, both documents are bound together and published as a EP-A1. If the search report is delayed, the specification only is published, and

Figure 3: EPO search report header

given the code EP-A2. The delayed search report will then be published separately, using the same publication number as the A2 to which it relates, but with the suffix changed to A3. Over the last few years, the workload at the EPO has increased to the extent that A2 documents, once a rarity, now form more than 60% of each year's publications, with the corresponding A3 documents following on within months or occasionally years. This delay has a knock-on effect upon final progress to grant, as an applicant is not obliged to file a request for the next stage – substantive examination – until 6 months after the publication of the search report. A header from a delayed search report is reproduced at Figure 3, showing the INID codes for the publication date of the report itself (88) and the corresponding A2 specification (43).

Despite these delays, the search reports of the European Patent Office are highly regarded for their completeness and quality. The citations in the report represent those parts of the prior art which the search examiner believes will represent the most significant hurdles during substantive examination. A system of relevance indicators is used, to denote whether the citation is particularly damaging on its own (category X, usually in relation to novelty) or when taken with one or more other documents (category Y, usually in relation to inventive step). The list of available codes is reproduced with each search report, and can be seen at the foot of the page in Figure 4.

Grant publication

Granted patents are also issued on Wednesdays – during 2004, an average of 1,100 per week. The applicant has the option to withdraw their application following publication of the search report, and may choose to do so if it appears that the effort and cost of proceeding to grant is no longer worthwhile. This can happen if the search report contains a number of X-citations which would require extensive modifications of the application

EP 1 128 027 A3

European Patent
Office

EUROPEAN SEARCH REPORT

Application Number

EP 01 10 4183

DOCUMENTS CONSIDERED TO BE RELEVANT

Category	Citation of document with indication, where appropriate, of relevant passages	Relevant to claim	CLASSIFICATION OF THE APPLICATION (Int.Cl.7)
X	US 5 558 051 A (YOSHIOKA MAMORU) 24 September 1996 (1996-09-24)	1	F01L1/344 F02D13/02 F01L1/34 F01L13/00
A	* column 1, line 11-14 * * column 1, line 64 - column 2, line 11 *	2	
X	US 5 293 741 A (UMEHARA KEN ET AL) 15 March 1994 (1994-03-15)	1	
A	* column 1, line 7,8 * * column 4, line 30-40 * * column 10, line 4-9 * * figures 2,5,6 *	2	
A	EP 0 937 865 A (TOYOTA MOTOR CO LTD) 25 August 1999 (1999-08-25) * paragraph '0001! * * paragraph '0012! * * paragraph '0035! * * paragraph '0036! * * paragraph '0046! * * paragraph '0061! * * figures 1-6,8,13-15,21 *	3-7,9-11	TECHNICAL FIELDS SEARCHED (Int.Cl.7)
A	EP 0 915 234 A (TOYOTA MOTOR CO LTD) 12 May 1999 (1999-05-12) * paragraph '0002! * * page 0079 * * figures 4-6 *	1	F02D F01L
A	US 5 893 345 A (HASEGAWA TADAO ET AL) 13 April 1999 (1999-04-13) * column 1, line 10-17 * * column 8, line 43-61 * * figures 2-8 *	3,9	

The present search report has been drawn up for all claims

Place of search	Date of completion of the search	Examiner
THE HAGUE	1 November 2001	Paquay, J

CATEGORY OF CITED DOCUMENTS

X : particularly relevant if taken alone
Y : particularly relevant if combined with another
    document of the same category
A : technological background
O : non-written disclosure
P : intermediate document

T : theory or principle underlying the invention
E : earlier patent document, but published on, or
    after the filing date
D : document cited in the application
L : document cited for other reasons

& : member of the same patent family, corresponding
    document

EPO FORM 1503 03 82 (P04C01)

Figure 4: Contents of European search report

in order to circumvent them. However, if the applicant chooses to persevere and argue their case, the contents of their application will be examined in detail. If they can satisfy the examiner that it fulfils the criteria for patentability, the application will be granted and published a second time. The same publication number as for the –A stage is retained, changed to a –B1. The official notice of grant is mentioned in the EPO Bulletin, available in paper form (until 2005) and electronically on disk and via the internet. With effect from April 2005, paper versions of EP-A and EP-B documents will cease to be published, and a new publications server will become the official source of supply for European Patent specifications.

Post-grant publications

Once a patent has been granted by the EPO, it is open for a period of 9 months for opposition. If third parties object to the grant within that period, the arguments are heard centrally before the Opposition Division of the EPO. This may result in the re-issue of an amended patent, with the same publication number but the KD code –B2. Alternatively, if the patent is upheld in its entirety, no further document is issued and the EP-B1 stands as published. A granted European Patent retains the body of the specification in the original language of the proceedings, but has 3 sets of claims, one in each of the official languages.

In order to enter into force in all the designated states, the applicant may be required (depending upon the countries concerned) to lodge translations of the entire specification, in accordance with Article 65 of the EPC. For example, if the granted specification is in English, and the patent holder has designated Italy, they must provide a translation into Italian within a fixed time period, usually 3 months. Failure to do so results in the patent being declared void for that country.

A number of the EPO member states have created special number series and/or KD codes for the publication of their Article 65 translations. For example, as shown in Figure 1, the grant of EP 455300-B1 (in English) became DE 6 91 10749-T2 in Germany, and similarly in Greece was re-published as GR 3017534-T3. However, the translation into Danish retained the original EP number and merely changed the code, becoming DK 455300-T3.

Other post-grant events

Provided that the Article 65 translations are duly lodged at the appropriate national patent offices, no further action is required for a granted EP to enter into force. The subsequent renewal fees are paid to the individual states, hence it is possible for a granted EP to lapse in one state but not in another. Similarly, the granting of licences, registration of re-assignments or other transactions in the patent must be carried out at the local level. For this reason, it is regarded as more a 'bundle' of national patents rather than a true unitary patent. Crucially, if the 9-month opposition period ends without objection being filed, anyone wishing to challenge the patent at a later date must do so at each national court individually. During litigation, the court findings in one country are not indicative of the status in another country.

At Table 6, the sequence of events leading up to a European Patent is illustrated. The example incorporates both a delayed search report and two correction documents. Table 7 summarises the full range of available KD codes, as of 2004.

Table 6: European Patent publication stages

	Number	Date / comments
European application	99107044	9 Apr 1999 ; Convention filing
European unexamined publication (no search report)	EP 953429-A2	3 Nov 1999 ; 18 months after original German priority
European search report	EP 953429-A3	5 Mar 2003
Correction to European unexamined publication	EP 953429-A8	19 Feb 2003 – corrects applicant data; new applicant added
European grant	EP 953429-B1	16 Jun 2004
Correction to European grant	EP 953429-B8	13 Oct 2004 – corrects inventor data; two new inventors listed

Table 7: Summary of current (2004) EPO document codes

Code	Definition
A1	Publication of unexamined specification with search report
A2	Publication of unexamined specification without search report
A3	Publication of search report
A8	Correction of front page of an A1, A2 or A3 document
A9	Complete reprint of an A1, A2 or A3 document
B1	Publication of grant of European Patent
B2	Re-publication of amended grant of European Patent after EPO opposition proceedings
B8	Correction of front page of a B1 or B2 document
B9	Complete reprint of a B1 or B2 document

► EUROPEAN CLASSIFICATION

The European Classification scheme (ECLA) is based upon the International Patent Classification (IPC), and the notation is very similar to it. The system is used within the EPO's search documentation, which covers multiple countries over many years. As a public search tool, it is available for use in certain files mounted on the free-of-charge esp@cenet ® system, as well as an increasing range of commercial search files. Some further aspects of ECLA are discussed in Chapter 12.

ECLA classes are not printed on the front page of any documents; they are retained solely as computer records. Unlike the US classification, ECLA is not reserved for publications from the EPO alone, but is applied to at least one family member from every patent family in the EPO master database, DocDB, irrespective of the publishing country.

In recent years, EPO examiners have added ECLA classes to a range of non-patent literature as well. Subject specialists scan the key journals in their field, and apply ECLA classes to individual articles which they believe will have value in the prior art for the future. At the time of writing, some 1,000,000 items of non-patent literature have ECLA classes, although not all of these will have been cited in a European search report. Conversely, some items of non-patent literature which have been cited in search reports do not carry ECLA classes, since classification is not obligatory or automatic at the time of citation.

► DATABASES AND DATABASE-SPECIFIC ASPECTS

This section refers to only those databases which are dedicated to European Patent data. Many multi-country databases include EP data within their coverage, and these are discussed in Chapter 7. The summary listing is shown in Table 8.

Since the EPO system is relatively new (1978 onwards), it has developed in parallel with the electronic information industry, and many databases cover the system from EP 0 000 001-A to the present day. However, character-coded full text of the specifications did not begin to be produced until the 1980's, and is generally not available for the granted documents until the 1990's. Prior to this, the documents were distributed in the form of image files, using a modified TIFF format, with only the basic (front-page) data being searchable. The initial CD-ROM based products were principally used for document delivery, and had only a very restricted number of searchable fields from the front page data set.

The searcher should remember that the full text databases listed will be in the three official languages of the EPO. In the case of granted documents, the claims are translated into all three languages, but the main part

Table 8: European Patent databases

Producer	Service name	Platform	Coverage
EPO	EPFULL (*)	STN	Bibliographic data 1978+ EP-A full text 1987+ P-B full text 1991+
EPO	EPAPAT (**)	Questel-Orbit	Bibliographic data 1978+ EP-A full text 1987+ (partial 1978–86)
EPO	EPBPAT (**)	Questel-Orbit	Bibliographic data 1978+ EP-B full text 1991+
EPO / INPI	EPPATENT	Questel-Orbit	Bibliographic data 1978+ Some legal status data 1978+
EPO	European Patents Fulltext (file 348) (***)	Dialog	Bibliographic data 1978+ EP-A full text 1987+ EP-B full text 1991+ Some legal status data 1978+
EPO	European Patents – Applications	Delphion	Bibliographic data 1978+ EP-A full text 1987+
EPO	European Patents – Granted	Delphion	Bibliographic data 1978+ EP-B full text 1991+
EPO	European Patents Fulltext	LexisNexis	Bibliographic data 1978+ EP-A full text 1986+ EP-B full text 1991+
MicroPatent/ EPO	PatSearch FullText	MicroPatent PatentWeb	EP-A full text 1978+ EP-B full text 1991+
EPO	EP- esp@cenet	esp@cenet	EP-A (current two years)
Minesoft/ EPO	PatBase	PatBase	Bibliographic data 1978+ EP-A full text
Lexis-Nexis Univentio	Total Patent	Total Patent	EP-A full text 1978+ EP-B full text 1980+
EPO	ESPACE-Bulletin	DVD	Bibliographic data 1978+ Legal status data 1978+
EPO	ESPACE-Access-EP-A	DVD	EP-A bibliographic data and abstracts 1978+
EPO	ESPACE-Access-EP-B	DVD	EP-B bibliographic data 1980+ EP-B first claim 1991+
EPO	ESPACE-EP-A (#)	DVD	EP-A bibliographic data 1978+ EP-A full text 2000+ Full page images 1978+
EPO	ESPACE-EP-B (#)	DVD	EP-B bibliographic data and all claims 1991+ Full page images 1991+
EPO	Register Plus	epoline	Procedural stages and legal status 1978+
EPO	Publications Server	https://publications. european-patent-office.org	Currently EP-B since beginning of 2005 – will be extended in due course (##)

(*) also available on the STN Easy platform
(**) also available on the QPAT platform
(***) also available on the DialogWeb platform
(#) these two products are due to be merged from January 2005
(##) the Publications Server is intended as a document delivery mechanism and has very limited search functionality

of the specification will remain in the same language as the corresponding EP-A document. Search files containing only EP-A documents must be searched in all three languages to ensure comprehensive retrieval.

For current information, the EPIDOS News publication (c.4 times per year) provides details of developments of all the EPO information products. Issues are released alternately on the EPO website and in paper form.

▶ RELATIONSHIPS WITH THE EUROPEAN UNION

As noted above, the EPO is not an EU body, and its membership is not synchronised with that of the EU. At the time of writing, Malta is the only EU state which does not belong to the EPO, and a larger number of states are EPO members but not belonging to the EU. Although the two bodies are independent, the EU is active in producing policies and international law which aim to stimulate and direct innovative capacity within its own member states. These policies have helped to shape certain revisions of the European Patent Convention. The EU also has a common interest with the EPO in seeking to promote the use of the patent system and related intellectual property protection regimes. The IPR Helpdesk<http://www.ipr-helpdesk.org/index.htm> is an EU initiative funded by the Directorate-General for Enterprise. Originally it focussed on IP support for actual or intended holders of research grants from the EU Framework programme, but latterly has developed into a more general advice centre. The website includes some helpful briefing documents, as well as tutorial material for training in the use of the EPO's esp@cenet search system.

The effect of European Regulations and Directives

When the European Commission and Parliament pass a new Regulation or Directive, it is intended for implementation amongst the EU member states. This could in theory lead to the anomalous situation of certain EPO member states being obligated to amend their national patent legislation in a fashion incompatible with their membership of the EPO and their commitments under the EPC. Hence, there is ongoing liaison between the two bodies. Specific examples include the Directive on certain aspects of biotechnology[2] and a proposal on software/computer-related inventions[3]. In the former instance, the EPO has incorporated key provisions of the Directive into the EPC and amended the Implementing Regulations and the EPO Guidelines for Examination. The EU has been responsible for the setting up of a unitary trade mark and design office in Alicante, Spain, and there has been discussion on a common EU utility model as well, but so far without progress.

Since the European Patent passes out of the jurisdiction of the EPO once the 9-month opposition period is over, any events relating to the end of the patent life are handled at a national level. Consequently, the two important Regulations on Supplementary Protection Certificates[4,5] for pharmaceuticals and agrochemicals have been implemented by the EU member states without the need for any amendment to the EPO's operating legislation. The EPO takes no part in the granting of these certificates, and no central record is maintained, even when it is a granted EP which is being extended; the case is treated entirely at the national level and records will be maintained in the national register(s) only.

The Community Patent

The principal driving forces for – and the chief stumbling blocks against – progress towards the European Community Patent are litigation and translation. The lack of a central patent court structure, capable of establishing decisions across all the EU states, has resulted in the situation with today's European Patent, which is examined centrally but litigated nationally. Translations, which have to be carried out at the applicant's expense for all the designated states, form a substantial part of the costs of getting a European Patent in force. Many argue that the majority of the Article 65 translations are never consulted, and that money could be saved by requiring only a smaller portion of the document – such as the claims – to be translated at the time of grant, instead of the entire specification. The language for the Community Patent has been at the heart of negotiations for many years.

The most recent proposal on the Community Patent was discussed during 2003 and early 2004, following a publication by the EU's Competitiveness Council which promised to break the deadlock[6]. However, the Council failed to reach agreement in May 2004 to support the compromise, so the matter was referred back to the President of the European Council in mid-2004 and seems to be stalled at the time of writing. The main stumbling block is the issue of the translation of the claims in the patent; the text under consideration proposes that the claims of a Community Patent (as opposed to the entire specification, with the European Patent) should be translated into all official EU languages. Although less complex and costly than having to lodge the complete document, it will still be a lengthy process. No agreement was reached on the length of the period for filing translations. Under the EP system, the basic deadline is 3 months after grant. Failure to lodge translations within an agreed deadline would result – like the EP – in the patent being declared void.

► **REFERENCES**

1. "Notice dated 1 October 2001 concerning new patent application numbering system for 2002". Official Journal of the European Patent Office, **24**(10), 465–467 (2001). See also the Guidelines for Examination in the EPO, Part A, Chapter II, sections 1a.1 and 1a.2.

2. "Directive 98/44/EC of the European Parliament and of the Council of 6 July 1998 on the legal protection of biotechnological inventions." Official Journal of the European Communities, **L213**, 13- 21 (30 July 1998).

3. "Proposal for a Directive of the European Parliament and of the Council on the patentability of computer-related inventions." COM (2002) 92 FINAL. Brussels: European Commission, 2002.

4. "Council Regulation (EEC) No. 1768/92 of 18 June 1992 concerning the creation of a supplementary protection certificate for medicinal products." Official Journal of the European Communities, **L182**, 1–5, (2 July 1992).

5. "Regulation (EC) No. 1610/96 of the European Parliament and of the Council of 8 August 1996 concerning the creation of a supplementary protection certificate for plant protection products." Official Journal of the European Communities, **L198**, 30–35 (8 August 1996).

6. European Commission, Report of the 2490th meeting of the Competitiveness Council. Document 6874/03 (Presse 59) pp.15–18 (3 March 2003).

3 The United States patent system

The United States Patent and Trademark Office (USPTO) was established in 1836, but the earliest patent legislation dates from 1790, making this one of the oldest continually operating patent systems in the world. Prior to the formation of the United States, several of the colonies had their own patent laws, such as Massachusetts in 1641, Connecticut in 1672 and South Carolina in 1691.

Between 1790 and 1836, some 10,000 patents were granted but not numbered. Many of the records were lost when the new Patent Office building was destroyed by fire in December 1836. Various attempts have been made to reconstruct the records from other collections, and these have been allocated a new number series starting with an X. As a result, the first US patent is not No.1, as might be expected, but No. X1, which was signed by George Washington himself.

The United States signed the Paris Convention shortly after it was completed, in May 1887, and joined the Patent Co-operation Treaty from the beginning, hence being able to be designated by this route from 1978. The standard country code for the United States is 'US'. Patents granted by the USPTO are valid in the 50 states of the Union, plus the US overseas territories and possessions such as American Samoa, Guam and Puerto Rico.

The terminology for patent documents under the US system is potentially confusing. The main patents for invention are termed 'utility patents', which should not be confused with 'utility models' for the lesser, patent-like, IP rights in other countries. The protection of designs, familiar in (e.g.) the United Kingdom as Registered Designs, are similarly termed Design Patents, which were introduced in 1842. Some plant material has been capable of protection by a special series of Plant Patents since 1930. For simplicity, it should be assumed in this chapter that references to 'patents' indicate US utility patents.

For many years, the US maintained a system of only publishing its patents once, after grant, in a single numbered series. This system continued for decades later than the other industrialised countries who progressively adopted deferred examination, with early publication at 18 months, from the mid-1960's. It was only in 2001 that the US changed its law, and it still has marked differences in practice from most other countries.

It is instructive to consider the rate with which patent issuing has increased over the lifetime of the Office. Table 9 shows the year of issue of each of the 'million' milestones, and the decreasing interval to the next million. Since passing US 6,000,000 in 1999, the Office is already well on the way to passing US 7,000,000 in less than 8 years – the first publication of 2005 was no. US 6,836,899.

There are two fundamental aspects of US patent practice which impact upon information work. These are the grace period and the 'first to invent' system.

The grace period is not unique to the United States, but due to the importance of US industry, their utilisation is perhaps the most significant. Within the US system, the grace period lasts for 12 months, and this duration is typical for other countries. The grace period allows that the inventor or their authorised representatives may publicly display or test an invention, including test marketing of a product, without jeopardising the novelty of the invention, for a period of 12 months prior to making a patent application. This means that an inventor can be more open concerning the details of their invention, confident that they will not be damaging their own application. By contrast, within most of the industrialised world, any such activities, even by the inventor, prior to patent application would constitute a novelty-destroying premature disclosure and could threaten the chances of a patent application proceeding to grant.

The operation of the grace period in the United States permits US inventors to be somewhat more relaxed about disclosures within the US than elsewhere, but only if the inventor has no intention of filing outside of the country. A disclosure under the grace period in the US can still

Table 9: Publication milestones in US patent history

Issue Year	Number	Interval (years)
1790	X1	
1911	1,000,000	121
1935	2,000,000	24
1961	3,000,000	26
1976	4,000,000	15
1991	5,000,000	15
1999	6,000,000	8

constitute a novelty-destroying act in respect of other patent-granting authorities. Perhaps the most famous example of this is the Cohen-Boyer patents, including US 4,237,224 on the fundamental processes of gene splicing. Stanley Cohen, an inventor based at Stanford University, published some details about the technique in a journal during 1973. The earliest US patent application was not filed until 1974, which was allowable within the grace period. However, the same journal article and a further disclosure in a US newspaper prevented corresponding applications elsewhere in the world for the same invention.

In terms of patent information work, the grace period needs to be recognised in the context of an invalidity search, when attempts are being made to cast doubt on the patentability of an invention. If apparent prior art is discovered in the United States, it may not affect a United States application, but could still affect other applications in different parts of the world. Consequently the same invention may be patentable in the United States but unpatentable elsewhere.

A second important aspect is the US's 'first-to-invent' system. This is sometimes confused with the grace period, since both aspects can lead to the same contrast in behaviour between a US inventor and an inventor elsewhere – namely, a pressure to file patent applications as soon as an invention is first recognised. Under the rest of the world's 'first-to-file' system, preference is given to the applicant who lodges their earliest (priority) application first. Although there is nothing guaranteed (each case has still to be examined), the earliest applicant has the best *a priori* claim to be granted the patent(s) on the invention. In the US 'first-to-invent' system, the presumption is that the person entitled to the patent is the one who first conceived the idea and reduced it to a workable form. This means that if two competing applications are filed for the same invention, the patent may be awarded to the inventor who can prove the earliest date of invention, rather than the one who lodged their papers at the patent office first. In information terms, this means that industry must take particular care to maintain records (for example, laboratory notebooks) showing the development of a research project, as they may be called upon for evidence of date of invention in the event of dispute.

▶ RECENT LAW CHANGES

The most significant development, from the information scientist's point of view, came in 1999 with the passing of the American Inventors Protection Act (AIPA). In common with US practice, this is now consolidated into a revised Title 35 of the United States Code (35 USC). The AIPA committed the United States to publishing its pending patent applications at 18 months from priority. The first of these documents appeared in March 2001, and they now publish regularly on each Thursday (the granted patents series continue to publish on Tuesday of each week).

An earlier significant hiatus in the legislation, important for the legal status searcher, came in 1995. The Uruguay Round Agreements Act (URAA) of 1994 was designed to bring the United States into line with the requirements of the TRIPS (Trade-Related Aspects of Intellectual Property) Agreement, which was part of the founding treaties of the World Trade Organisation. TRIPS required a minimum term of 20 years from filing for patents. Up to this time, the United States, with its single-publication policy, had calculated patent term from the date of issue (grant) of the patent, for 17 years. Under the URAA, patents in force on 8th June 1995, and granted patents based on applications pending before the same date, were allowed a term of 17 years from grant or 20 years from application, whichever was the longer. Applications filed after this date have a uniform term of 20 years from application.

Further term adjustments were brought in under the AIPA, from 29th May 2000, and may be applied if the USPTO takes excessive time in prosecution of an application. The intention is to ensure that the effective life of a patent is not reduced below the old Act term of 17 years, even if the prosecution takes longer than 3 years.

The implications of the AIPA for the information specialist were reviewed in a symposium of the Chemical Information (CINF) of the American Chemical Society[1] in 2002.

▶ US PATENT DOCUMENTS

Application procedure

In common with other patent offices, an application for a patent in the United States is allocated a serial number on receipt. However, unlike other offices which usually recycle to number one at the start of each new year, US serial numbers are in blocks of approximately one million. On each occasion when it appears that, during the course of the current calendar year, there will be a need to allocate a serial number in excess of 999,999, the sequence reverts to 000,001. This means that, in recent decades, the same serial number has been given at approximately 8–10 year intervals. In order to distinguish between potentially conflicting serial numbers, the full citation of a US application number has two parts – a so-called "series code" which identifies the cycle, and the actual serial number itself. Table 10 shows the application number series which have been used so far for utility patents.

Table 10: US application number series codes

Series code	Start year	Final year
01	1915	1934
02	1935	1947
03	1948	1959
04	1960	1969
05	1970	1978
06	1979	1986
07	1987	1992
08	1993	1997
09	1997 (*)	2001
10	2001 (**)	2004 (#)

* Series 09 started on 30th December 1997, rather than 1st January 1998 as previous practice.
** Series 10 started on 5th December 2001, rather than 1st January 2002 as previous practice.
# Serial numbers allocated under series 10 were in excess of 750,000 by mid-2004, and a new series 11 was commenced, which runs concurrently with series 10 at the present time.

The series code is a necessary part of the input format for some search systems, but unfortunately is often lost in document citations. However, if the article or patent cites (a fictitious example) 'US patent application 345,678' and it is clear from the context that this is dated in the early 1980's, then reference to the above table or the more detailed concordance on the USPTO website at <http://www.uspto.gov/web/offices/ac/ido/oeip/taf/filingyr.htm> will confirm that this number must fall within series 06, and the correct citation would be 06/345678.

The application series code assumed additional importance from 1995, when the United States began using a provisional application system. This allows the applicant to lodge an 'informal' application, which is not required to be as complete as a conventional first filing. The provisional application must be converted into a regular utility patent filing within 12 months and – perhaps more importantly for information purposes – can be used to claim foreign priority under the Paris Convention. This means that the serial number from a US provisional application may appear on the front page of (for example) a European corresponding filing. The serial number, just like the regular numbers, ranges from 000,001 to just under one million, but the series code is 60. However, this creates potential for confusion if the series code is lost, either from the front page citation or any corresponding database records. In at least one year since 1995, the serial number portion of the provisional series 60 and the regular series 09/10 have been overlapping, and the only way of distinguishing documents is by determining which series is intended in the citation. Recently, some commercial databases have begun to reformat US provisional application numbers, using additional letters to distinguish the two series.

Examination, early publication and grant

The USPTO examiners are divided into subject-matter groups called Art Units, with each examiner within the Art Unit having responsibility for a specific area of technology. Newly received patent applications are classified and allocated to an Art Unit, where the process of examination commences. This includes a search by the examiner of the previous literature (patents and non-patents). Under the new US procedure, the processes of examining a patent and of publishing the specification as filed at 18 months operate in parallel. This contrasts with the process at (e.g.) the EPO where search and examination are strictly sequential, with no progress being made on examination until the search report has been published and the applicant has filed a request for examination.

As a consequence of these differences, there are distinct aspects of the US patent documentation which differ compared to other major systems. One difference, illustrated by the example in Table 11, shows that it is possible for the two publications to leap-frog one another. The normal sequence would be for the appearance of the unexamined publication as a Kind of Document US-A1, followed later by the granted patent, issued as a US-B2. However, if the examination time required for a particular application is less than 18 months, the first publication is the granted patent, which retains the –B suffix for grant, but distinguishes it by using a '1' meaning first publication. The corresponding unexamined publication may then publish a number of weeks or months after the grant, still using the

Table 11: US publication sequence

	As printed	Typical database entry
Pre-AIPA legislation		
US application	08/732,862 (15 Oct 1996)	1996US-0732862
US publication / grant	US 5,953,748 (14 Sep 1999)	US 5953748-A
Under AIPA – 'conventional' order		
US application	10/85,973 (28 Feb 2002)	2002US-0085973
US unexamined publication (pre-grant publication, PGP)	US 2003/0169420-A1 (4 Sep 2003)	US 2003169420-A1
US granted patent	US 6,839,103-B2 (4 Jan 2005)	US 6839103-B2
Under AIPA – 'reverse' order		
US application	09/454,725 (4 Dec 1999)	1999US-0454725
US granted patent – first publication	US 6,234,712-B1 (22 May 2001)	US 6234712-B1
US unexamined publication	US 2001/0028824-A1 (11 Oct 2001)	US 2001028824-A1

–A1 suffix. Note that the number formats for early publication and grant differ; the early published cases have a 4-digit year followed by a 7-digit serial number, which recycles to 0000001 every year, whereas the granted patents continue to be published in the running series, now around the 7,000,000 mark.

Under previous legislation, when there was only one publication, the granted patent bore the KD code US-A in the databases, although this was not actually printed on the front page of the documents for many years, and rarely used in contemporary discussions of US patent documentation.

In cases where the provisional application processes has been used, this data is captured at INID field (60) under the title "Related U.S. Application data". Depending upon the database, this earliest priority may be captured and searchable, or lost. If lost, the earliest searchable application data will be the regular US application based upon the earlier provisional, which appears at INID field (21). An example of this is shown in Figure 5.

One further major difference between the US and rest-of-the-world practice is in the area of search reports. These appear at INID field 56, entitled "References cited", but only on the granted patent, not on the US-A1 documents. As a consequence, the literature which appears on a US patent is, by definition, prior art which has failed to result in the rejection of the patent application. By contrast, the search report on an EP-A or GB-A

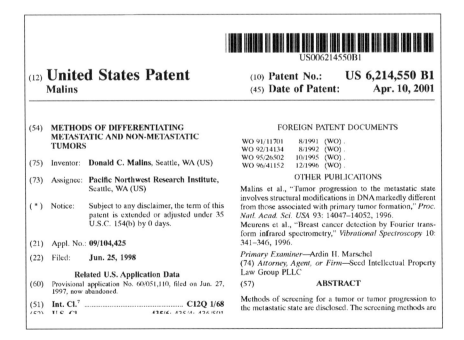

Figure 5: US front page showing provisional filing data (INID 60)

document is untested at the time of publication, and may result in the rejection or substantial modifications to the text of the granted patent. This difference in the purpose of the search reports for different documents can have important consequences when these data fields are used in citation searching. In recent years, it has been noticeable that US lists of references cited have increased in length and (according to anecdotal evidence) decreased in relevance. This is probably due in part to the requirement under US law to lodge an Information Disclosure Statement (IDS) as part of the application procedure. This is a list of all the relevant prior publications which the applicant knows about. Failure to disclose known relevant prior art is treated very severely by the USPTO, and as a consequence these IDS's tend to err on the side of generosity. Much, if not all, of the IDS is transferred to the list of 'References cited', which tends to dilute the precision of these lists and affect their usefulness for citation searching even more.

Prior to the new procedure under the AIPA, a small number of patent applications were published. The main schemes for these were the Statutory Invention Registration process and the so-called NTIS (National Technical Information Service) publications.

The Statutory Invention Registration process is a mechanism whereby a US applicant can request that the contents of their application are laid open to the public, even after the USPTO has indicated that they will not permit the granting of a patent on the same application. This procedure was useful if an inventor applied for a small incremental advance in technology, which may be insufficient to merit a patent in its own right, but nonetheless commercially important. The inventor, by deliberately laying open their invention, will ensure that the information is in the public domain and unpatentable in other jurisdictions as well. A Statutory Invention Registration document appears similar to a patent, but has none of the enforceable rights of a patent. They are published in a separately numbered series, with a KD code of –H. Since the introduction of 18-month publication from 2001, it is likely that this procedure will decrease in use, since applicants will be able to allow their case to publish as a US-A1 document and then withdraw from further processing of the case. An example of the header information from an S.I.R. is shown at Figure 6.

The second process of 'early publication' under the old legislation applied only to patent applications arising from Federally-funded research. In order to facilitate the process of licencing of any patents arising from such work, the patent applications were published prior to grant. The co-ordinating body for this was the well-established Department of Commerce NTIS, who already produced large numbers of US Government reports in regular series, and a corresponding bibliographic database. Patent applications published under this system were allocated a dummy US 'patent' number, which consisted of the application number preceded by the series

(19) **United States**
(12) **Statutory Invention Registration** (10) Reg. No.: **US H2074 H**
Lundquist et al. (43) **Published:** **Jul. 1, 2003**

US00H002074H

Figure 6: Title header of a US Statutory Invention Registration

code. For example, if application 345,678 in series 07 was published as an NTIS case, the dummy US number allocated would be 7345678. During the period from the 1960's to the 1980's, this system did not create any problems, but once the regular granted patent series exceeded around 6,000,000, it was possible to get conflicts, with the same apparent publication number being issued twice. As a result, commercial database producers have had to modify the number formats in order to distinguish between NTIS published applications and regular patent grants. Some have applied a dummy KD code of US-A0 (A-zero) to the NTIS cases, whilst others have used a letter N prefix and/or suffix to the publication number, e.g. USN 7532327-N. If an application which had been published under the NTIS scheme subsequently proceeded to grant, it would be allocated a proper grant number in the conventional sequence.

In addition to the NTIS series and the SIR series, a small number of applications were published under various procedures such as the Trial Voluntary Protest Program (TVPP), using the application number as a dummy publication number, with a B prefix, hence US B123456-A, and the Defensive Publication procedure (1969–1985), using a T- prefix. Further details on number formats and coverage for these minority document types can be found in the documentation produced by the commercial database producers such as Chemical Abstracts Service (CAS) and Thompson Scientific (for the WPI database). Searchers may also sometimes see reference to the publications of the Office of the Alien Property Custodian (APC). These were foreign-owned patents and pending applications confiscated during wartime by the US government. The bulk of documents relate to German and Japanese inventions seized during World War II. The information aspects of the APC's activities are dealt with in a detailed paper by White[2].

In the last few years, the USPTO has started to use the WIPO ST.50 corrections standard, which provides for new KD codes to be allocated to documents which correct earlier faulty publications. In the case of the US, two new KD codes are used: US-A8 for a republication of a front page of a specification, and US-A9 for the complete republication. Unfortunately, the USPTO has chosen to adopt a different practice to the EPO and WIPO on this standard. Instead of re-using the publication number and changing only the suffix, the US practice is to publish under a totally new number. This means that it is substantially more difficult to determine whether these correction documents have been produced. For example, the corrected version of US 2003/0003092-A1 is not US 2003/0003092-A9, as might be expected, but US 2004/0086498-A9.

Post-grant activities

Under the US system, there is no equivalent to the opposition procedure handled by the granting office, as in Europe. The majority of post-grant events surrounding patents will be handled by court action. However, a limited number of activities can take place in the life of the granted patent, which do result in a new or revised publication entering the bibliographic record.

The most common procedures are re-issue and re-examination. Under the re-issue procedure, the USPTO withdraws a granted patent which is in some way defective "through error without any deceptive intention", such as due to minor typographical errors or the like. A new document is issued in place of the old one, which is not permitted to contain any new subject matter. The new document totally replaces the original from the legal point of view, and the claims in the re-issue become the enforcable claims for the invention. A re-issue document has a new number, preceded by the letters Re, and a KD code of US-E. Although the majority of re-issue documents replace utility patents, they are occasionally issued to replace Design Patents or Plant Patents as well. Some example publication sequences are shown in Table 12.

By contrast to a re-issue, the re-examination process more commonly results in a substantive change in the subject matter protected by a patent. The re-examination process can be initiated by the Director of the USPTO or by a third party. This procedure is designed to address issues where "a substantial new question of patentability" has been raised in respect of

Table 12: US Re-issue publications

Application	Grant	Re-issue application	Re-issue
07/789,361 (8 Nov 1991)	US 5276208-A (4 Jan 1994)	08/324,620 (17 Oct 1994)	US Re 37,208-E (5 Jun 2001)
29/50,713 (23 Feb 1996)	US D378692 (1 Apr 1997)	29/102,729 (30 Mar 1999)	US Re 38,467-E (23 Mar 2004)**
746,477 (1 Dec 1976)	US PP 4,146 (8 Dec 1977)	878,330 (16 Feb 1978)	US Re 29,912-E (13 Feb 1979)

** Note : some database entries will change this prefix to US RD38467, but the actual printed document retains the Re prefix in common with re-issues of utility patents.

Table 13: Summary of current US KD codes

Code	Definition
A1	Publication of unexamined application (Pre-Grant Publication, or PGP)
A2	Re-publication of unexamined application
A9	Complete reprint of an A1 document (with new number)
B1	Publication of grant of patent without prior A1 publication
B2	Publication of grant of patent following prior A1 publication
C1, C2, C3	Re-examination certificate
E	Re-issue patent
H	Statutory Invention Registration
P1	Publication of unexamined Plant Patent application
P2	Granted Plant Patent without prior P1 publication
P3	Granted Plant Patent following prior P1 publication
P4	Re-publication of unexamined Plant Patent application
P9	Complete reprint of a P1 document
S	Design Patent

a granted patent. The new document which emerges after re-examination frequently has a different number of claims with different scope. Under the old (pre-AIPA) legislation, the re-examination certificate used the same number as the original patent, but changed the KD code to US-B. In the (rare) event of multiple re-examinations, US-B2, US-B3 etc. certificates could be issued. Once the AIPA procedure started, this KD code was needed for the normal granted sequence, so re-examinations from 2001 were allocated the code US-C1. Corresponding multiple re-examinations would result in US-C2, US-C3 etc. certificates. Since a re-issue document can itself be re-examined, it is possible to see combinations of prefixes and suffixes such as US Re 35,860-C1, which was a re-examination of US Re 35,860-E which was a re-issue of US 5352046-A (old Act).

It is worth pointing out that the USPTO only began to print the official KD code on its documents from January 2, 2001. Prior to this, although a plain-text designation of the type of document was included (e.g. the words 'Re-examination Certificate'), no code was included. Any bibliographic records prior to 2001 with KD codes will have been added by the database producer.

▶ DATABASES AND DATABASE-SPECIFIC ASPECTS

The main USPTO website can be found at <www.uspto.gov>, although some direct access web addresses are used for particular services within the site. Since the opening of the site, this has included some search capability.

Initially, two files were available, one of abstracts and second containing full texts. However, the former has now been removed and the full text version expanded. Since the introduction of pre-grant publications in the United States, a separate file containing the full texts of US-A documents has also been added to the website. In addition to the public web-based file, the USPTO has a public reading room in its headquarters outside Washington DC, from which it is possible to access an enhanced system called EAST (Examiner Automated Search Tool). This contains full text from 1920 to the present, including OCR scanning of the 1920–1970 segment. Since this service cannot be considered 'public' in quite the same sense as other electronic services, due to its restricted access means and times, it will not be considered further in this section.

There are substantial numbers of databases available on the internet which contain subsets of US data, usually dedicated to specific subject areas: examples include the DNA Patent Database (DPD), a collaborative project of Georgetown University and the Foundation for Genetic Medicine, available at <http://dnapatents.georgetown.edu/>, the US Department of Energy's patent database (part of its invention licensing programme) at <http://www.osti.gov/gencoun/search.easy.jsp> or the US National Agricultural Library (NAL) selection of biotechnology patents at <http://www.nal.usda.gov/bic/Biotech_Patents/>. The latter illustrates the problem with many of such sources – they do not tend to be updated as efficiently as the main USPTO site, and in the case of the NAL example, are missing several year's worth of data.

The USPTO's publication programme on optical disk operates under the CASSIS label, and produces a wide range of different products covering not just patents but trademarks. In recent years, much of this material has migrated to the internet site and the corresponding disk products have been discontinued. The programme is administered by the Office of Electronic Information Products, and current products and prices can be found at <http://www.uspto.gov/web/offices/cio/cis/pricelist.htm>. The newsletter "CASSIS Currents" is also useful to maintain awareness of the product range; this can be found via <http://www.uspto.gov/web/offices/ac/ido/oeip/catalog/products/cassis.htm> or the index at<http://www.uspto.gov/web/offices/ac/ido/oeip/cc/index.htm>.

In addition to many files based on 'first-level' data, the professional searcher should become familiar with the IFI Claims ® database. This was one of the earliest electronic databases covering US patents, and started life as an industry collaboration, before developing into the commercial product (now owned by the WoltersKluwer publishing organisation) which is now mounted on a range of commercial hosts. The coverage is most extensive for chemistry, and includes a range of value-added indexing. Coverage is from 1950 to the present day for chemistry, and from 1963 for electrical and mechanical patents. Design Patents are also included in the file, as well as the newer Pre-Grant Publications since 2001.

Table 14: United States patent databases

Producer	Service name	Platform	Coverage (#)
USPTO	eOG:P	http://www.uspto.gov/web/patents/patog/	Weekly Official Gazette data on new grants: current 52 weeks only
USPTO	Annual Index of Patents	DVD	Annual cumulation of bibliographic data on grants + image + exemplary claim
USPTO	Patents Full Text	http://www.uspto.gov/patft/index.html	US grants full text 1976+ US grants – number, class only, 1790–1975
USPTO	Applications Full Text	http://www.uspto.gov/patft/index.html	US pre-grant publications 2001+
USPTO	PAIR / IFW	http://portal.uspto.gov/external/portal/pair	Legal status and images of file wrappers
USPTO	Assignment Database	http://assignments.uspto.gov/assignments/q?db=pat	US patent assignment and re-assignment 1980+
USPTO	United States Patents – Granted; United States Patents – Applications	Delphion	US grants full text 1971+ US grants – images only, 1790–1969 US pre-grant publications full text 2001+
Micro Patent	US (Granted)	MicroPatent	US grants full text 1836+
Micro Patent/ USPTO	US (Applications)	MicroPatent	US pre-grant publications full text 2001+
EPO/ Micro Patent	MPI-INPADOC Plus	MicroPatent	US bibliographic data 1920+ (some 1859–1919)
USPTO/ Lexis	LEXPAT/XPAT; LEXPAT/OLDPAT; LEXPAT/CURPAT	LexisNexis	US grants; images 1790–1835, claims and abstracts 1836–1970, full text 1970+
USPTO	USPATFULL/ USPAT2	STN	US grants full text 1971+ (complete from 1976+); US pre-grant publications full text 2001+
IFI Claims	IFIPAT ; IFIREF ; IFICDB	STN	US grants (chemical) 1950+, (electrical/mechanical) 1963+ US pre-grant publications 2001+; bibliographic + claims
IFI Claims	IFIPAT ; IFIUDB ; IFICDB	Questel	US grants (chemical) 1950+, (electrical/mechanical) 1963+ US pre-grant publications 2001+; bibliographic + claims

Table 14: *continued*

Producer	Service name	Platform	Coverage (#)
USPTO	USPAT	Questel	US grants full text 1971+
USPTO	USAPPS	Questel	US pre-grant publications full text 2001+
IFI Claims	Claims/ US Patents (file 340); Claims/Uniterm (file 341); Claims/ Comprehensive (file 941)	Dialog	US grants (chemical) 1950+, (electrical/mechanical) 1963+ US pre-grant publications 2001+; bibliographic + claims
USPTO/ IFI Claims/ Dialog	US Patents Fulltext (files 652, 654)	Dialog	US grants full text 1971–75 (file 652) US grants full text 1976+ and US pre-grant publications full text 2001+ (file 654)
IFI Claims	Claims/Citation (files 220–222)	Dialog	Citations to US granted patents, 1790+ (citing document 1947+)
IFI Claims	Claims/US Patents (files 340, 341, 942)	Dialog	US grants (chemical) 1950+, (electrical/mechanical) 1963+ US pre-grant publications 2001+; bibliographic + claims
USPTO	Claims/Current Patent Legal Status (file 123)	Dialog	US post-issuance legal status
USPTO	US Patents	QPAT	US grants full text 1971+; US pre-grant publications full text 2001+

(#) Note: this listing does not include details of additional document kinds, such as re-examined patents, defensive publications, SIRs and reissue patents. Consult provider documentation for details.

The added value indexing in the CLAIMS file is based upon strictly controlled thesauri of general concepts, chemical names and patent assignees. The subject indexing is formalised into the so-called Uniterm system, which can be searched as text strings or corresponding numerical codes. The system provides extremely detailed subject retrieval capabilities, beyond what can be achieved by text searching in either applicants' or customised abstracts. Additional fragmentation coding for chemical structures is only available on a subscriber-only basis. The file is updated weekly with new material, and completely reloaded on an annual basis to incorporate changes in the US patent classification. A companion legal status file (CLAIMS/Current Patent Legal Status) is also available on the same hosts. One particularly useful, quasi-legal, feature in the main bibliographic file is the linking together of related divisionals, continuations and continuations-in-part via the standardised patent application number field. This facilitates quick retrieval of conceptually related documents which may be missed under some other forms of patent family search. The website for the file producer can be found at <http://www.ificlaims.com>.

The US patent information industry has involved many takeovers and mergers in recent years, including the acquisition of Corporate Intelligence's Patintelligence service by Information Holdings Inc. (IHI), the owners of MicroPatent, and the incorporation of Current Patents, Delphion and IHI itself into the Thomson Corporation.

▶ THE US PATENT CLASSIFICATION

Unlike virtually all other national patent offices, the USPTO has retained a fully-functional national classification. All US patents (and since 2001, all unexamined applications) bear the national classification on the front page, at INID code 52.

The US system at the time of writing has approximately 130,000 subdivisions (possible valid class marks), grouped within some 430 main classes. The notation system is mainly numerical, although some alphabetical suffixes are used after sub-classes. The notation 73/597, for example, refers to main class 73, sub-class 597. When included in patent databases, some reformatting may take place, to standardise the length of the field.

The system was started in 1836, and underwent its first revisions in 1898. In contrast to the IPC, the US system is updated much more rapidly, which makes it a very suitable tool for searching in areas of fast-moving technology. The drawback is that it is only applied to US documents, so any search with this system will be limited to only a portion of the prior art which a true patentability search requires.

There are a number of tools available for helping in the use of the system:

- Index to the US Patent Classification System – a broad, back-of-book style keyword index to assist users in identifying one or more candidate classes for a subject.
- The Manual of Classification – containing the full class schedules in a hierarchical fashion
- Classification Definitions – expanded scope notes and examples of the use of each class, with cross-references to related classes

Each of these tools is now available via the USPTO website, at the address <http://www.uspto.gov/go/classification/>. In addition, users may need to refer to the Classification Orders, which are printed instructions outlining the creation of a new class or the modification of a definition of an existing class. Unfortunately there is no central electronic index to these, although they can be obtained via the public search services at the USPTO once an

Order number has been identified. Issuance of new Classification Orders is noted in the Official Gazette.

A separate classification scheme exists for use with Design Patents. It is permissible for utility patents for inventions with an aesthetic element to them to be classified using the Design Classes, and likewise some Design Patents may carry utility patent classification as well as Design Classes. A Design classification has a D prefix to the number. The number and title of each of the utility classes as at January 2005 is given in Annex A. It is worth noting in particular that the system has developed in the class 700 series, to allow for recent trends in patenting of software and computer-assisted business methods within the United States. Neither the IPC nor corresponding classifications in Europe (ECLA) or Japan (FI) have been updated in this subject area, due to the differing patentability requirements under these jurisdictions. This does not, of course, means that valid prior art to software applications can only be found in previous US patents – merely that such prior art is somewhat more easy to locate.

▶ REFERENCES

1.   "Living with AIPA: Impact of the American Inventors' Protection Act after a year." Proc. Symposium of the Chemical Information (CINF) Division of the American Chemical Society, held at the 223rd National Meeting, Orlando, Florida, USA, 7–11 April 2002. Papers CINF 41–43, 48–52.

2.   "Patents for Victory: Disseminating enemy technical information during World War II". M. White. Science and Technology Libraries, **22**(1/2), 5–22 (2001).

4 The Japanese patent system

► HISTORY OF JAPANESE PATENTS

The modern patent system in Japan dates back to the Rules of Monopoly in 1871, shortly after the Meiji restoration of 1868. A trademark registration office was established by 1884, followed by a new patent law the following year. Modifications to the law were made at various times in the early twentieth century, with a substantial revision in 1959 and again in 1971. The latter brought in the deferred examination system, with early publication at 18 months. From the searcher's point of view, it is worth noting that a further revision in 1976 introduced patent protection for medicines and chemical products *per se* (as opposed to methods for their production) which had previously been excluded. Readers interested in following up details of earlier Japanese patents are referred to the work by Drazil[1]. A more modern guide, which focuses on the procedural stages, is published by the Japanese branch of the AIPPI (Association Internationale pour la Protection de la Propriété Intellectuelle), and it helpfully formats the discussion text in columns, parallel to the actual law provision covering that stage, allowing rapid cross-referencing. The most recent English edition appears to be from 1994, which will not incorporate some more recent law changes[2], although a related publication was produced in 2004[3].

Japan signed the Paris Convention in 1899, and joined the Patent Co-operation Treaty from the beginning, hence being able to be designated by this route from 1978. The standard country code for Japan is now 'JP', but prior to 1978 the code 'JA' was used, and may be still found in older printed material.

Japan has historically used a dating system based upon the Imperial calendar for all its official government documents, including patents. Since Japanese patents make use of dates both for recording filing details and as a component of the publication numbers themselves, it is worth getting familiar with this system from the beginning. The basic function is identical with the citation method for United Kingdom Acts of Parliament, which can be referred to according to the session of Parliament in which they were passed, which are in turn identified by the regnal year(s) of the monarch. Hence the old United Kingdom Patents Act 1949 can be cited as "12, 13 & 14 Geo. 6. c. 87", meaning chapter 87 of the Public & General Acts passed in the Parliament during the 12th, 13th and 14th years of the reign of George VI. The Japanese calendar system is similar, based upon the Emperor's regnal year.

During the modern period in Japan, there have only been four Emperors. Each is referred to in official documents by his Era name, rather than his personal one. Year one of the new Era commences when the Emperor accedes to the throne, and ends at December 31st of that year. This means, for example, that the final year of Hirohito's reign (Showa year 64) was actually only just over a week long, since he died on 8th January 1989. His son's first regnal year, commencing on 9th January, was thereby 51 weeks long. Table 15 indicates the Eras since the Meiji restoration.

Provided that a searcher knows the Western year coverage of a database, it is relatively straightforward to deduce which calendar is being used in the database records. For example, when using the JAPIO database, we know that coverage starts from 1976. Hence, a record which contains the year prefix 62 cannot be using the Western year 1962, but must refer to an Imperial year. Since only one Emperor has reached his 62nd regnal year during the period of the database, the document must have been published in Showa 62, corresponding to Western year 1987. The difficulty comes as databases expand to cover wider year ranges: for example, a publication with year 15 could refer to Heisei 15 (2003), Showa 15 (1940), Taisho 15 (1926) or even Western year 1915 in some circumstances.

There is an unfortunate added dimension to the case of Japanese patents, which occurred during the changeover in 1989 from Showa to Heisei. Although legal electronic records will show the year component of publication numbers reverting to Heisei 01 from 9th January, the printed documents continued to bear the Showa 64 year for the following three

Table 15: Japanese Imperial Era and calendar dates

Emperor Name	Era Name	Accession year (Western)	Abbreviation	Year range (Western)	Year range (Japanese)
Matsuhito	Meiji	1867		1867–1912	1–46
Yoshihito	Taisho	1912		1912–1926	1–15
Hirohito	Showa	1926	Sho. or S.	1926–1989	1–64
Akihito	Heisei	1989	Hei. or H.	1989–date	1–

months, until the changeover was completed on 11th April 1989. Hence, for example, JP 01–020000-A, published on 24th January 1989, actually has 64–020000-A printed on the front page, although retrievable by the correct legal number. Clearly this can cause problems in some document supply services if the actual and official numbers are not correctly matched.

▶ JAPANESE PATENT DOCUMENTATION AND RECENT LAW CHANGES

One striking aspect of Japanese patents is their quantity. Many thousands of unexamined applications are published each week, resulting in an annual output in excess of 400,000 documents per year. Some of this is due to legal differences – for many years, Japanese patent applications could only contain one claim, resulting in an inflated application and publication rate – and some of it is cultural. Japanese industry regards numbers of patent filings as a measure of research effort, and there are pressures similar to the academic 'publish or perish' syndrome. It has been estimated that up to one-third of the entire annual growth in the Chemical Abstracts Service (CAS) bibliographic file is due to new Japanese patent applications in the field of chemistry. Since CAS only abstract the first family member, this only accounts for unexamined applications, and in a restricted subject field. To get the full picture, we need to consider that over 2,000 cases are granted per week in Japan, adding a further 120,000 documents to the bibliographic record, together with a smaller number of utility models. It can be seen that Japanese documents are adding considerable volumes of technical knowledge to the state-of-the-art, which need to be consulted in order to establish patentability in other parts of the world, despite the language difficulties. Some of the key databases which assist this process will be discussed in later sections.

Normal progress to grant

The main sequences of publication under the pre-1995 legislation and at the present day are illustrated in Table 16 below. For filings up to 1st January 1996, the normal route was for an unexamined case to be published (with KD code A) around 18 months after priority filing. This is often referred to as the 'Kokai' stage, after the Japanese language designation. The applicant had up to 7 years in which to defer the search and examination, which meant that the second stage publication (JP-B, the 'Kokoku') frequently did not appear until well after the grant in most other countries. This second stage was the examined specification, but was not yet granted. Both of these stages had a publication number with the Emperor year prefix, but unlike (e.g.) the European Patent Office system, the same number was not retained between the publication stages. In any given year, the same serial number 12345 could be applied to the 18-month stage of one invention and the examined stage of an earlier-filed one. To distinguish for document delivery purposes, it is therefore necessary to know the KD code of the required document.

Following publication as an examined case, it was open for a period of 3 months of 'pre-grant opposition', during which the final grant could be opposed by a third party. If no such opposition occurred, a grant certificate was issued. This certificate had a third publication number, in a continuous running sequence. Few databases collated the information on this third stage – the European Patent Office's internal EPODOC search file was one exception, and other databases which draw upon these data (such as Questel's PlusPat file).

After 1995, the system of pre-grant opposition was abolished, and the grant and publication of examined documents were near-simultaneous. The granted publication is the 'Toroku' stage, replacing the earlier

Table 16: Japanese patent publication stages and number formats

	As printed	*Typical database entry*
Pre-1995 legislation		
Japanese application	58–188564 (11 Oct, Showa 58 (1983))	1983JP-0188564
Japanese unexamined publication	JP 59–88455-A (22 May 1984)	JP 59–080455-A2
Japanese examined publication	JP 3–37541-B2 (5 Jun 1991)	JP 03–037541-B4
Japanese registration	JP 1674848-B	JP 1674828-C
After 1995		
Japanese application	63–331710 (27 Dec, Showa 63 (1988))	1988JP-0331710
Japanese unexamined publication	JP 2–174499-A (5 Jul 1990)	JP 02–174499-A1
Japanese granted publication	JP 2764982-B2 (published 11 Jun 1998, grant date 3 Apr 1998)	JP 2764982-B2
After 2000		
Japanese application	11–142970 (24 May, Heisei 11 (1999))	1999JP-0142970
Japanese unexamined publication	JP 2000–327531-A (28 Nov 2000)	JP 2000–327531-A1
Japanese granted publication	JP 3500421-B2 (published 23 Feb 2004, grant date 12 Dec 2003	JP 3500421-B2

Figure 7: Japanese publication and grant dates

'Kokoku', and the number format changed to a running sequence, which started at 2,500,001 dated 29 May 1996, with a KD code of B2. Technically, there is a post-grant opposition period which dates from the publication of the granted specification, but the actual date of grant is some weeks earlier. Note in Figure 7 the different dates associated with the two INID codes concerned: field (45) represents the date of publication of the granted patent, but the date from which the patent rights have effect is shown at field (24), in this case some 2 months earlier.

After the year 2000, there were two further changes to the system. Firstly the Emperor's year was dropped as the prefix to the unexamined stage publication number, in favour of a 4-digit Western year. The Japanese form of the year is however still retained for the application numbers. Secondly, the deferment period was reduced from seven years to three.

Japanese B1 publications

In addition to the 'conventional' route to publication, proceeding from JP-A1 to JP-B2, small numbers of patent applications in Japan make use of an accelerated examination process. This has the effect of passing over the early published stage at 18 months and proceeding directly to the granted document, which is given the code JP-B1. The details of the process were described by O'Keefe[4] in 2000, reviewing the effects since the law change in 1996. According to this article, cases which publish as a JP-B1 will never appear in the Patent Abstracts of Japan (PAJ) file, which is devoted to published unexamined applications (JP-A documents), and hence may be missed in a search of Japanese prior art unless additional sources are consulted. The Derwent WPI file and INPADOC are two sources which capture these additional records. However, there is some evidence that even when cases are granted rapidly via this route, a corresponding Kokai is still produced. In the example in Table 17, the grant stage was published in August 2000, only 15 months after filing, but the corresponding Kokai appeared as expected 3 months later, at 18 months from filing.

The user should note that there are some special aspects to the numbering system applied to Japanese patent documents re-published under the PCT system; more details of these can be found in the user documentation on the Patolis web-site.

Table 17: A Japanese accelerated examination process in chronological order

	Number	Date
Japanese application	11–134723	14 May 1999 (Heisei 11)
Japanese registration	JP 3076559-B1	14 Aug 2000 (publication), 9 Jun 2000 (in force)
Japanese unexamined publication	JP 2000–316501-A	21 Nov 2000

The importance of utility models

Japanese law allowed application for utility models from 1905, and until a significant law change in 1994 they formed a substantial part of the body of intellectual property literature emerging from Japan. Although designed to protect only small innovative developments, they were examined just as the main patent system, and had a term of approximately 15 years. Since the law change, in which the examination phase was dropped and the term reduced to 6 years, they have become much less popular as a protection tool and numbers of utility model applications have fallen significantly in

Table 18: Japanese utility model publication stages and number formats

	As printed	Typical database entry
Pre-1994 legislation		
Japanese utility model application	54–61418 (8 May, Showa 54 (1979))	1979JP-U61418
Japanese unexamined utility model	JP 55–162379-U (21 Nov 1980)	JP 55–162379-U
Japanese examined utility model	JP 60–15427-Y2	JP 60–015427-Y
Japanese registration	JP 1621538-U	Not recorded
Cases filed after 1994		
Japanese application	16–172 (19 Jan, Heisei 16 (2004))	2004JP-U00172
Japanese granted utility model (no examination)	JP 3102877-U (published 15 Jul 2004, grant date 28 Apr 2004)	JP 3102877-U
Cases pending in 1994		
Japanese application	2–401403 (21 Dec, Heisei 2 (1990))	1990JP-U401403
Japanese unexamined utility model	JP 4–91338-U1 (10 Aug 1992)	JP 04–091338-U1
Japanese granted utility model	JP 2500002-Y2 (published 5 Jun 1996, grant date 21 Feb 1996)	JP 2500002-Y

recent years. In response to this, a further law change in 2005 has increased the term again, to 10 years from filing, but this will not affect pending cases.

The sequence of publication under the pre-1994 legislation and at the present day are illustrated in Table 18 above. The number format for the old Act sequence followed that for patents closely. However, under the new system, there is only a single publication, which takes place a few months after filing and runs in a single continuous series from 3,000,001 upwards. Since it is unexamined, it retains the conventional first level publication code of U. Cases which were pending when the 1994 legislation entered into force were still examined as under the old system, but the Y2 stage was abolished in favour of a single examined/registered document, with numbers starting at 2,500,001 as for the patents.

▶ DATABASES AND DATABASE-SPECIFIC ASPECTS

This section will discuss a number of databases which contain only Japanese information. For multi-country databases which include Japan within their coverage, refer to Chapter 7.

The main JPO website can be found at <www.jpo.go.jp/index.htm>. Large portions of the site are available in English, for non-Japanese speaking users.

Although the situation has changed markedly in recent years, it is still the case that substantial numbers of information services covering Japanese patent documents operate solely in Japanese. For the non-Japanese speaker/reader, such services are effectively invisible, and it can be quite difficult to obtain information about the content and range of search facilities available. The following Table is not therefore a comprehensive survey of all available Japanese sources, but concentrates upon those which have at least some English-language elements to them.

The major domestic patent database suppliers are the JAPIO (Japan Patent Information Organization) and the Patolis Corporation, both of which are well-known outside Japan as well. The Japan Patent Data Service Co. <www.jpds.co.jp> is less recognised, although it operates the JP-NET internet service, in Japanese, <www.jprom.co.jp> with a comprehensive range of publications available. Unlike the other two services, JP-NET requires an additional browser plug-in before the web service can be used.

The Patolis Corporation provides a range of services based upon JPO data, in addition to the main search site in Japanese and English. This includes back-files in CD-ROM formats compatible with the main JPO disk series. The English-language web search interface, Patolis-e, provides bibliographic searching, search report citations and additional legal status compared to the free JPO site. Additional technical keywords and deep

Table 19: Japanese patent databases

Producer	Service name	Platform	Coverage
JAPIO	Patent Abstracts of Japan	Internet (*) Command line (**) CD-ROM/DVD	See Table 20 ; JP-A abstracts only
Patolis Corporation	PATOLIS-E	Internet	JP-A 1955+ JP-U 1960+
Japan Patent Data Service	JP-NET	Internet	JP-A 1993+ JP-B 1994+ Legal status 1989+
Japanese Patent Office	Patent Gazette	JPO website	JP-A 1971+ JP-B 1922+
Japanese Patent Office	Utility Model Gazette	JPO website	JP-U 1971+ JP-Y 1922+
Japanese Patent Office	Patent Concordance	JPO website	Applications from 1921+
Japanese Patent Office	Utility Model Concordance	JPO website	Applications from 1913+
Paterra Inc.	Protys (#)	Internet	JP-A full-text (rolling file, most recent 5 weeks); current awareness tool

(*) via esp@cenet, Delphion, JPO
(**) via STN (file JAPIO), Questel-Orbit (file JAPIO), Dialog (file 347), MicroPatent
(#) this service has been temporarily withdrawn as of early 2005; the parent web-site is <www.paterra.com>

indexing are applied by the database producer. These are listed in the Patolis Search Guide, which is a free-of-charge resource on many aspects of Japanese documentation, and is available at <http://search.p4.patolis.co.jp/search_en.html>. The main Patolis-e interface is at <http://www.p4.patolis.co.jp/patolis-e.html>.

Some additional aspects of Japanese document searching have been discussed in the regular "East meets West" conferences held by the EPO's Japanese information section. Proceedings of these meetings are distributed via the website at <http://www.european-patent-office.org/epidos/conf/jpinfo/>.

The Patent Abstracts of Japan (PAJ) service is by far the best known source of English-language material covering the Japanese patent system. However, it is available in a number of different editions, not all being updated to the full file content. The policy on coverage changed during the life of the database, and not all hosts have loaded the missing data which have been subsequently released by the JAPIO Corporation. There are two significant changes in the coverage, both being implemented in 1989. The first was the decision to include all published JP-A documents, irrespective of origin. During the period 1976–1989, English abstracts were only

Table 20: Subject coverage of PAJ

IPC class / sub-class	Coverage start year
Chemical sections	
A01 (excluding A01N: Preservation of bodies of humans or animals or plants or parts thereof; biocides e.g. as disinfectants, as pesticides, as herbicides; pest repellants or attractants; plant growth regulators)	1989
A01N	1976
A21, A22, A23, A24, A41, A42, A43, A44, A45, A46, A47	1989
A61 (excluding A61K: Preparations for medical, dental or toilet purposes)	1989
A61K	1976
A62, A63	1989
B01	1976
B02	1989
B03, B04, B05	1976
B06, B07, B08	1989
B09	1976
C01, C02, C03	1976
C04, C05, C06	1989
C07, C08, C09, C10	1976
C11	1989
C12	1976
C13, C14	1989
C21, C22, C23, C25, C30	1976
D01	1976
D02, D03, D04, D05	1989
D06 (excluding D06N : Wall, floor or like covering materials e.g. linoleum, oil-cloth, artificial leather, roofing felt, consisting of a fibrous web coated with a layer of macromolecular material; flexible sheet material not otherwise provided for)	1989
D06N	1976
D07, D21	1989
Physical / Electrical sections	
G01, G02, G03, G04, G05, G06	1976
G07, G08, G09, G10	1989
G11	1976
G12, G21	1989
H01 (excluding H01F, J, L, M, P, Q and S)	1989
H01F, H01J, H01L, H01M, H01P, H01Q, H01S	1976
H02 (excluding H02K, M, N and P)	1989
H02K, H02M, H02N, H02P	1976
H03, H04	1976
H05 (excluding H05G: X-ray technique)	1989
H05G	1976

Table 20: *continued*

IPC class / sub-class	Coverage start year
General / Mechanical sections	
B21, B22, B23, B24	1976
B25, B26	1989
B27 (excluding B27N: Manufacture by dry processes of articles, with or without organic binding agents, made from particles or fibres consisting of wood or other lignocellulosic or like organic material)	1989
B27N	1985 (*)
B28	1989
B29, B30	1976
B31, B32	1989
B41	1976
B42, B43, B44	1989
B60	1976
B61	1989
B62 (excluding B62D: Motor vehicles; trailers)	1989
B62D	1976
B63	1976
B64	1989
B65 (excluding B65G and H)	1989
B65G, B65H	1976
B66, B67, B68	1989
E01	1989
E02	1976
E03, E04, E05, E06, E21	1989
F01, F02, F03, F04, F15	1976
F16 (excluding F16C, D, F, G, H, J, K and N)	1989
F16C, F16D, F16F, F16G, F16H, F16J, F16K, F16N	1976
F17	1976
F21, F22	1989
F23	1976
F24	1976
F25, F26, F27	1989
F28	1976
F41, F42	1989

(*) sub-class B27N was introduced with the 4th edition of the IPC from 1st January 1985. Some subject material in the new sub-class was previously classified under sub-class B29J, which was included in JAPIO from 1976.

produced for cases originating within Japan; all other publications deriving from Convention filings into Japan from elsewhere in the world were assumed to have published in at least one Western language, and hence substantially more accessible than the domestically-filed applications.

The second major change was one of subject selection. Between 1976–1989, only a subset of JP-A documents was chosen for abstracting, based upon the primary IPC sub-class. This was biased to select mainly chemical and some electrical patents, leaving substantial numbers of mechanical cases not abstracted and missing from the database. There do not appear to be any plans to create a back file to fill in these gaps. Table 20 shows the breakdown according to IPC on coverage; for definitions of the IPC classes, refer to Annex C.

It is worth pointing out that all Japanese-language sources which have been translated into English suffer from the same weakness, namely the difficulty of transliterating from Japanese characters into Western letters. For the searcher, this is a particular problem when attempting to search on names, such as assignee or inventor fields. The level of inconsistency in rendering Japanese personal names into English is such that the JPO has taken the decision to remove this field from its search files altogether. Similarly, the Derwent World Patent Index file did not record Japanese inventors at all until 2005. For more information on the challenges facing the Japanese translator, see the paper by Huby et al.[5].

▶ THE JAPANESE PATENT CLASSIFICATION AND INDEXING SYSTEMS

For a substantial part of the twentieth century, Japan used its own system of patent classification to assist retrieval. By 1969, this was based upon 136 classes (not all introduced from the beginning) using a numerical system, with further alphanumeric suffixes. For example, Figure 8 shows the front page of a 1970 granted patent, with a range of classification marks drawn from group 16 (Organic Compounds). They appear under the INID code 52 at the top left of the front page.

The Japanese classification was phased out from the early 1970's in favour of the International Patent Classification (IPC). However, this soon became insufficient for the JPO's searching needs, and was supplemented by two further subject retrieval schemes. The FI (File Index) classification is based upon the IPC but elaborates it further, while the F-Term (File Forming Term) indexing codes are used in some areas of technology to provide an enhanced multi-dimensional retrieval. Since both of these systems are essentially in-house, the corresponding codes have not been printed on the front pages of the patent documents until quite recently (2001 for FI classes). Relatively few public search systems provide access

Figure 8: Japanese national classification (INID field 52)

using these systems, and most search files are still limited to the IPC. However, in recent years there has been a resurgence in interest in these detailed systems, and a variety of Western databases, such as PlusPat and Chemical Abstracts, have either implemented them or are investigating how to do so. Search systems such as Patolis, produced within Japan, have contained these search features for a longer time range. In the case of Patolis, the English-language interface Patolis-E is providing more Western searchers with their first exposure to FI and F-terms. Some more information on FI is provided in Chapter 12.

For further background on the old Japanese national classification, users are referred to the books by Drazil[1] and Finlay[6]. The main structure of the JPO system as at 1969, shortly before it started to be phased out in favour of the IPC, is shown in Annex B. The system was abandoned in 1980.

▶ REFERENCES

1. "Guide to the Japanese and Korean patents and utility models". J.V. Drazil. London: British Library, Science Reference Library, 1976. ISBN 0–9029–1421–9.
2. "Guide to Industrial Property in Japan". Tokyo: AIPPI Japan and the Japanese Patent Office, 1994.
3. "Japanese Laws Relating to Industrial Property". Tokyo: AIPPI Japan, 2004. Two loose-leaf volumes.
4. "Japanese submarine patents: examined patents within a year of filing!" M. O'Keeffe. World Patent Information **22**(4), 283–286 (2000).
5. "Some problems in the translation of Japanese patents." R. Huby; V.T. Schenk. World Patent Information **16**(3), 154–158 (1994).
6. "Guide to foreign-language printed patents and applications." I.F. Finlay. London: Aslib, 1969. ISBN 0–85142–001-X.

5 Major national and regional patent systems

▶ NATIONAL SYSTEMS

Canada

Historical aspects and current law

The Canadian patent system is relatively unusual amongst major patent offices, in that its publications reflect the bilingual nature of Canada itself. All bibliographic data are identified in both English and French, and a small proportion of Canadian patents have the entire specification written in French.

The first true Canadian patent system was not formed until 1869, shortly after the British North America Act 1867, under which the Dominion of Canada was created. Prior to this date, various of the individual provinces – New Brunswick, Nova Scotia, Newfoundland, Prince Edward Island, Upper and Lower Canada – had their own patent laws and published patent specifications or numerical lists of patents. The province of Newfoundland retained some independent legislation until as recently as 1949, at least in the area of trademarks.

For much of the twentieth century, Canada's patent legislation and publication sequence was modelled closely upon that of the United States. A single document was published after substantive examination and grant, and the term of 17 years was calculated from the date of publication. Canada also used the 'first to invent' system, equivalent to that of the United States, and still maintains a 'grace period' system. This means that an inventor can disclose their invention in public within Canada up to 12 months before they file their application, without losing their Canadian rights. However, such disclosure will prejudice their applications outside of Canada in countries which do not recognise this grace period.

Canada is a long-term signatory to the Paris Convention, having signed in 1925, but was relatively late amongst major industrial countries in joining the Patent Co-operation Treaty, not becoming a member state until January 1990. Around the same period – 1989 – there was a major revision of domestic legislation which affected patent granting and publication. This introduced the 'first-to-file' system, but retained the general 12-month grace period. The standard country code for Canada is 'CA'.

Patent applications filed in Canada after 1st October 1989 are treated under a deferred examination system with dual publication. The specification is published unexamined at 18 months after national filing (or from priority if claiming it), and is allocated a number in the 2,000,000 series. Pre-1989 filings had reached approximately 1,300,000, so there is a break in the sequence where the new law becomes the predominant publishing mechanism.

After filing, an applicant may request a search and examination at any point up to 5 years later – this was reduced in 1996, from the original seven-year deferment under the 1989 legislation. From an information point of view, this means that Canadian applications can appear inactive for a substantial period after the publication of the unexamined document, yet still have the potential to proceed to grant. Careful checking of the legal status is required before assuming that an application has lapsed or been withdrawn. Since the 1989 legislation, renewal fees (annuities) have been payable to maintain Canadian patents in force after grant. Unlike the United States, Europe and Japan, at the time of writing Canada does not provide for extension of patent term for pharmaceuticals or agrochemicals.

A further similarity with the United States system was the persistence of a national classification system. After the new law in 1989, this was gradually phased out, and modern Canadian specifications carry only the International Patent Classification. However, the Canadian system has been retained as a searchable field in the databases mounted on the Canadian Patent Office website, and it is still of use for retrieving older specifications.

National patent documentation

Prior to the introduction of the 1989 publication sequence, granted Canadian patent documents did not carry Kind-of-Document (KD) codes, since they were only published once. However, for the sake of uniformity, various of the major databases assigned a dummy code A. Re-issue documents carried a KD code of E on the published version, but the same databases assigned a code B to them, reflecting the fact that they were second-stage publications after grant.

When the new system was developed, the published documents began to be assigned an official code A, which was potentially confusing with the existing dummy database form. Consequently, some databases assigned a second dummy code, this time AA, to distinguish new Act A documents from their old Act counterparts. The documents can also be distinguished by the range of their publication number – new Act documents are always greater than CA 2000001. Applications which proceed to grant carry a KD code of C on their front page, and also in the database record.

One particular aspect of Canadian documents is worth noting. Since the accession to the Patent Co-operation Treaty (PCT), an international application has been capable of maturing into a national filing and – subject to national examination – a granted Canadian patent. The PCT is a major entry route into the Canadian system, and a substantial proportion of the unexamined cases published each week represent transfers from the PCT. During the early years of Canada's membership of the PCT, there were no announcements in the *Canadian Patent Office Record* to show that these cases had entered Canada. Consequently, a number of major database producers, such as the Derwent World Patent Index (WPI) file, failed to pick up this data in order to add the Canadian members to the file's family system. Searchers should note that it is often necessary to supplement family searches with a separate interrogation of the Canadian national data in order to locate the corresponding Canadian member.

Table 21: Canadian patent databases

Producer	Service name	Platform	Coverage
CIPO	Canadian Patents Database	Internet ; via main CIPO website	Granted patents 1920–1978 (bibliographic only) Granted patents 1978+ (bibliographic, claims and abstracts and page images) Unexamined applications 1989+ (bibliographic, claims and abstracts and page images) Legal status and post-grant actions also available
CIPO	Canadian Patent Office Record	Internet ; via main CIPO website	PDF version of weekly Gazette, available since 1999. Annual indexes also available
CIPO	Patent Documents on CD-R	CD-ROM (MIMOSA compatible)	Granted patents 2000+ (bibliographic and abstracts + page images) Unexamined applications 1999+ (bibliographic and abstracts + page images)
CIPO	Patent Documents on CD-R	CD-ROM back-file	Bibliographic data only, 1978–2000 ; annual, monthly or weekly updates by subscription
Health Canada	Patent Register	Internet <www.patentregister.ca/>	Selective coverage of Canadian patents protecting pharmaceuticals; in-force patents only

Databases and database-specific aspects

Canada was one of the earliest national patent offices to load a substantial amount of its back-file of documents onto the internet. Whilst many offices tended to limit their offering to the most recent few years, Canada opted to digitise the entire backfile to 1920, and this is available from the website. The main website for the Canadian Intellectual Property Office (CIPO) is found at <http://www.cipo.gc.ca>. The site is bilingual throughout.

France

Historical aspects and current law

France has had a patent system since 1791, shortly after the French Revolution, and patents of importation (allowing a French citizen to have rights over the importation into France of an invention patented elsewhere) were introduced by a Napoleonic decree of 1810. There were further modifications of the law in 1844 and again in 1901 when the patent office (today the *Institut National de la Propriété Industrielle*, or INPI) was founded. The term of a patent was modified from 5, 10, 15 and eventually to 20 years.

Until a major revision of the law in 1968, French patent applications were not examined for novelty and did not include any claims as such. Cases were only examined for unity of invention, and normally granted around 9 months after filing. Abridgements were published around 1 month after grant, and specifications published around 3 months later. This process meant that effective decisions on patent protection could only be decided after the issue of the document, by means of court action. Prior to 1968, the only applications subject to search were a special series of documents covering pharmaceuticals, the *Brevet Spécial de Médicament* or BSM series. These were issued between 1961 and approximately 1973, after which time such applications were handled under the normal law.

The 1968 legislation required the inclusion of claims in an application, and also introduced utility models into the French system. These are termed *certificat d'utilité* and use a different KD code to distinguish them, but are published in the same numerical series as regular patents. Their term is 6 years. Under the normal patent application procedure, a request for a search report must be filed within 18 months of the priority, but if no such request is received, the patent application is automatically transformed into an application for a *certificat d'utilité*.

The current legislation is the Intellectual Property Code, which dates from 1992 and 1995. This uses a so-called Search Report procedure. Following issue of the search report compiled by the French Patent Office, the applicant has three months in which to either file new claims or submit arguments showing why the claims should be retained as originally filed. If no reply is received, the application may be rejected for "manifest lack of novelty". After the deadline for response to the search report, the patent is granted and published. This search report procedure is not properly speaking an examination, and except in cases of manifest lack of novelty, the patent is always granted and with the claims last filed by the applicant.

French patents are valid in the mainland of France, plus the Overseas Départments and territories of Réunion, New Caledonia, French Polynesia, Saint-Pierre and Miquelon, Wallis and Futuna, and the French Southern and Antarctic Territories.

As with Italy, France instituted a supplementary protection certificate system (known in French as the Certificat Complémentaire de Protection, or CCP) under a national law of 1990, which pre-dated the EU legislation. Term extensions for pharmaceuticals were available under the national law between 1990 and 1992, and allowed a maximum 7-year extension, or a term of 17 years from marketing authorisation. The EU legislation replaced this system from 1993, allowing only a maximum 5-year extension.

In 1977, France became a founder member of the European Patent Office. As with many of the national patent offices of the member states, the advantage of the parallel EPO procedure made a significant impact upon the numbers of applications being filed in France under the national system. An approximate measure of the balance between the two systems shows that in any given year, applications filed at the EPO designating France, plus applications filed under the PCT designating France via the EPO route, come to around 100,000 cases, whereas direct national filings are fewer than 20,000. France is one of a number of EPO countries which has not permitted applicants to use the PCT route to enter its national patent system directly. It has opted to 'close the national route'. An applicant wishing to obtain patent protection in France via the PCT must do so by designating an EPO application covering France.

France was a founder signatory to the Paris Convention, as it entered into force in 1884. It is also a founder member of the European Patent Office, from 1977, and joined the Patent Co-operation Treaty system in 1978. The standard country code for the France is 'FR'.

National patent documentation

Applications filed in the French national system may be deposited in Paris, or at a number of regional centres (Lille, Nancy, Strasbourg, Lyon, Grenoble, Sophia Antipolis, Marseille, Toulouse, Bordeaux, Nantes, Rennes or Baie-Mahault in the Overseas Département of Guadeloupe). These centres can receive documents and allocate an application number.

Under the current legislation, France publishes its patent applications at 18 months, as an FR-A1 document (*Demande de Brevet*), followed by the granted patent using the same number but with the suffix changed, as an FR-B1 grant (*Brevet*). An application for a utility model is numbered in the same series, but with a code FR-A3 (*Demande de certificat d'utilité*), which is followed if granted by the grant FR-B3 (*Certificat d'utilité*). The current publication number series commenced at FR 2,000,001 when the 1968 legislation came into force, and is currently around the 2,800,000 mark (number FR 2857556-A1 published in January 2005). The old BSM series mentioned above used a distinct KD code of FR-M.

Contrary to common practice, the French Patent Office recommends the use of the application number, or *numéro d'enregistrement national* found at INID 21, for the purposes of document ordering, rather than the conventional *numéro de publication* at INID 11. Bibliographic databases usually give prominence to the latter. The front page of a recent FR-A1 document showing both fields is at Figure 9.

Databases and database-specific aspects

The French Patent Office has chosen to develop some internet-based tools independently of the EPO-wide esp@cenet service. Consequently, the expected file of national patents under the address <http://fr.espacenet.com> is not the preferred route to access French documents – this provides access to the Worldwide file instead. The main search engine, Plutarque, is accessible via the main INPI website or directly from <http://www.plutarque. com>. This gives access to a range of search services, including patents, trade marks, designs and models, but only the most recent two years-worth of data (FR, EP and WO documents) are freely accessible. Prior registration is required to access the larger back-files, which contain abstracts and page images. Viewing the full text is a chargeable extra feature.

A feature of the Plutarque system is its use of natural language input to derive IPC class marks, which are presented to the user as alternative search terms.

Figure 9: Front page data – French unexamined publication

Table 22: French patent databases

Producer	Service name	Platform	Coverage
INPI	Plutarque	Internet	FR-A 1966+ EP-A 1978+ WO-A 1978+
INPI	FRANCEPAT	STN	FR-A bibliographic data 1966+, abstracts and images 1978+ FR-M 1961–1978 Legal status including SPC data 1969+
Univentio	FRFULL	STN	FR-A full text 1980+
INPI	FRPATENT (*)	Questel	FR-A bibliographic data 1966+, abstracts and images 1978+ FR-M 1961–1978 Legal status including SPC data 1969+
INPI/ Univentio	FRFULL	Questel	FR-A full text 1980+
INPI	File 371	Dialog	FR-A bibliographic data 1966+, abstracts and images 1978+ FR-M 1961–1978 Legal status including SPC data 1969+
INPI/EPO/ MicroPatent	French Published Applications	MicroPatent	FR-A bibliographic data and full text 1971+, images 1992+
INPI	BREF	CD-ROM/ DVD	FR-A 1966+ ; EP-A 1978+ ; WO-A 1978+ (bibliographic data only)
INPI	COSMOS-A	CD-ROM/ DVD	FR-A full page images 1989+
INPI	COSMOS-B	CD-ROM/ DVD	FR-B full page images 2000+ (MIMOSA compatible)
INPI	Bulletin Officiel de la Propriété Industrielle (BOPI)	Internet	Weekly PDF format of Gazette with indexes

(*) the same file is also loaded on the QPAT platform

The early disk-based products from INPI were developed outside of the EPO's PATSOFT/MIMOSA programme, and are incompatible with these application packages. The most recent offering, COSMOS-B, is MIMOSA compatible.

Germany

Historical aspects and current law

The modern state of Germany was not formed until the Reich was proclaimed in 1871 at Versailles, in the aftermath of the Franco-Prussian war. The first patent law for the entire country was in force by 1877, replacing the patent systems of the constituent kingdoms and principalities which made up the new country. Many of these had already passed patent laws, such as Prussia (1815), Bavaria (1825), Württemberg (1836) and Saxony (1843). The German act initially provided for a term of 15 years, revised in 1936 to 18 years.

Patents were granted in an essentially continuous numbered sequence until the Patent Office was closed in 1945, having reached approximately 768,000. A new law was enacted in 1949 and publication resumed at number 800,001 from 1950. These documents were termed *Erteilten* or *Patentschriften*, and the document type was sometimes designated by PS. A new system allowing pre-grant opposition was brought in from 1957, causing another jump in the numbering, to 1000001. Under this system, documents were published twice; initially as an *Auslegeschrift*, examined but not yet granted and open to a 3 month period of pre-grant opposition. After any opposition proceedings, the document was republished as a granted patent, the *Patentschrift*. Although it is not much help to the present-day searcher, these documents could be distinguished by the colour of paper; *Auslegeschriften* were printed on pale green paper and *Patentschriften* on white. In cases where the opposition proceedings had caused a change in content between the two documents, the granted patent bore an endorsement "*Weicht ab von Auslegeschrift*" or "*Patentschrift weicht von der Auslegeschrift ab*".

Germany used a national patent classification from the late 1800's until it was replaced by the IPC in 1975. A number of other countries, including Austria and Denmark, utilised the same or a slightly modified system.

With the proclamation of the German Democratic Republic on 7th October 1949, a new patent law for East Germany was promulgated in 1950. The country continued to grant its own forms of patent documents until the re-unification effective 3rd October 1990. The so-called Extension Act of 1992 allowed for patent applications filed in either of the two former countries prior to re-unification to be extended to have effect in the entire territory.

As noted above, many patent offices started to experience difficulties with backlogs during the 1960's, and Germany swiftly adopted the deferred examination model pioneered by the Dutch. Applications filed after 1st October 1968 were allocated a new form of application number, starting at 18 00001, which the document carried through all the stages of examination and publication. The publication number retained an appearance similar to the old continuous series, but in fact was a discontinuous system. The publication number was preserved throughout all stages, and retained the same format as the application number, which was in two parts; the first two digits were the calendar year of application minus 50, hence publication number DE 20 04000-A was the first publication stage based upon the 4000th application filed in 1970. The new publication stage, the unexamined application (*Offenlegungsschrift*), was laid open at 18 months after priority, and printed on yellow-brown paper. It was possible to defer both search and examination for a period of 7 years. In 1976, the patent term was extended to 20 years. In 1981, the intermediate *Auslegeschrift* series was abolished, leaving a two-stage publication sequence, *Offenle-gungsschrift* followed by *Patentschrift*. In some cases, even this sequence can be amended (see below.)

One aspect of the current law in Germany is the existence of the utility model or *Gebrauchsmuster* system. These patent-like rights require a lesser degree of inventive step and are not examined initially. Following a change in the law in 1990, they can be obtained for products, but not methods or processes. These document types have always been an important part of the prior art for the mechanical and electrical fields, and since this change, small numbers of utility models covering chemical compounds are also being published each year.

Germany is a long-term signatory to the Paris Convention, having signed in 1903. It is a founder member of the European Patent Office, from 1977, and joined the Patent Co-operation Treaty system in 1978. The standard country code for the Federal Republic of Germany since 1978 is 'DE'. The code 'DT' was used prior to this. For the former East Germany, the codes were 'DL' (pre-1978) and 'DD' (1978–1990). Certain other code variations can be observed, representing different document stages, such as DE-OS for *Offenlegungsschrift,* and PAS for *Patentschrift,* but these are rarely encountered in databases, only as page headers in the printed documents.

National patent documentation

As a result of the various changes in procedure, Germany has a number of quite complicated KD codes and numbering systems. As with many intellectual property offices, the *Deutsches Patent- und Markenamt* has responsibility for a number of rights other than patents, such as trade marks, designs, computer chip topographies and so on. Unlike other offices, the Germans have adopted a unified intellectual property numbering system, where each type of right is denoted by a code embedded in the publication number. This system was adopted for all document types from 1994, but was introduced gradually from 1989 onwards. These numbers are retained from application through to grant, so appear as publication number formats in searchable databases.

The most recent form of these numbers came into effect from 1st January 2004. The overall format is wholly numerical, in segments 2+4+6+1. The first 2 digits represent the type of intellectual property right. The next 4 digits represent the year of *application*, but this part remains the same throughout the process; hence cases published in 2006 may have 2004 at this position. The third segment of 6 digits is a running serial number, and

Table 23: German Intellectual Property Right numbering codes

Type of right	Number (2004+)	Number+Serial Range (1994–2004)
National patent application	10	1 + 00001 to 74999 **
PCT application designating Germany	11	1 + 80001 to 99999
Supplementary Protection Certificate	12	1 + 75001 to 79999
Utility model application	20	2 + 00001 to 74999
Utility model application by means of PCT application	21	2 + 80001 to 99999
Semiconductor topography application	22	2 + 75001 to 79999
Trade mark application	30	3 + 00001 to 99999
Registered design application	40	4 + 00001 to 49999
Typographical font application	41	4 + 50001 to 59999
EP Patent designating Germany granted in German language	50	5 + 00001 to 99999
EP Patent designating Germany granted in English or French language	60	6 + 00001 to 99999

** note ; initially, the range 00001–89999 was reserved for national applications and 90001–99999 for PCT transfers. The separate range for SPC applications was introduced from 1994. Other sources list the range up to 79999 for national patents, from 80001 to 89999 for SPC's and 90001 to 99999 for PCT transfers.

the final single digit, separated by a decimal point, is a computer check-digit. This final digit is often omitted from database records of publication number.

The earlier form of these numbers, between 1994 and 2004, was similar but used only one digit to represent the right, the last two digits of the year and 5 digits for the serial portion, giving a 1+2+5+1 format. In order to denote certain document kinds, the 1994–2004 system preserved specific number ranges in combination with a type of right code. In the current system, the two-digit ranges 13–19, 23–29, 31–39, 42–49, 51–59 and 61–69 are un-used.

Examples of use of these codes are:

DE 1 00 46981-A1   Published unexamined patent application, applied for in 2000

DE 2 95 00440-U1   Published utility model application, applied for in 1995

DE 4 01 00134   Application for registered design, applied for in 2001

DE 5 00 00339-T2   Registration of granted European Patent published in German, filed at the EPO in 2000

DE 6 99 12443-T2	Registration of granted European Patent published in English, filed at the EPO in 1999
DE 11 2004 123456-B3	Granted national patent, applied for in 2004 (fictitious example)
DE 20 2004 000123-U	Published utility model application, applied for in 2004 (fictitious example)

Due to the various numbers of publication stages at different times, new KD codes have been introduced over the years to try to prevent duplication of the meaning. Broadly, the sequences are as shown in Table 24.

Databases and database-specific aspects

The national gazette for Germany, the *Patentblatt*, forms the basis for a number of electronic products, both internet and non-internet based. In addition, from the late 1940's, a commercial company, Wilhelm Lampl Verlag (later WILA Verlag and now part of the Thomson Group), produced a range of abstract journals covering German patent and utility model applications. These form the basis for several bibliographic databases which, until recently, were available on the STN service, as the PATOS series of files (PATOS-DE covering German national documents, PATOS-EP covering EP documents and PATOS-WO covering PCT publications.

A wide variety of disk-based products have been produced covering Germany, and some of these have been ported to an online web-based service (PATONbase) at the PATON server, based at the University of Ilmenau in eastern Germany. The same organisation provides the PATONLine system, with enhanced coverage of former East German documents (1950–1990). Part of this is open-access, but a wider collection is available to registered users within the German academic community.

After the re-unification of Germany in 1989, complicated transitional procedures were put into place to handle the merging of the two national patent systems. The European centre for the STN host, located in Germany,

Table 24: German KD codes and sequences

1968–1981	Normal sequence	*Offenlegungsschrift* (A1) followed by *Auslegeschrift* (B2) followed by *Patentschrift* (C3)
	Accelerated examination	*Auslegeschrift* (B1) followed by *Patentschrift* (C2)
	Rare cases	*Patentschrift* only (C1)
1981–2003	Normal sequence	*Offenlegungsschrift* (A1) followed by *Patentschrift* (C2)
	Accelerated examination	*Patentschrift* only (C1)
2004+	Normal sequence	*Offenlegungsschrift* (A1) followed by *Patentschrift* (B4)
	Accelerated examination	*Patentschrift* only (B3)

Table 25: German patent databases

Producer	Service name	Platform	Coverage
Bundesdruckerei	DEPAORDER	Internet	<www.depaorder.de> ; document supply, by publication number only
Bundesdruckerei	DEPATISNet	Internet	<www.depatisnet.de> ; German coverage included, start date undetermined
Deutsches Patent- und Markenamt (DPMA) / Bundesdruckerei	Publications server	Internet	<publikationen.dpma.de> Document delivery and legal status; searchable by publication number. Searchable weekly *Patentblatt,* also accessible via <www.patentblatt.de>
DPMA	German Patents – Applications	Delphion	DE-A bibliographic data and claims 1968+; full text 1987+
DPMA	Germans Patents – Granted	Delphion	DE granted patents and utility models, bibliographic data and first claim, 1968+; full text 1987+
DPMA	DEPANet	Esp@cenet	<de.espacenet.com> ; bibliographic data DE-A and utility models (most recent 2 years)
DPMA	DPINFO	Internet	<https://dpinfo.dpma.de> Legal status register (registration required)
DPMA	PATDPA	STN	DE-A, granted patents and utility models; bibliographic data 1968+; front page images 1983+
DPMA	PATDPASPC	STN	German Supplementary Protection Certificates for drugs and agrochemicals, bibliographic data 1992+
DPMA	PATDD	STN	DD (East Germany) ; bibliographic data 1981+
DPMA / FIZ Karlsruhe	PATDPAFULL	STN	DE-A full text 1987+; DE granted patents full text 1987+ Translations of European patent documents, full text 1992+ Utility models, bibliographic data and claims 1999+
DPMA/University of Ilmenau	PATOS	PATON	<www.paton.de> DE-A and utility model, bibliographic data 1980+
DPMA/University of Ilmenau	DE-T2	PATON	German translations of EP; bibliographic data 1992+
DPMA/ Bundesdruckerei	DEPAROM-ACT	CD-ROM	DE-A, granted patents and German translations of EP ; bibliographic data, abstracts, page images, 1995+
DPMA/ Bundesdruckerei	DEPAROM-T2	CD-ROM	German translations of EP ; bibliographic data, page images,

Table 25: *continued*

Producer	Service name	Platform	Coverage
DPMA/ Bundesdruckerei	DEPAROM-U	CD-ROM	Utility models, full page images,
DPMA/ Bundesdruckerei	DEPAROM-KOMPACT	CD-ROM	Bibliographic data (index disk) for all document kinds covered by other DEPAROM disks (1991+)
EPO	ESPACE-DE	CD-ROM	German applications, bibliographic data, page images 1991–1994 (closed series)
MicroPatent	German Published Applications; German Granted Patents; Translations; Utility Models/ Gebrauchsmuster	Micro-Patent	DE-A full text 1989+; DE granted patents full text 1989+; Translations of granted EP designating DE, abstracts 1989+, full text 2004+; Utility models abstracts 1989+, full text 2004+
Univentio	File 324	Dialog	DE-A, granted patents and utility models; bibliographic data 1967+; full text 1980+ in original and machine-translated into English
Wila Verlag	DEPAT	Questel	DE-A bibliographic data 1968+ DE-*Auslegeschriften* bibliographic data 1968–1981 (closed series) DE granted patents, bibliographic data 1980+ DE utility models bibliographic data 1983+

had already mounted a file of East German patents (PATDD), and subsequent bibliographic data relating to pending applications continued to be added to this file, even though the data itself was published from Munich by the new Federal agency for the re-unified state.

Italy

Historical aspects and current law

Italy was one of the founder signatories of the Paris Convention, which entered into force on 7th July 1884. It was an early member of European Patent Office, from 1978, but only joined the Patent Co-operation Treaty system in 1985. Italy has opted to close the national route under the PCT, so that a PCT application may only designate Italy by way of a European Patent, not directly. The standard country code for Italy is 'IT'.

The region has a distinguished history in patent information, having been responsible for what is probably the world's first patent law in Venice in 1474, and several of the states within 19th century Italy, such as Sardinia and Lombardy, had their own laws. By 1864, the first moves were made to a united Italian patent law. Today, patents granted by the Italian Patent Office (the UIBM, or *Ufficio Italiano Brevetti e Marchi*) have effect in the Republic of Italy and the Holy See (Vatican City), although the latter has its own standard country code (VA), and applies the laws of Italy on patents subject to them "*not being contrary to precepts of divine right, the general principles of canon law or the 1929 Lateran treaties*". San Marino (code SM) promulgated its own patent laws in 1997 and their patent office started work in 1999, but an existing bilateral treaty with Italy still holds – industrial property rights obtained in Italy are binding and enforceable in San Marino and vice versa.

Despite this background, Italian patent documentation is poorly developed, and both sources of documents and their coverage in databases create considerable problems for the searcher. The official gazette (*Bollettino dei brevetti per invenzione, modelli e marchi*) is nominally a monthly publication, but often appears at irregular intervals, and most library stocks of both bulletin and specifications have large gaps.

Italy uses a regional approach for its national patent applications. Each of the Chambers of Commerce in the provincial capital can act as a receiving centre for lodging a patent application, and preserves its own format of application number. Designated provincial offices act as a collection and processing centre for data from the other provincial offices in the same region, so that data can be input into the overall information system. A substantial proportion of the patents in force in Italy appear to be not national patents, but European Patents designating Italy, hence a comprehensive legal status check will require consideration of both routes of protection.

One issue for the pharmaceutical industry is the question of patent term extension. Italy, as a member of the EU, has operated an SPC system under the 1992 and 1996 Regulations for some years, but it also had its own national law on term extension (Italian Law No. 349 of 1991), which operated between November 1991 and January 1993, when it was replaced by the EU system. The national law was considerably more generous than the later EU provisions, allowing up to 18 years extension, and later laws have been brought in to gradually reduce these extensions until they are in line with the maximum permitted (5 years) under the EU system. Consequently, calculation of the actual term of any given pharmaceutical patent is an extremely complex business.

Italy operates a utility model system, with a term of 10 years from date of application.

National patent documentation

As indicated above, Italy uses a regional approach for patent application. From 1991, the method for allocating these application numbers changed. Prior to that date, each Chamber of Commerce was allocated a fixed range of numbers to be used within a given year, resulting in a discontinuous but all-numeric series. After 1991, a two-letter code representing the Chamber of Commerce was used, with each Chamber starting at number 1 in a new year. This created problems for database producers who were set up to load application numbers in a numeric form only. To circumvent the problem, the INPADOC database adopted a set of 2-digit codes corresponding to the Chamber of Commerce codes, and used these instead. For example, application number 91 RM 0011 (the 11th application received at the Rome chamber in 1991) becomes 91 73 0011, as Rome is the 73rd province in alphabetical order. To complicate matters, a further 8 provinces were created during 1997, forcing INPADOC to insert additional 3-digit codes to take account of this. The full listing is shown in Table 26.

The current law (from 1997) in Italy provides for publication at 18 months (IT-A1 document kind, re-using the application number format), followed by grant, again re-using the same number, but with the code –B1. Utility models are similarly published as IT-U1 followed by IT-Y1 when granted. It is possible to transform an original utility model application into a patent application whilst still pending, and vice versa – the resultant documents are allocated the codes IT-A4 (started as utility model, published as patent application) and IT-U4 (started as patent application, published as utility model), respectively.

Unfortunately, these new kind codes conflict with the earlier codes –A and –U which were used for granted cases, before the early publication system came into place. Therefore, databases may contain a mixture of early published applications and grants. It may be necessary to compare the publication date to determine which legislation was in force at the time, and the consequent status of the document. However, the granted documents under the older legislation were numbered in a single running series, which reached around 1,320,000, so the number format can be a clue to the status.

Translations into Italian of granted European Patents designating Italy are not published in the normal bibliographic record (as for Germany), but appear as a notice in the gazette, retaining the original EP number.

Databases and database-specific aspects

As noted above, the issue of obtaining timely and accurate data from the Italian Patent Office for inclusion in any databases (country-specific or multi-country) is a vexed one for the information professional. The few dedicated sources available are frequently out of date, and the limited legal

Table 26: Italian province codes

Chamber of Commerce	Code	INPADOC equivalent	Chamber of Commerce	Code	INPADOC equivalent
Agrigento	AG	01	Messina	ME	49
Alessandria	AL	02	Milano	MI	50
Ancona	AN	03	Modena	MO	51
Aosta	AO	04	Napoli	NA	52
Arezzo	AR	05	Novara	NO	53
Ascoli Piceno	AP	06	Nuoro	NU	54
Asti	AT	07	Oristano	OR	55
Avellino	AV	08	Padova	PD	56
Ban	BA	09	Palermo	PA	57
Belluno	BL	10	Parma	PR	58
Benevento	BN	11	Pavia	PV	59
Bergamo	BG	12	Perugia	PG	60
Biella	BI	991	Pesaro	PE	61
Bologna	BO	13	Pescara	PS	62
Bolzano	BZ	14	Piacenza	PC	63
Brescia	BS	15	Pisa	PI	64
Brindisi	BR	16	Pistoia	PT	65
Cagliari	CA	17	Pordenone	PN	66
Caltanissetta	CL	18	Potenza	PZ	67
Campobasso	CB	19	Prato	PO	995
Caserta	CE	20	Ragusa	RG	68
Catania	CT	21	Ravenna	RA	69
Catanzaro	CZ	22	Reggio Calabria	RC	70
Chieti	CH	23	Reggio Emilia	RE	71
Como	CO	24	Rieti	RI	72
Cosenza	CS	25	Rimini	RN	996
Cremona	CR	26	Roma	RM	73
Crotone	KR	992	Rovigo	RO	74
Cuneo	CN	27	Salerno	SA	75
Enna	EN	28	Sassari	SS	76
Ferrara	FE	29	Savona	SV	77
Firenze	FI	30	Siena	SI	78
Foggia	FG	31	Siracusa	SR	79
Forli	FO	32	Sondrio	SO	80
Frosinone	FR	33	Taranto	TA	81
Genova	GE	34	Teramo	TE	82
Gorizia	GO	35	Terni	TR	83
Grosseto	GR	36	Torino	TO	84
Imperia	IM	37	Trapani	TP	85
Isernia	IS	38	Trento	TN	86
L'Aquila	AQ	39	Treviso	TV	87
La Spezia	SP	40	Trieste	TS	88
Latina	LT	41	Udine	UD	89
Lecce	LE	42	Varese	VA	90
Lecco	LC	993	Venezia	VE	91
Livorno	LI	43	Verbania	VB	997
Lodi	LO	994	Vercelli	VC	92
Lucca	LU	44	Verona	VR	93
Macerata	MC	45	Vibo Valentia	VV	998
Mantova	MN	46	Vicenza	VI	94
Massa Carrara	MS	47	Viterbo	VT	95
Matera	MR	48	UIBM Dep.Post.	DP	96

Table 27: Italian patent databases

Producer	Service name	Platform	Coverage
Justinfo Ltd, Slovenia	ITALPAT	Questel	Patent applications and utility models, bibliographic data 1983–1993
Italian Patent Office/EPO	ESPACE-IT	CD-ROM	Patent applications 1993–1995. Utility model applications 1995 only. Bibliographic data and document images
Italian Patent Office	UIBM	Public internet (http://www.uibm.gov.it)	Unknown – experimental system only
InfoCamere (IT)	SIMBA	Fee-based internet (https://telemaco.infocamere.it)	Some data from 1980. Full details unknown – currently only available to Italian subscribers
FILDATA Srl (IT)	FILPAT	Public internet (http://www.fildata.it)	Utility models, bibliographic date 1990–date. Six-month rolling file of patent bibliographic data.

status for Italy in the INPADOC file is devoted to European Patents designating Italy, not national patents. The recent launch of the SIMBA service holds out some prospect of improvements in the future, and the newly-formed user group, the AIDB (Associazione Italiana Documentalisti Brevettuali) has made it a priority to start discussions with the Italian Patent Office in order to improve the situation. The list of current files available is given at Table 27.

United Kingdom

Historical aspects and current law

Some form of patent protection for inventions has been available in various parts of the United Kingdom since at least the 15th century, and as noted in the introductory chapters, the English Statute of Monopolies of 1623 was instrumental in the development of the modern system. By the Industrial Revolution period, patenting – and the commercial advantages gained by it – was well established, at least in England.

The United Kingdom could be regarded as an early experiment in the development of regional patent systems. Prior to 1852 it was necessary to file for protection separately in England (which included Wales), Scotland and Ireland. After the foundation of the Patent Office, completed under the Patent Law Amendment Act the year after the Great Exhibition of 1851 and reflecting a new-found interest in the reform of patent law to match industrial development on a global scale, patents were granted for the entire United Kingdom. However, even today the situation is not quite as simple as may appear. Coverage is automatic for Great Britain, Northern Ireland and the Isle of Man, but not for some other close territories such as the Channel Islands. A number of the dependent territories, Crown colonies and even some independent Commonwealth member nations can be brought within the coverage of a UK patent by a process of re-registration. In territories such as Hong Kong, Malaysia and Singapore, which today have their own national patent systems, a substantial portion of the protection in force is still in the form of re-registered British documents.

Further legislation was passed in 1883, 1902, 1919 and 1949, by which time a UK patent had a term of 16 years from the date of filing of the complete specification. Under the 1949 Act, publication was in a single numbered series. Detailed abstracts, called abridgements, were prepared by the examiners for each case, and published in groups according to the British classification key. These summaries were highly regarded for their content and quality, and have recently been loaded onto the EPO's esp@cenet search system, as a unique data set. From 1916 until the most recent law change, patents were published in a single numerical series, starting at 100,001.

The United Kingdom was one of the founder signatories of the Paris Convention, which entered into force on 7th July 1884. It was also a founder member of both the European Patent Office, from 1977, and the Patent Co-operation Treaty from 1978. The standard country code for the United Kingdom is not, as might be expected from the familiar Internet top-level domain, uk, but 'GB'.

Following a Government investigation into patent law reform in 1970[1], the United Kingdom followed the lead of the Netherlands and Germany by introducing a system of deferred examination with early publication. This came into force as the 1977 Patents Act, which is still the primary legislation today, albeit modified by some provisions of the Copyright, Designs & Patents Act 1988 and the Patents Act 2004.

The new legislation in 1977 was specifically designed to be compatible with the European Patent Convention, and the two documents are very similar, at least in the way in which they lay out the procedure for examining and publishing patents. The system provided for a sequential process of search and substantive examination, with the applicant required to file a request for substantive examination once the search stage had been completed and the specification published at 18 months after priority. This delay allowed for third parties to review the published unexamined application and to bring new prior art to the attention of the examiner. If an applicant decides to proceed to substantive examination and the case reached grant, it is republished using the same publication number, but with the KD code GB-B. There is no opposition period as such, although provision does exist for the publication of an amended document after grant, with a code GB-C; these are rarely seen. Patent term is now 20 years from the UK application date, and the patent has to be maintained in force by payment of annual renewal fees for the entire term.

Publications under the 1977 Act are numbered in the range of 2,000,001 upwards, from 1979. For many years after the new series began, a few pending cases continued to be published each year under the old 1949 Act, which reached approximately GB 1,605,000 by 2003. The only cases to publish in recent years were those whose subject matter was delayed due to national security considerations at the time of filing. These published for the record and immediately expired.

In common with other member states of the EPO which are also members of the EU, the United Kingdom operates the EU's supplementary protection certificate scheme. Term extension may be granted within the United Kingdom on the basis of either a granted UK patent or a granted European Patent designating the UK. As a result of this, the status registers available on the internet have to cope with both GB and EP publication numbers. The current range of GB publication numbers has just passed 2,404,000, which means that the UK office has published some 404,000 unexamined cases. Considering that in the same time period, the EPO has published over 1,400,000 unexamined cases, this illustrates the extent to which the EPO has impacted upon the number of cases handled by the national offices of its member states. Substantial numbers of applications are still filed in the United Kingdom, but many (perhaps more than 75%) are only used as a means of obtaining a priority date in order to enter the European system, and never publish as GB-A documents.

The British classification key was started in 1888, but underwent a major revision in 1963, applied from specification number GB 940,001 onwards. At this time, the system was regrouped into approximately 400 subject headings under the same 8 main sections as the fledgling IPC, lettered A to H. The hierarchical structure is thus Section (letter) – Division (Number) – Heading (Letter), followed by the individual alphanumeric code mark. An example classification may thus be:

Section C	Chemistry, Metallurgy
Division C3	Macromolecular compounds
Heading C3A	Cellulose derivatives
Code mark C3A 7C	Articles made from cellular and porous.

The classification undergoes regular revision, and new Classification Keys are issued. These were initially produced every 20,000 specifications, then every 50,000 and in recent years new editions have been released on calendar dates. The system is still applied to United Kingdom national patents, and appears on the front pages of the documents. Initially, both EP cases and PCT cases designating the United Kingdom were also classified by the British system, to assist searching within the United

Kingdom, but in recent years the resource has not been available to do this and the effort ceased. Few electronic systems utilise the British classification as a search tool; one is the disk-based product ESPACE-ACCESS-Europe, produced by the European Patent Office, which includes bibliographic information from 1978 to the present for United Kingdom documents.

National patent documentation

Since 1997, the official gazette of the United Kingdom Patent Office has been entitled the *Patents & Designs Journal*, although in previous years it was called the *Official Journal (Patents)*, and is still commonly referred to by many searchers as 'the OJ'. The gazette is published weekly and back-copies are available in PDF format on the main website of the Office, at <http://www.patent.gov.uk>.

Under the 1977 legislation, an applicant resident in the United Kingdom was required to file first in the UK, and then wait for a period of approximately 6 weeks before filing elsewhere in the world. This provision was to enable a national security check to take place. After the 6-week period had elapsed, the *Patents & Designs Journal* (PDJ) publishes a short entry for the application, consisting of the title as filed, the application number and the applicant's name. These listings of newly-filed applications are amongst the earliest public records anywhere in the world of patent filings. Although this national security provision has been amended by section 7 of the recent Patents Act 2004, it is believed that the listings of new applications will continue to be provided in the Journal.

The same listing includes details of applications entering the United Kingdom claiming foreign priority, which means that the record appears at approximately 13½ months from priority. INPADOC is one of the few databases to collate the information from this stage. Since no formal publication of the specification takes place, the database producer generated a dummy KD code of GB-A0 (A-zero), and re-used the application number as the publication number.

After the initial listing in the PDJ, the next public event is the publication of the specification at 18 months after priority, carrying a KD code GB-A (early in the life of the 1977 Act) or GB-A1. Unlike the EPO, the UK Patent Office does not issue specifications without a search report (corresponding to the EP-A2) or delayed search reports (corresponding to the EP-A3). The GB-A1 document consists of the entire specification as filed, except in those instances where the applicant is proceeding via the PCT and entering the British national system. In these circumstances, the GB-A1 document is a single sheet with abstract and drawing, but the body of the specification is not re-published. An example of this republication is shown in Figure 10; note INID code 87 showing the data for the corresponding PCT publication.

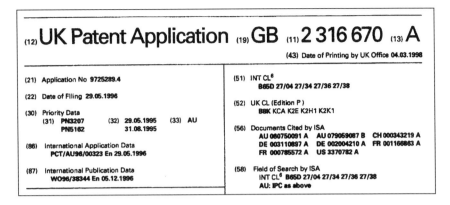

Figure 10: UK republication of a PCT application entering national phase

At the present time, a substantial proportion of the GB-A documents never proceed to grant, so there is never a corresponding GB-B document. If the case does go to substantive examination, it is eventually republished using the same publication number but with the new KD code GB-B2. Provision does exist for the issue of an amended document as a GB-B2, but this does not happen very often. Many database producers drop the numerical suffix and record British grants simply as GB-B. The full sequence for a typical grant therefore appears as Table 28.

One further function of the PDJ is in the monitoring of European Patents granted and effective in the United Kingdom. The Journal notes the grant date of all cases which designate the United Kingdom, irrespective of language, and a separate listing of the Article 65 translations into English of patents originally granted in French or German. This latter listing is important, as failure by the patent holder to lodge the required translation within a fixed time period results in the European Patent being declared void in the UK. Unlike Germany, these translations are not accorded a new UK number. The United Kingdom exercised its Article 65 rights from 1987, so that cases which were granted as an EP-B up to 1986 do not have to have the translations lodged.

Table 28: Typical GB grant sequence

Stage	As printed	Typical database entry
Application in the UK	7836675 (13 Sep 1978)	GB19780036675-A0
Unexamined publication	GB 2029757-A (26 Mar 1980)	GB 2029757-A1
Granted patent	GB 2029757-B (28 Jul 1982)	GB 2029757-B2

Table 29: Application process for Supplementary Protection Certificate in the UK

Event	Publication
Patent application in UK	Application number GB8332598.5, filed 7 Dec 1983
Published unexamined	GB 2133788-A1, published 1 Aug 1984
Published granted	GB 2133788-B, published 15 Jul 1987
Application for SPC	SPC/GB95/009, filed 15 May 1995, citing GB 2133788-B
SPC granted	SPC/GB95/009, granted 21 Jul 1995
Patent expiry	GB 2133788-B, expired 6 Dec 2003
SPC entered into force	SPC/GB95/009, in force 7 Dec 2003
(SPC expires)	SPC/GB95/009, expires 6 Dec 2008

The United Kingdom operates the SPC provisions under current EU Regulation. The application process, grant and entry into force of these certificates is a process independent of the main patent granting stream, and new formats of numbers are adopted. Table 29 shows the sequence of events.

Databases and database-specific aspects

Until the mid-1990's, the only publicly available electronic access to British national patents was via the multi-national databases such as Derwent WPI or INPADOC. Searchers interested in using country-specific aspects, such as the British national classification, were limited to working at the reading rooms of the British Library or the UK Patent Office. However, the UK Patent Office has been a partner in the esp@cenet ® system since its launch in 1999, initially with a 2-year file of GB-A documents, subsequently expanded to all cases published under the 1977 Act (earliest date January 1979). More recently still, the old abridgements for early 20th century patents have been loaded into the esp@cenet Worldwide file, creating a substantial and informative abstract field for many of these older documents. The Univentio organisation, which specialises in OCR creation of full-text databases from paper masters, has completed scanning the 1977 Act documents, and has plans to extend the coverage back to older patents as well. MicroPatent has also created an OCR-scanned file, back to 1916. Earlier bibliographic data for GB documents may be found in some of the multi-country databases, discussed elsewhere in this book. The current list of dedicated files is given at Table 30.

Searchers wishing to undertake historical research in pre-1977 Act patents are referred to the book by van Dulken[2] which includes more details on the various paper indexes and how to use them at the British Library.

Table 30: United Kingdom patent databases

Producer	Service name	Platform	Coverage
UK Patent Office	Esp@cenet Level I server	Public internet (http://gb.espacenet.com)	Patent applications 1979–date, bibliographic data and images. Granted patent images 2002–date (planned)
UK Patent Office/EPO	Esp@cenet Level 2 server (Worldwide file)	Public internet (http://gb.espacenet.com)	Patents 1900–date, bibliographic data and images.
UK Patent Office	ESPACE-UK	CD-ROM	Patent applications 1976–date, bibliographic data and images.
UK Patent Office/ Univentio	GBFULL	STN International	Patent applications 1979–date, bibliographic data and full text. Some clipped images available.
UK Patent Office/ Univentio	GBFULL	Questel Orbit	Patent applications 1979–date, bibliographic data and full text. (forthcoming file).
UK Patent Office/ MicroPatent	PatSearch Full Text GB(A)	Fee-based internet (http://www.micropat.com)	Patents and patent applications, 1916–date, bibliographic data and full text.

Russian Federation

Historical aspects and current law

The patent system of the Russian Federation came into being soon after the dissolution of the Soviet Union on 25th December 1991. This was the latest chapter in a series of political changes in this part of the world since the decree of Alexander I in 1812 governing the protection of inventions. This remained in force until 1896, when the first Russian patent law as such was passed. This only lasted until 1919, when Lenin signed the Statute on Inventions which effectively abolished all previous patent legislation and declared useful inventions to be 'public property'.

New legislation in 1924, 1931, 1959, 1974 and 1978 meant that the Soviet Union gradually restored some semblance of Western protection. Two parallel systems of patent-like documentation developed. These were the 'inventor's certificate' system, which was open to residents of the Soviet Union, and provided a remuneration to the inventor in return for assigning all rights in the use of the invention to the State, and a more conventional 'patent' which was open to applicants from outside of the Soviet Union, with a 15 year term.

From 1st July 1991, the inventor's certificate system was closed to new filings, although pending cases continued to be processed or optionally converted to a patent application. Some further cases which, under the old Soviet legislation, would not be published have also been laid open.

Soviet patents in force at the dissolution of the Union automatically became Russian Federation patents, without the need for the re-registration process used by some other of the states of the former USSR. A similar process was used for Soviet inventor's certificates, although deadlines were imposed.

Within days of the formal dissolution of the Soviet Union, a new Provisional Agreement on the Protection of Industrial Property was signed in Minsk, by representatives from Armenia, Belarus, Moldova, the Russian Federation, Tajikistan and the Ukraine. This had the appearance of the beginnings of a supra-national patent system, but after a number of years of negotiation, only 9 out of the 15 countries from the former Soviet Union eventually agreed to form a new Eurasian Patent Office (EAPO) – this is discussed in more detail under 'Regional Patent Systems' elsewhere in this chapter. The EAPO does not replace the national offices of the member states, but like the EPO operates in parallel with them. The headquarters of both the Russian Federal Institute of Industrial Property (ROSPATENT) and the EAPO are in Moscow. ROSPATENT was inaugurated on 1st February 1992 as the successor to the Patent Office of the USSR.

The Russian Federation system today operates both a patent and a utility model system, with terms of 20 years and 5 years respectively. The utility model may be extended for up to a further 3 years on application.

The Soviet Union acceded to the Paris Convention in 1965, and the Russian Federation, as successor state to the USSR, is still a signatory. It was an early signatory to the Patent Co-operation Treaty in 1978, and a founder member of the new Eurasian Patent Office when that agreement entered into force in 1995. The standard country code for the Russian Federation is 'RU', succeeding the previous 'SU' for the Soviet Union.

National patent documentation

One of the complicating factors when dealing with current Russian documents is the transitional arrangements for handling cases still pending at the dissolution of the Soviet Union. In general, pending patents and inventor's certificates which had not been laid open as of the date of the new Russian law, have been published with a number format in keeping with the old Soviet Union series, but using the country code 'RU' and a distinct KD code.

There have been a number of amendments to patent law, affecting application and publication number formats. These changes are analysed in detail by Höhne[3]. Essentially, application numbers have been amended in three series; 1991–1992, 1992–1994 and 1995 to date. The present system incorporates a 'kind of right' code, similar in style to the current German numbers. Applications are published at 18 months as a RU-A1 document, with a publication number in the same format as application number.

After substantive examination and grant, applications are republished in a single running series, with a number greater than 2,000,001 e.g. RU 2239295-C2. However, it appears that a substantial proportion of cases are processed to grant very rapidly and by-pass the unexamined stage, appearing as RU-C1 documents with number formats as for the C2.

Some cases which were not published as of the new law are being published as RU-C documents (note the absence of the final digit) and with publication numbers in a running format below 2,000,001, for example RU 1896741-C (fictional example). These are valid Russian patents based on old USSR inventor's certificates which were still in force as of 1992 and have been published at the holder's request.

Databases and database-specific aspects

The Russian Patent Office has cooperated in the development of a combined CD-ROM search product, CISPatent, covering patent applications from 8 of the former USSR states (Armenia, Belarus, Georgia, Moldova, Russian Federation, Tajikistan, Uzbekistan, Ukraine) plus the Eurasian Patent Office.

As mentioned above, many Russian cases by-pass the RU-A1 stage and appear in databases only at the granted stage. However, in cases where pendency is longer, the RU-A1 document is a potentially valuable piece of intelligence, but few databases cover these. One which does is the Patent Abstracts of Russia (PAR) file, mounted on the PATON service at the German patent information centre in Ilmenau. More details of this service are provided in the paper by Höhne[3]. The public internet services of the Russian Federation patent office are distributed under the umbrella of the Federal Institute of Industrial Property website (http://www.fips.ru).

The 2004 Annual Report of the Russian Patent Office notes that work was completed on a MIMOSA-compatible backfile on DVD of Russian/ Soviet Union patents from 1924–1993. It would appear that this collection has now been made available as the RUPAT OLD file mentioned in Table 31. The same report notes that many of the periodical publications of the Office have been issued in electronic form on CD or DVD, as well as on paper.

Russia is a prominent member state of the Eurasian Patent Office, and further Russian national bibliographic information can also be found in the internal registries and information system (EAPATIS) of the EAPO. At present, this system is not publicly available, as it is mainly concerned with information exchange between the offices of the EAPO member states.

Table 31: Russian patent databases

Producer	Service name	Platform	Coverage
Russian Patent Office	CISPatent	CD-ROM	Patent publications of the members of the Commonwealth of Independent States, 2002–date
Russian Patent Office	Abstracts of Patents and Utility Models	CD-ROM	Approximately biweekly production
Russian Patent Office	PAR	PATON	English abstracts of Russian patents, 1994–date
Russian Patent Office	RussiaPat	STN	English abstracts of Russian patents, 1994–date, plus legal status.
Russian Patent Office	RUPAT	Public Internet <www.fips.ru>	Full text of granted patents 1994–date (*). Some coverage of RU-A documents.
Russian Patent Office	RUPAT OLD	Public Internet <www.fips.ru>	Bibliographic records of Soviet Union / Russian patents 1924–1993. Full text OCR only. (*)
Russian Patent Office	RUABEN	Public Internet <www.fips.ru>	English abstracts of Russian patents, 1994–date
Russian Patent Office	RUABUl	Public Internet <www.fips.ru>	Russian abstracts of utility models, 1996–date
Russian Patent Office	Electronic Patent Bulletin	Public Internet <http://www.fips.ru/el bl/default_en.htm>	Recent issues of RUPO Gazette, including PDF images of complete documents.
Russian Patent Office	Register of Abstracts of Russian Inventions in English ; Register of Russian Utility Models	Public Internet <http://www.fips.ru/cdfi/index_en.htm>	Register, including legal status, for Russian patents and utility models.

(*) pre-registration required for access

▶ THE PATENT CO-OPERATION TREATY (PCT)

The PCT is an extremely important system for the specialist in patent information, as it has become one of the most popular routes by which newly-filed applications are laid open to public inspection. In recent years, over 100,000 cases per year have been published, corresponding to many millions of pages of technical intelligence.

Operation of the PCT started in 1978, based upon the Treaty which had been signed in Washington DC in 1970. The main distinguishing feature of the PCT is that it does not grant any patents. It is principally an administrative system, which handles applications centrally from the time of their filing, through the prior art search process, until they are forwarded to national patent offices for substantive examination. This process includes a centralised publication of the application at 18 months after priority, and may optionally include the preparation of an international non-binding opinion on patentability.

PCT documentation

It is very important to realise that, as presently constituted, the PCT system will never examine nor grant any applications. Consequently, many of the legal status questions asked of national applications do not have any relevance in respect of the PCT. For purposes of comparison, we should remember that although the EPO only publishes a single granted document, it too is not a true supra-national patent system. Legally, the outcome is a bundle of national patents which happen to have been examined separately under one statute (the EPC), and accepted by all the member states concerned. In a similar fashion, the outcome of a PCT application is that each individual patent office takes on the task of examining its own national application which has "matured" from a PCT international application. The case will be examined under national legislation and be either granted as a national patent or rejected. The overall picture is still a bundle of national patents, but this time they have been examined under local statute, not according to a single procedure.

The great benefit of the PCT is that it allows the applicant to defer the considerable cost of translation of their patent application into multiple official languages, until they have at least had a chance to assess the search report produced at 18 months (the so-called Chapter I procedure). Documents published at eighteen months can appear in English, French, German, Japanese, Russian, Spanish or Chinese. All documents carry a country code 'WO' code prefix to identify them.

The following Figure 11 illustrates a typical sequence of events using the PCT procedures. There are a number of points to note here:

- The priority filing in the United States was used to pursue patent protection in the US via the national route and also as a basis for filing the International Application which led to all the other patents in the family. This is not uncommon – the presence of a PCT publication in a patent family should never lead to the assumption that all protection for the invention worldwide derives from the PCT system.
- All the national applications (Canada, Australia, UK, EPO) derived from the PCT International Application are accorded a filing date which is the same as the date of filing of the

Figure 11: Publication sequence under the PCT system

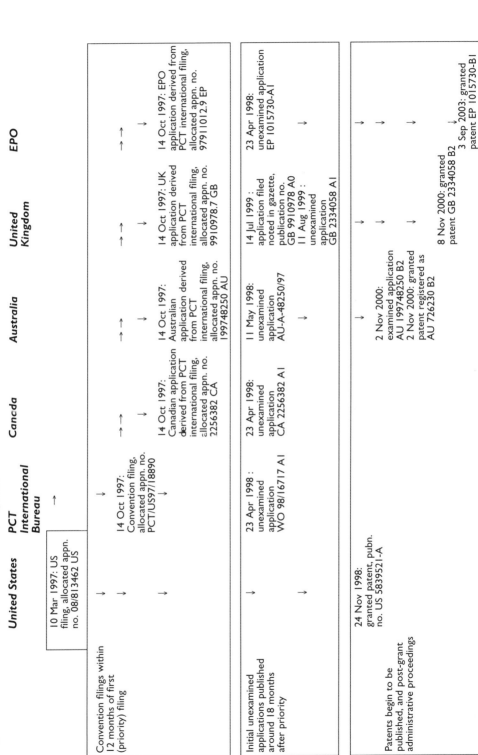

International Application itself (in this case, 14 Oct 1997), even though the file will not actually be sent to these national patent offices until some while later. This can cause an apparent mismatch between the eventual national application number and the application date. For example, the UK application number has a 99 prefix, showing that it was allocated in 1999, but the filing date is from 1997.

- National authorities differ in their policy concerning publication of unexamined cases corresponding to a previously published WO document. Some (e.g. Australia and most EPO) allocate a dummy –A publication number for issue in the gazette, and do not republish any document. Others (e.g. UK) issue a single page in the normal GB-A format, cross-referring to the corresponding WO document.

The PCT documents (officially referred to as 'pamphlets') published at 18 months can be in any one of seven official languages: English, French, German, Japanese, Russian, Spanish or Chinese. Some 70% are in English at present. The front page data will always carry English language equivalents, but the body of the specification will be entirely in a single language chosen by the applicant.

Applicants can file an international application at their national patent office (leading to an application number in the format PCT/CCYYYY/NNNNNN, where CC is the country code of the place of filing, YYYY is the year of application to the PCT system and the NNNNNN is a serial number) or directly at the headquarters of the PCT administration, which is the International Bureau of WIPO based in Geneva. If they choose the latter route, the CC used is the two letters 'IB', for International Bureau. In order to encourage patent applications from less-developed countries, it is now possible to *apply* in any language, but a translation must be supplied in order for the pamphlet to be *published* in one of the seven official publication languages.

During the application process, the applicant is invited to designate one or more of the member states of the PCT, in a similar fashion to the EPO system. At the time of writing, there are 125 member states in the treaty. However, unlike the EPO designation process, inclusion on the front page of a PCT application does not indicate that the applicant is definitely seeking protection in all the states listed. On the contrary, since new regulations came in during 2003, designation of a single member state is regarded as valid designation of all member states. Since examination is only done at the local level, a listing at INID field 81 or 84 is no guarantee at all that there will be eventually a granted patent corresponding to the invention – see Figure 12 for an example of a designated states listing.

The pamphlet is usually accompanied by an official search report, which is drawn up by one of the International Search Authorities (ISA's).

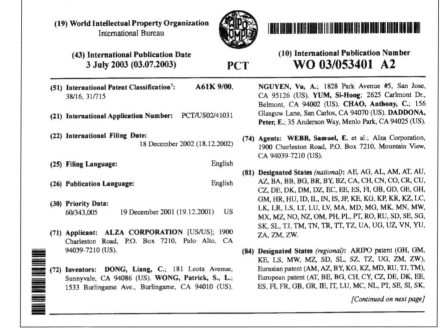

Figure 12: Designated states listing on PCT front page

These are a group of patent offices who have been sub-contracted to search PCT cases on behalf of the International Bureau. Each ISA has to prove that they have access to a specific body of prior literature, the so-called PCT Minimum Documentation (defined in the text of the PCT and its Regulations), before they are affirmed as a search authority. At the time of writing, there are 11 ISA's; the European Patent Office plus the national patent offices of Austria, Australia, Canada, China, Japan, the Russian Federation, South Korea, Spain, Sweden and the United States. The national patent office of Finland has been provisionally accepted as an ISA but has not yet started to operate as such.

After the pamphlet has been published, the applicant has a choice of routes. He may opt for Chapter I, which means that the International Bureau ceases to have responsibility for the case and it is forwarded to the national patent office(s) designated by the applicant. The alternative, Chapter II, route involves one additional step, the creation of a non-binding opinion on patentability, before the application is forwarded. This opinion is prepared by an International Preliminary Examination Authority (IPEA), drawn from the same authorities as the ISA's. In either case, Chapter I or Chapter II procedure, the application is put into a state where it can be forwarded to the designated offices within 12 months of the publication of the pamphlet (technically, 30 months from priority).

The standard KD codes for WO documents are the same as for the EPO i.e. WO-A1 is a published International Application with search report, WO-A2 is the same without search report, and WO-A3 is the delayed search report. Although no PCT cases as such go to grant, there are a number of additional KD codes which are confusingly similar to those used for examined patents:

- WO-C1 modified first page
- WO-C2 complete corrected document
- WO-B1 publication of amended claims

The International Bureau has also recently started to use the ST.50 correction codes on its own documents, generating WO-A8 and WO-A9 types equivalent to those in use by the EPO. The same publication number is re-used, with the changed suffix.

Prior to some rule changes during 2003, the Chapter I procedure did not include any establishment of a written opinion – this was all left as an optional process under Chapter II. However, the new procedures mean that this element of the old Chapter II procedure will now be incorporated into the international search procedure under Chapter I, effective for applications filed after 1 January 2004. The ISA will in future provide a written opinion on patentability, as well as a search report, although the former will not be published. The International Bureau converts this opinion into an "International Preliminary Report on Patentability (Chapter I of the PCT)", or IPRP (Chapter I) for short, supplied to the applicant. If the applicant requests to proceed via Chapter II, the same written opinion will be used as the basis for a corresponding – but still not binding – IPRP (Chapter II) in place of the original International Preliminary Examination Report. Details of the operation of the system under these new rules were laid out in the PCT Newsletter[4] – the section of most relevance to information scientists is "Enhanced International search and preliminary examination system". The Newsletter is well worth monitoring for other changes in the system.

As at the beginning of September 2005, there were 128 member states of the PCT. They are listed in Table 32, in chronological order of joining.

Databases covering the PCT system

One of the characteristics of the PCT system, being only involved in the early stages towards publication, is the lack of a centralised legal status register. The amount of information available to third parties is very limited until a case is forwarded to the appropriate national or regional patent office for further examination, leading to grant or refusal. It is only once

Table 32: Member states of the PCT, as of September 2005

State	Date on which State became party to the Treaty
Cameroon, Central African Republic, Chad, Congo, Gabon, Germany, Madagascar, Malawi, Senegal, Switzerland, Togo, United Kingdom, United States of America.	1978–01–24
France	1978–02–25
Russian Federation	1978–03–29
Brazil	1978–04–09
Luxembourg	1978–04–30
Sweden	1978–05–17
Japan	1978–10–01
Denmark	1978–12–01
Austria	1979–04–23
Monaco	1979–06–22
Netherlands	1979–07–10
Romania	1979–07–23
Norway	1980–01–01
Liechtenstein	1980–03–19
Australia	1980–03–31
Hungary	1980–06–27
Korea (North)	1980–07–08
Finland	1980–10–01
Belgium	1981–12–14
Sri Lanka	1982–02–26
Mauritania	1983–04–13
Sudan	1984–04–16
Bulgaria	1984–05–21
Korea (South)	1984–08–10
Mali	1984–10–19
Barbados	1985–03 12
Italy	1985–03–28
Benin	1987–02–26
Burkina Faso	1989–03–21
Spain	1989–11–16
Canada	1990–01–02
Greece	1990–10–09
Poland	1990–12–25
Côte d'Ivoire	1991–04–30
Guinea, Mongolia	1991–05–27
Armenia, Belarus, Georgia, Kazakhstan, Kyrgyzstan, Moldova, Tajikistan, Turkmenistan, Ukraine, Uzbekistan	1991–12–25
Ireland	1992–08–01
Portugal	1992–11–24
New Zealand	1992–12–01
Czech Republic, Slovakia	1993–01–01
Viet Nam	1993–03–10
Niger	1993–03–21
Latvia	1993–09–07
China	1994–01–01
Slovenia	1994–03–01
Trinidad and Tobago	1994–03–10
Kenya	1994–06–08
Lithuania	1994–07–05
Estonia	1994–08–24
Liberia	1994–08–27

State	Date on which State became party to the Treaty
Swaziland	1994–09–20
Mexico	1995–01–01
Uganda	1995–02–09
Singapore	1995–02–23
Iceland	1995–03–23
Macedonia	1995–08–10
Albania	1995–10–04
Lesotho	1995–10–21
Azerbaijan	1995–12–25
Turkey, Israel	1996–01–01
Cuba	1996–07–16
Saint Lucia	1996–08–30
Bosnia and Herzegovina	1996–09–07
Serbia and Montenegro	1997–02–01
Ghana	1997–02–26
Zimbabwe	1997–06–11
Sierra Leone	1997–06–17
Indonesia	1997–09–05
Gambia	1997–12–09
Guinea-Bissau	1997–12–12
Cyprus	1998–04–01
Croatia	1998–07–01
Grenada	1998–09–22
India	1998–12–07
United Arab Emirates	1999–03–10
South Africa	1999–03–16
Costa Rica	1999–08–03
Dominica	1999–08–07
Tanzania	1999–09–14
Morocco	1999–10–08
Algeria	2000–03–08
Antigua and Barbuda	2000–03–17
Mozambique	2000–05–18
Belize	2000–06–17
Colombia	2001–02–28
Ecuador	2001–05–07
Equatorial Guinea	2001–07–17
Philippines	2001–08–17
Oman	2001–10–26
Zambia	2001–11–15
Tunisia	2001–12–10
Saint Vincent and the Grenadines	2002–08–06
Seychelles	2002–11–07
Nicaragua	2003–03–06
Papua New Guinea	2003–06–14
Syria	2003–06–26
Egypt	2003–09–06
Botswana	2003–10–30
Namibia	2004–01–01
San Marino	2004–12–14
Comoros	2005–04–03
Nigeria	2005–05–08
Libya	2005–09–15

a case is being handled by these offices that a third party can see the corresponding national file wrapper and hence gain access to at least some of the correspondence between applicant and the International Bureau. Any subsequent legal processes are handled on the national or regional level, resulting in additions to the file wrapper and subsequent gazette notifications or publications. Once granted, a national patent which matures from a PCT international application is indistinguishable from one filed directly, through the national route.

The fundamental problem with searching any source covering PCT documents is the multiple publication languages. The most complete systems to date only cover the full texts of those documents published in English, French, German or Spanish. Texts published in Japanese, Chinese or Russian are only retrievable via the supplementary abstract in English; no full-text searching is possible. According to the 2004 review of the PCT system, published by WIPO[5], this would mean that 16.4% of publications are not searchable by the same criteria as the remaining 83.6% – the full breakdown is given in Table 33.

In mid-2005, WIPO launched a new 'micro-site' on the internet, under the name of PatentScope, <http://www.wipo.int/patentscope/en/>, which collates a great deal of information on the PCT system. It includes an Online File inspection module, including access to selected documents of the PCT international phase file. The bulk of the service (1978–1998) comprises only searchable bibliographic information plus images of published pamphlets. Progressively more information is available from 1998 to date, including priority documents and some declarations. The content of the PCT Electronic Gazette remains as in Table 34.

Since the PCT has grown to be such a significant first-publication route for many industries, notably pharmaceuticals, a number of niche database have grown up which contain substantial numbers of PCT documents, but are not complete collections; one such example is the Current Patents

Table 33: Publication language breakdown under the PCT, 2004

Publication language	Number of applications published in 2004	Percentage of applications
English	75,106	66.7
Japanese	16,835	15.0
German	13,999	12.4
French	4,254	3.8
Chinese	1,096	1.0
Spanish	758	0.7
Russian	510	0.4
Total	**112,558**	**100.0**

alerting service which is cumulated into the DOLPHIN database. The following table (Table 34) is limited to search files which contain complete collections of PCT documents from the given start date.

Table 34: PCT databases

Producer	Service name	Platform	Coverage
WIPO	PCT Electronic Gazette	Public internet <http://www.wipo.int/ipdl/en/>	Bibliographic date Jan 1997–date. Claims and full text Apr 1998–date (Eng/Fre/Ger/Spa only)
WIPO	ESPACE-WORLD	CD-ROM/DVD	Facsimile images of PCT publications, 1978–date. Searchable bibliographic data and abstracts only.
WIPO/ including EPO	ESPACE-FIRST	CD-ROM/DVD	Searchable front-page data abstracts (Eng/Fre/Ger/Spa only), 1978–date
EPO	ESPACE-ACCESS	CD-ROM/DVD	Bibliographic information, including searchable abstracts in English and French, 1978–date. Cross-index to facsimile disk series and esp@cenet.
WIPO/ Bundesdruckerei	PCT Gazette	CD-ROM	Bibliographic information, including searchable abstracts, 1997–date. Includes all 4 parts of the Gazette.
WIPO/Univentio	WIPO PCT Publications	Delphion	Bibliographic data, images and full-text, 1978–date.
WIPO/ MicroPatent	PatSearch FullText	MicroPatent	Bibliographic data and full-text, 1978–date. Images 1997–date
WIPO/Univentio	Total Patent	Total Patent	Bibliographic data and full-text, 1978–date.
WIPO/Univentio	PCTFULL	STN	Bibliographic data and full-text (Eng/Fre/Ger/Spa only), 1978–date.
WIPO/FIZ Karlsruhe	PCTGEN	STN	Data on nucleic acid and protein sequences from PCT applications, 2001–date.
WIPO/Questel	WOPATENT	Questel-Orbit	Bibliographic data, abstracts (Eng/Fre only) and some legal information, 1978–date.
WIPO/Univentio	PCTFULL	Questel-Orbit	Bibliographic data and full-text (Eng/Fre/Ger/Spa only), 1978–date.
WIPO/Univentio	WIPO/PCT Patents Fulltext (file 349)	Dialog	Bibliographic data and full-text (Eng/Fre/Ger/Spa only), 1978–date.

▶ REGIONAL PATENT SYSTEMS

Up to this point, most of the discussion about patent documents has concentrated on the 'one country, one patent' model – i.e. there will be as many patents for an invention as there are countries in which the applicant has sought and obtained protection. The exception has been the European Patent Office. However, the EPO is not the only regional system in operation, and a number of further groups of countries are moving towards regional co-operation in patent granting. The political landscape changes quite quickly, so any comment upon this situation is likely to be out of date soon. However, the following systems are in force or developing at the time of writing.

The Eurasian Patent Office

As mentioned earlier in this chapter, moves to institute a regional system for patent granting across the former USSR were started very soon after the Union dissolved in 1991. The European Patent Office was instrumental in helping to draft the new regional agreement, and it bears many similarities to the European Patent Convention.

The Eurasian Patent Convention was eventually signed in Moscow on 9th September 1994[6], by 10 of the former Soviet states, and entered into force from 12th August 1995 after the necessary three signatories had ratified it – Belarus, Tajikistan and Turkmenistan. The Russian Federation, Kazakhstan, Azerbaijan, Kyrgyzstan, Moldova and Armenia joined over the next 6 months, bringing the total membership to 9. There are no apparent moves at present for Georgia, the Ukraine or Uzbekistan to join the EAPO, and the remaining three former Soviet republics (the Baltic states of Estonia, Latvia and Lithuania) have decided to join the European Patent Office instead. The country code for the EAPO is 'EA'. The Office started operations on 1st January 1996, with headquarters in Moscow.

The operation of the EAPO is very similar to the EPO, using deferred examination with early publication at eighteen months, followed by substantive examination leading to a grant of patent with a term of twenty years from filing date. The EAPO has only a single official language – Russian – as opposed to the three used by the EPO. The first unexamined documents were issued in October 1996, and the first patent was granted in April 1997.

One significant difference from the EPO practice is that it is not possible to designate individual member states. All nine states are by default included in the coverage of any granted patent, and the only way of withdrawing protection is by subsequently not paying the renewal fees for any un-necessary countries.

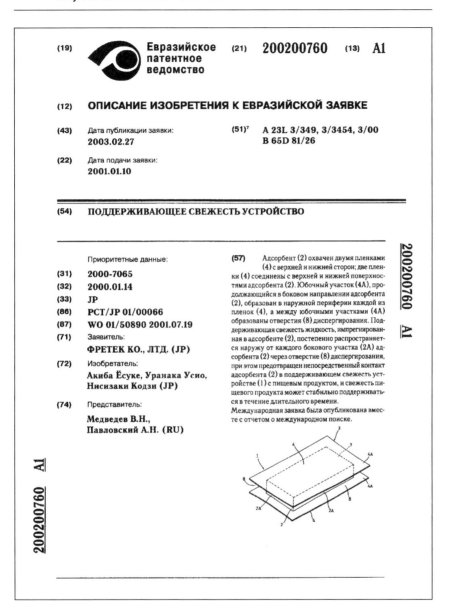

(19) **Евразийское патентное ведомство**

(21) **200200760**

(13) **A1**

(12) **ОПИСАНИЕ ИЗОБРЕТЕНИЯ К ЕВРАЗИЙСКОЙ ЗАЯВКЕ**

(43) Дата публикации заявки:
2003.02.27

(51)⁷ A 23L 3/349, 3/3454, 3/00
B 65D 81/26

(22) Дата подачи заявки:
2001.01.10

(54) **ПОДДЕРЖИВАЮЩЕЕ СВЕЖЕСТЬ УСТРОЙСТВО**

Приоритетные данные:

(31) **2000-7065**
(32) **2000.01.14**
(33) **JP**
(86) **PCT/JP 01/00066**
(87) **WO 01/50890 2001.07.19**
(71) Заявитель:
ФРЕТЕК КО., ЛТД. (JP)
(72) Изобретатель:
Акиба Ёсуке, Уранака Усио, Нисизаки Кодзи (JP)
(74) Представитель:
Медведев В.Н., Павловский А.Н. (RU)

(57) Адсорбент (2) охвачен двумя пленками (4) с верхней и нижней сторон; две пленки (4) соединены с верхней и нижней поверхностями адсорбента (2). Юбочный участок (4A), продолжающийся в боковом направлении адсорбента (2), образован в наружной периферии каждой из пленок (4), а между юбочными участками (4A) образованы отверстия (8) диспергирования. Поддерживающая свежесть жидкость, импрегнированная в адсорбенте (2), постепенно распространяется наружу от каждого бокового участка (2A) адсорбента (2) через отверстие (8) диспергирования, при этом предотвращен непосредственный контакт адсорбента (2) в поддерживающем свежесть устройстве (1) с пищевым продуктом, и свежесть пищевого продукта может стабильно поддерживаться в течение длительного времени.
Международная заявка была опубликована вместе с отчетом о международном поиске.

200200760 A1

200200760 A1

Figure 13: Eurasian Patent Office – unexamined application

Figure 13 shows the front page of an unexamined Eurasian application, and Figure 14 the header of a granted patent, which uses a single running series of publication numbers. A substantial proportion of all granted EA-B documents derive from transfers via the PCT system, but the number of locally filed inventions is also rising slowly.

Figure 14: Eurasian Patent Office – granted patent

The documentation from the Eurasian Patent Office is being incorporated into a number of multi-national patent databases, such as INPADOC. In addition, the Office produces CD-ROM products covering the complete specifications as published, in the form of EA-A and EA-B documents. The main website of the Office is <http://www.eapo.org>, which contains details of additional search services and electronic information. It is hoped that at least some of the content of the internal EAPATIS system will become publicly available in due course.

The documentation of the EAPO was reviewed in a conference presentation by Dzegelenok in 2005[7].

Africa – ARIPO and OAPI

There are two operating regional systems in Africa, one for a number of the former French colonies which operates in French, and the other covering a number of former British colonies with English as its working language.

The Francophone organisation OAPI (the *Organisation Africaine de la Propriété Intellectuelle*) is based in Yaoundé, in the Cameroon. It has seventeen member states and dates its origins from 1962, when the Malagasy Republic and eleven other states concluded the Libreville Agreement, to form the African and Malagasy Patent Rights Authority (OAMPI). Subsequently, the Malagasy Republic (Madagascar) withdrew and additional members joined a new arrangement, founded on the Bangui Agreement of 1977. The members at the time of writing are: Burkina Faso, Benin, Cameroon, Central African Republic, Chad, Congo, Côte d'Ivoire, Djibouti, Equatorial Guinea, Gabon, Guinea, Guinea-Bissau, Mali, Mauritania, Niger, Senegal, and Togo.

The Bangui Agreement entered into force on 8th February 1982, and is unlike any other operating treaty in intellectual property anywhere in the world. By contrast with systems such as the EPO, this Agreement creates a single authority, which is empowered *both to grant and litigate* in the patents arena. The Agreement becomes the controlling legislation for the member states, and although they do retain a national patent office presence, they are to all intents and purposes sub-offices of the OAPI headquarters in Yaoundé. A single patent is granted by OAPI, carrying the 'OA' code prefix, which has effect in all the member states, and (most significantly) the Organisation uses a centralised court structure which enables a single case to establish validity or order revocation for all the territories.

The parallel English-speaking organisation to OAPI is ARIPO, the *African Regional Industrial Property Organization*. Membership is determined by accession to the Lusaka Agreement of 9th December 1976. At the time of writing there are fifteen member states: Botswana, the Gambia, Ghana, Kenya, Lesotho, Malawi, Mozambique, Sierra Leone, Somalia, Sudan, Swaziland, Tanzania, Uganda, Zambia and Zimbabwe. Within the framework of OAPI, there are separate treaties on patents and industrial designs (the Harare Protocol of 10th December 1982, which entered into force on 25th April 1984) and on trade marks (the Banjul Protocol). All ARIPO states apart from Somalia have ratified the Harare Protocol.

Under this system, the applicant can file an application with either their national office or directly with the ARIPO office in Harare. As with other regional offices, a single application can have effect in all designated member states, but the ARIPO system – unlike OAPI and the EAPO – allows the applicant to designate fewer than the maximum number. Applications which are filed at a national office are forwarded to Harare for examination after the preliminary formal stages. After substantive examination is completed, copies of the application are sent to each designated state, which reserves the right to make a pre-grant declaration that the ARIPO patent will not have effect upon its territory.

In recent years, a revision of the Harare Protocol has made a link between it and the Patent Co-operation Treaty. Under this system, designation of "ARIPO" in a PCT application is taken to mean automatic designation of all states party to both the Harare Protocol and the PCT. The country code for ARIPO is 'AP'.

Neither of the two African systems has made much of its information resources available to the public as electronic files at present. They each have a website (<http://www.aripo.wipo.net/index.html> for ARIPO and <http://www.oapi.cm> or <http://www.oapi.wipo.net/index.html> for OAPI) but these are devoted to procedural aspects of the respective Offices' work. Publications from both OAPI and ARIPO are included in data feeds derived from INPADOC, and there is a disk-based product in the ESPACE series covering OAPI publications on CD (see chapter 7).

The Gulf Co-operation Council (GCC)

The Patent Office of the Co-operation Council for the Arab States of the Gulf, to give it its full title, was established in 1995 and is based in Riyadh, Saudi Arabia. The implementing Regulations were passed in the following year and the operational Rules in 1998. It has six member states: Bahrain, Kuwait, Oman, Qatar, Saudi Arabia and the United Arab Emirates. The first patent applications were received in October 1998, and the first issues of the official gazette were produced in 2000. From issue 2, this included bibliographic details, including a title, abstract and drawing, of applications received. The GCC Office is a regional alternative to the national patent offices of its member states, although two – Oman and Qatar – had no patent laws at all prior to their membership. The original term of the GCC patent was fifteen years, but this was revised in 2000 in order to bring the regional law into compliance with the TRIPS agreement, and now allows for a 20-year term from filing date.

At the time of writing, issues of the bilingual (English and Arabic) Gazette have included a section listing 'Applications approved for grant by decision, subject to completion of processing'. Each application has an application number in the form GCC/P/YYYY/NNN where YYYY is the Western year and N is a serial number. Corresponding entries in the Gazette have a so-called 'Number of the decision to grant the patent' listed at INID field 11, in the form P/NNNN. It appears that these announcements are equivalent to publication for opposition prior to grant. Entries for the same documents in subsequent issues of the Gazette have amended this format to a simpler, running number series, which is being used by the INPADOC database as the publication number. It is not clear whether this definitive grant number is issued at the end of the 3-month opposition period. Although the country code 'GC' has been allocated to the office, it is not used in the Gazette – instead, a plain language designation of the office name appears at INID field 19. A sample page from the Gazette is shown at Figure 15.

In December 2004, the EPO announced that they would begin to load the complete collection of all GCC granted patents (KD code GC-A), starting from GC-0000001-A granted 2002, into its INPADOC database. The GCC website is at <http://www.gulf-patent-office.org.sa>, from which Microsoft Word versions of the Gazette can be downloaded, but there appears to be no searchable index so far.

Future developments in regional patent systems

In addition to the systems discussed in this chapter, there are moves to establish regional patent systems in other parts of the world. These often develop out of regional economic cooperation agreements, or free-

[19] *PATENT OFFICE OF THE
COOPERATION COUNCIL FOR
THE ARAB STATES OF THE GULF*

مكـتب بـراءات الاختــراع [19]
لجلس التعاون لدول الخليج العربية

[12] Patent

[11] Number of the Decision to Grant the Patent: P/5162	
[45] Date of the Decision to Grant the Patent: 12/01/2002	

[21] Application No. GCC/P/1999/290	[51] Int. Cl.[7]: F21B 47/00
[22] Filing Date: 19/09/1999	[56] Documents Cited:
	- US 4932005 A (BIRDWEEL) 05 June 1990 .
[30] Priority:	- GB 2146126 A (NL INDUSTRIES INC.) 11 April
[31] Priority No. [32] Priority date [33] State	1985.
98117831.2 21/09/1998 EPO	- US 3700049 A (TIRASPOLSKY et al.) 24
	October 1972.
[72] Inventor: Douwe Johannes Runia	
[71] Applicant: SHELL INTERNATIONALE RESEARCH MAATSCHAPPIJ B. V. of Carel van Bylandtlaan 30 , 2596 HR The Hague , The Netherlands.	
[74] Agent: Suleiman Ibrahim Al-Ammar	

[54] THROUGH-DRILL STRING CONVEYED LOGGING SYSTEM

[57] Abstract: A system for drilling and logging of a wellbore formed in an earth formation is provided. The system comprises a logging tool string and a drill string having a longitudinal channel for circulation of drilling fluid, the drill string including a port providing fluid communication between the channel and the exterior of the drill string, the channel and the port being arranged to allow the logging tool string to pass through the channel and from the channel through the port to a position exterior of the drill string. The system further comprises a removable closure element adapted to selectively close the port, wherein the logging tool string is provided with connecting means for selectively connecting the logging tool string to the closure element.   No. of claims: 10   No. of figures: 4

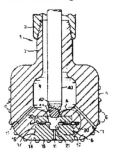

Note: The grant decision shall be finalized, and the patent shall be handed over to the applicant only three months from the date of this gazette, if no objection to this patent has been filed by any individual interested in the patent to the Grievance Committee in the office.

Figure 15: Gulf Cooperation Council Patent Office – gazette entry

trade blocs. Some of the areas which could see developments in the next decade are:

- The Andean Community (ANCOM) – member states Bolivia, Colombia, Ecuador, Peru and Venezuela, who have formed a common customs union for trade. The Community is guided by the Cartagena Agreement, which includes certain common provisions on industrial property.

• The Arab League – twenty-two member states in North Africa and the Middle East, which would have a likely headquarters in Cairo.

• The Association of South-East Asian Nations (ASEAN) – ten members, which have been working towards common intellectual property regulations, assisted by the EPO. It is possible that regional co-operation may extend to the 'ASEAN+2', including South Korea and China.

• Mercosur – the second 'common market' in South America (Argentina, Brazil, Paraguay and Uruguay, with Chile as associate member), which is investigating harmonisation in the copyright area, but so far has made little progress in patents.

• Caricom (the Caribbean Community) – a grouping of fourteen countries in the Caribbean, Central and South America.

▶ REFERENCES

1.   "The British Patent System; report of the committee to examine the patent system and patent law." Chaired by M.A.L. Banks. Cmnd. 4407. London: HMSO, 1970.

2.   "British Patents of Invention, 1617–1977: a guide for researchers." S. van Dulken. London: British Library: 1999. ISBN 0–7123–0817–2.

3.   "Efficient access to Russian patent documents." M. Höhne, J. Ludwig, R. Schramm. World Patent Information **22**(1), 23–33 (2000).

4.   "Overview of changes to the PCT system as of 1 January 2004". PCT Newsletter No. 11/2003, 1–5, (November 2003) and "New enhanced international search and examination procedure." PCT Newsletter No. 12/2003, 13–15 (December 2003). ISSN 1020–072X, available from the WIPO website.

5.   "The International Patent System in 2004; Yearly Review of the PCT". Geneva: WIPO, 2005. Available at <http://www.wipo.int/pct/en/activity/pct_2004.pdf>.

6.   "Eurasian Patent Convention – done at Moscow on September 9, 1994". WIPO Publication No. 222 (R/E/F). Geneva: WIPO, 1995. ISBN 92–805–0615–3.

7.   "Patent information from the Eurasian Patent Office." P. Dzegelenok :in Proc. Annual Conference of the PIUG, 21–26 May 2005, Crystal City, Alexandria, VA, USA.

PART II – databases and search techniques

6 Patent guides and libraries

▶ GENERAL DIRECTORIES AND REFERENCE WORKS

Given the large numbers of publications on patents which are targeted at the legal community, it is perhaps surprising that relatively few works exist which provide a comprehensive survey of patent information sources. Part of the problem is that such compilations are out-of-date almost as soon as they are published. Nonetheless, even older works retain some usefulness. An early attempt at a list of electronic sources was published by Kulp[1], and a European effort was completed by Rimmer[2]. Somewhat out of date, but still useful as listing, are the Aslib publication edited by Sibley[3] and the WIPO directory[4], although the latter is more a listing of library stocks rather than databases. More recently, one highly-regarded survey was published by Simmons *et al.*[5] as part of a major chemical encyclopaedia, and a revised version appeared in the latest edition of the Manual of Online Search Strategies[6]. The fifth edition of the Kirk-Othmer encyclopaedia is under preparation at the time of writing, and will include an updated version of Simmons' review. The work by Armstrong[7], although large, appears to have been produced semi-automatically and includes many databases with only peripheral coverage of patents, and many which are essentially in the marketing and licensing areas rather than bibliographic records of patents as such.

Other than these tools, the information specialist wishing to maintain awareness of developments in patent databases is reliant upon well-established industry magazines and journals, such as Online, Database, Searcher (US) and World Patent Information. Several countries have independent user groups, including the UK (PATMG), US (PIUG), Italy (AIDB), Netherlands (WON), France and Denmark. Several of these publish some form of newsletter or periodical publication, covering developments in local patent documentation and information services.

In addition to primary sources, the secondary and tertiary literature on patent information search techniques is relatively sparse. However, older books, if they can be located, still provide a useful context to developing skills. The earlier first edition of the current work was a welcome addition[8] and, as mentioned previously, the work by Liebesny is widely regarded as a classic[9]. Also of note are the books by Newby[10], Finlay[11] – which concentrates on the language skills for reading front pages of non-English documents – and Eisenschitz[12]. The British Library in London has for many years had skilled staff in its patents section, and they have produced a number of introductory guides[13,14] and a larger work by Rimmer which concentrates on countries covered by the British Library stocks[15]. A similar foundational work existed in German for many years[16] but it appears that this was superseded by a CD-ROM version which unfortunately recently ceased production[17]. Finally, readers will find it useful to browse the "Bibliography" section of the Patent Information Knowledge Base, which forms a part of the website of the PIUG (Patent Information Users' Group, Inc.) <http://www.piug.org/pikb.html>.

In addition to works describing patent documentation as such, there are a number of useful directories of patent information sources. Two which can be recommended are the British Library's collection of links, within the Patents part of the website, at <http://www.bl.uk/collections/patents/keylinks.html> and <http://www.bl.uk/collections/patents/othlinks.html>, or the Australian-based IPMenu website, particularly the country subsection <http://www.ipmenu.com/country.htm>, which provides a country-by-country listing in a standard layout, including links to national patent office websites and searching sites where they exist. The British Library site places a heavy emphasis on web-based services, including a comprehensive listing, with comments, of the many free-of-charge services available. IPMenu also includes commercial information suppliers in its coverage.

▶ UNITED KINGDOM PATENT LIBRARIES

The United Kingdom has had a network of libraries with notable patent holdings for many years, which used to operate as the Patent Information Network (PIN) libraries. More recently, they have adopted the PATLIB label from the wider European network, and operate as PATLIB UK. The libraries vary quite widely in the range of services which they can offer, and the staff expertise available. Contact details for each library can be obtained via the British Library website at <http://www.bl.uk/collections/patents/patentsnetork.html> or directly from the EPO website at <http://patlib.european-patent-office.org/directory/overview.pl>. At the time of writing, the UK centres are based in Aberdeen, Belfast, Birmingham, Bristol, Glasgow, Leeds, Liverpool, London, Manchester, Newcastle-upon-Tyne, Plymouth, Portsmouth, Sheffield and Swansea.

▶ UNITED STATES PATENT LIBRARIES

In the United States, the corresponding network of libraries operates under the title of the Patent and Trademark Depository Library (PTDL) Program. This is fully supported by the USPTO, and details of the Program can be found on the USPTO website at <http://www.uspto.gov/go/ptdl/>, which includes a full listing by state of the network. Each state has at least one library, and the more populous ones have up to six; there are more than 120 in the whole Program. As with the PATLIB UK, these libraries operate in a variety of environments – some are university based, others reside in parts of a general or public library serving the city. A few of the larger libraries are given 'Partnership' status, which means that they have access to a wider range of resources and search tools, and become regional focal points for patent information. Some of the larger libraries are subscribers to the WEST bibliographic system, a web-browser based search tool. All libraries in the programme maintain a core collection of at least 20 year's-worth of US patents, plus additional fact sheets and help materials for inventors, directories of patent agents and attorneys in the United States and trademark support. A range of optical disk (CD, DVD) products from the USPTO's own CASSIS service are available for searching by visitors to the PTDLs. Librarians at the PTDLs are not encouraged to run searches for visitors, but to help and instruct them in running the searches for themselves.

▶ GERMAN PATENT LIBRARIES

As with the United Kingdom, the German library network for patent dissemination was established before the PATLIB programme under the EPO, and provided contacts for industry to use patent information. The libraries are informally known as the PIZ (Patentinformationszentren) network and the administration has been formally incorporated as the *Arbeitsgemeinschaft Deutscher Patentinformationszentren e.V.* The centres are commonly based upon universities or local chambers of commerce. Their dedicated website is at <http://www.patentinformation.de>, showing contact details for the 24 libraries in the current network, and a good collection of additional basic help for the would-be patent information user in Germany. One of the most well-known centres outside of Germany is the Technical University at Ilmenau, which hosts the web-based PATON search service, including a number of commercial full-text files. The website for the Ilmenau centre can be found at <http://www.patent-inf.tu-ilmenau.de>. Several of the centres organise periodical courses for industry or searchers.

▶ THE EUROPEAN PATLIB NETWORK

The European Patent Office, through its sub-office in Vienna, has always been a strong supporter of the development of national patent libraries in its member states. In recent years, the EPO has sponsored an annual conference for the librarians from the so-called PATLIB network, allowing staff to meet and exchange ideas and support. Each of the member states has at least one library with stocks of patent material, and obtains access to the CD-ROM products of the EPO to assist patent information use.

The listing of members of the European PATLIB network can be found at the dedicated micro-site within the main EPO website, at <http://patlib.european-patent-office.org/index.en.php>. By 2004, there were approximately 300 libraries in the network, and a searchable directory is included on the website. More members are expected to join the network as the new member states of the EPO start to organise their libraries within the system. The network envisages that the member libraries will become more pro-active in the future: to quote from their website,

> *"The future will see PATLIB centres moving away from their former role as "patent libraries" and becoming first-point providers of quality information in the area of patents and intellectual property, and prime movers in the provision of information to local government institutions, the general public, companies and academic circles."*

▶ JAPANESE PATENT LIBRARIES

For many years, the Japanese Patent Office disseminated its information products via the quasi-autonomous National Center for Industrial Property Information (NCIPI). This organization provided online access for the public file data to the regional bureaux of MITI (the Japanese Ministry of International Trade and Industry), and CD-ROM products to local libraries. Electronic data were provided to the Japan Patent Information Organization (JAPIO), who produced a variety of products, including the bibliographic file of the same name, mounted on a variety of online hosts, and the Patolis online system.

By the late 1990's, the JPO sought to take advantage of the internet to create a direct access route for its data, in the form of the Industrial Property Digital Library (IPDL) mounted on the main JPO website. The NCIPI has recently taken over responsibility for managing the IPDL on behalf of the JPO, and it is now accessible via their own website <http://www.ncipi.go.jp/english/index.html> as well as the main JPO site.

A direct network connection to the NCIPI provides access to some 59 IP Centers around Japan, in each prefecture. Some of the more populous prefectures such as Tokyo, Kanagawa, Hiroshima and Fukuoka have several centres. A list (in Japanese) is provided at the JPO website at <http://www.jpo.go.jp/torikumi/chiteki/chiran.htm>. These Centers offer free assistance with patent information matters, particularly document supply for small and medium-size enterprises. Some of the larger ones also have consultants that advise on patent technology transfer, searches on the JPO's IPDL and other matters relating to patent filing and searching.

By 2001, JAPIO was split into two; a non-profit corporation under the old name, charged with responsibility for making official Japanese data (including gazette and file wrapper data) available at marginal cost to third parties, and a new commercial Patolis Corporation, which has continued to develop the paid-for databases, and to market the Patolis-E web-based search system. Over the past few years, this new commercial freedom for Patolis has resulted in more links with academia, to develop advanced multi-lingual search systems based on dynamic machine-translation between Japanese and English.

▶ REFERENCES

1. "Patent databases; a survey of what is available from Dialog, Questel, SDC, Pergamon and INPADOC." C.S. Kulp. Database, **7**(3), 56–72 (August 1984).
2. "Patent Information and Documentation in Western Europe – an inventory of services available to the public". (ed.) Brenda Rimmer. 3rd. edn. Munich: KG Saur, 1988. ISBN 3–598–10744–7.
3. "Online patents, trade marks and service marks databases." J.F. Sibley. London: Aslib, 1992. ISBN 0–85142–289–6.
4. "World Directory of Sources of Patent Information." WIPO Publication No. 209(E). Geneva: WIPO, 1993. ISBN 92–805–0109–7.
5. "Patents, Literature". E.S. Simmons; S.M. Kaback in Kirk-Othmer Encyclopaedia of Chemical Technology, 4th edition. pp.102–156. New York: Wiley, 1996.
6. "Patents" E.S. Simmons. Chapter 3, pp.23–140 in Manual of Online Search Strategies, volume II: Business, Law, News and Patents. (eds.) C.J. Armstrong; A. Large. Aldershot: Gower Press, 2001. ISBN 0–566–08304–3.
7. "World Databases in Patents". (ed.) C.J. Armstrong. London: Bowker-Saur, 1995. ISBN 1–8573–9106–3.
8. "Information Sources in Patents." (ed.) C. P. Auger. London: Bowker-Saur, 1992. ISBN 0–86291–906–1.
9. "Mainly on patents; the use of industrial property and its literature." F. Liebesny (ed.) London: Butterworths, 1972. ISBN 0–408–70368–7.
10. "How to find out about patents." F. Newby. Oxford: Pergamon Press, 1967.

11. "Guide to foreign-language printed patents and applications." I.F. Finlay. London: Aslib, 1969. ISBN 0–85142–001-X.

12. "Patents, trade marks and designs in information work." T.S. Eisenschitz. London: Croom Helm, 1987. ISBN 0–70990–958–6.

13. "Introduction to patent information." S. Ashpitel; D. Newton; S. van Dulken (ed). (4th edition). London: British Library, 2002. ISBN 0–7123–0862–8.

14. "How to find information: patents on the Internet". D. Newton. London: British Library, 2000. ISBN 0–7123–0864–4.

15. "International Guide to Official Industrial Property Publications." B. Rimmer; S. van Dulken (3rd revised edition). London: British Library, 1992. ISBN 0–7123–0791–5.

16. "Grundlagen der Patentdokumentation: die Patentbeschreibung, Schutzrecht und Informationsquelle." A. Wittman; R. Schiffels. Munich: Oldenburg Verlag, 1976. ISBN 3–4862–0521–8.

17. "Das Handbuch der Patentrecherche." A. J. Wurzer (ed.) Munich: NATIF® GmbH, 2002. ISBN 3–00–008724–9.

7 National and international patent information sources

The chapters in Part I of this book have examined the patent documentation of the G8 member states. However, other industrially important countries outside this grouping, such as China, South Korea, India, Australia and so on, also have their own patent information resources. Patent documents from these countries can be retrieved either by dedicated local resources (such as their own national patent offices) or as part of a multi-national patent database. Both types of source will be examined in more detail in this chapter. The structure of the following sections will try to place the wide range of different resources into context, by listing them according to the medium of distribution rather than country-by-country. Users wishing to locate resources for a specific country can do so via some of the guides and reference works discussed in chapter 6.

It should be clear even from a short perusal of the holdings of any of the national patent libraries, that patent information at the beginning of the 21st century is still produced in a wide range of different media. Each medium has its strengths and weaknesses, and it is worthwhile becoming familiar with the available suppliers. A short summary of some of the major tools in each medium follows.

▶ PAPER SOURCES

Surprisingly enough, some patent information still persists in paper form, both in the private sector and public products. Typically, this includes information which is prepared by a library (and is therefore a non-official product) or is produced for the specific purpose of current awareness, and therefore has a limited life-time. An example of the former would be the card indexes of British patent filings and re-assignments and the Register of Stages of Progress for UK applications, both maintained by the British

Library in London. An example of the latter would be the customised bulletins (Tailor-Made Profiles) from Derwent Information (now part of Thomson Scientific) and the paper version of the Current Patents Gazette, a current awareness product from Current Patents. In the United States, some of the support documentation is still best examined at the public reading rooms in Washington DC – for example, it is one of the few places which maintains a collection of the paper Classification Orders, which form an audit trail for the development of the USPTO classification system.

Clearly, as time goes on, more and more patent information is being digitised. However, in the rush to electronic products, some niche paper-based services are at risk of being discarded without the development of a correspondingly efficient electronic service. Patent information user groups are a good mechanism by which searchers can liaise with (and if necessary, lobby) their national library and patent office, to preserve products which continue to deliver useful information.

► OPTICAL DISK (CD-ROM, DVD)

The Trilateral offices (EPO, USPTO, JPO) have been instrumental since the early 1990's in developing optical disks for use in dissemination of patent information. At a time when most information providers were only using CD-ROM for storing bibliographic information, the EPO developed the DOS-based 'Patsoft' software to distribute images of the complete texts of their unexamined applications. These were modified TIFF format files, and a week's production (some 1,500–2,000 documents) filled at least one CD-ROM. The product range was christened 'ESPACE' ®, from the French for 'space', since it was designed to save the many metres of shelf-space occupied by the paper equivalents.

The Patsoft software was replaced by a more flexible Windows-based product called MIMOSA (from MIxed MOde Software) in the mid-1990's. This application has become the *de facto* standard for CD-ROM and DVD-ROM authoring in the patent information field, and is used by a number of national patent offices for their own disk-based products, as well as by the EPO. The principal development of MIMOSA was the introduction of so-called mixed-mode searching, enabling the text to be stored for searching and the drawings to be retained separately. The two parts of the document are re-assembled dynamically to view. For printing purposes, the corresponding PDF format files are on the same disk.

The ESPACE series has continued to develop, and now includes a range of single-country and multi-country products, plus a number of directory-type databases. Some are collations of text-based front-page data, whilst others continue the original function of the ESPACE series as a distribution medium for the entire specifications, in a facsimile format including all diagrams and drawings. Some of the ESPACE disks from 2000 onwards have included searchable full text of the applications or the granted patents. Table 35 lists the active optical disk products from the EPO at the time of writing, including a selection of the ESPACE series products – note that in cases where a product is dedicated to documents from one of the major authorities reviewed elsewhere in this book, the product is listed in the section covering databases for that authority. Additional MIMOSA-compatible test disks have been prepared using data from a range of national patent offices (Table 36), although in some cases these have not been further developed due to supply difficulties with data. Some other patent offices and commercial publishers have developed optical disk products which are not compatible with MIMOSA (Table 37) – some of the more recent developments dispense with a separate applications program entirely, and operate within a standard browser without the need for additional software. In some cases, the entire product has been further developed into a search service based on a remote website, using the same format.

CD-ROM remains a popular medium for distributing other patent-related information, such as legal texts, directories of patents available for licensing and so on.

One of the largest co-operative efforts in publishing patent information on disk is the GlobalPat service. It is derived from the European Patent Office's First Page Data Base (FPDB) and is produced in cooperation with WIPO, after the USPTO pulled out to concentrate on web-based publishing. The FPDB is an English-language collection containing a substantial proportion of the world's patent literature. Coverage dates from the 1970's (varying for each country) to the present day, and includes documents from the US, PCT, EPO and the UK, German, French and Swiss national offices. As such, it represents a large proportion of the minimum documentation set defined for the use of PCT search authorities. Contents are presented as in the form of a mock-up front page, which includes basic bibliographic details, including title and abstract, with some clipped images. No full-text is provided, as the search tool is intended as a basic document identification mechanism rather than to permit full screening for relevance. The Trilateral Offices (USPTO, EPO and JPO) jointly financed the project and the translation of the non-English abstracts. GlobalPat is produced in subject-based sub-sets, consisting of 69 technology groups based upon the IPC. This enables a search department with a limited range of subject interest to subscribe to just the portions of the file which they require, and not to all technologies. The backfile (data from the beginning to 2000) has been released as 144 disks for the entire subject range. The frontfile is currently in production. Although substantial parts of the content have been superseded by internet-based files, GlobalPat is still a valuable way for smaller patent offices and industrial information departments to obtain a low-cost but comprehensive search tool.

Table 35: EPO disk-based products

Product name	Content	Form
EPO Official Journal	Content of the Official Journal of the EPO from 1978	Searchable PDF
ESPACE-First	EP-A1, -A2, -A3, A8, A9; WO-A1, -A2, correction publications since 1978	Bibliographic data and abstracts in language of publication
ESPACE-Legal	EPO Board of Appeal decisions, Guidelines for examination, treaties and official forms	Bibliographic; some searchable and editable PDF
ESPACE-World	WO-A1, -A2, correction publications since 1978	Bibliographic data and abstracts
GlobalPat	US, WO, EP, GB, DE, FR and CH from 1971	Bibliographic data, abstract, representative drawing. Collection available in 69 subject groups according to IPC.
AseanPat	Brunei, Indonesia, Malaysia, Philippines, Singapore, Thailand, Vietnam (start date ranging from early 1980's)	Bibliographic data, some English abstracts
ESPACE-OAPI	OAPI patents 1966–1992	Bibliographic data
ESPACE-ACCESS-Europe (*)	BE, NL, LU, CH, PT, GB (start date ranging from 1978)	Bibliographic data, some English abstracts
ESPACE-AT	AT-B, AT-U from 1990	Bibliographic data, images of complete specifications
ESPACE-BENELUX	BE-A, NL-A and -C, LU-A from 1991	Bibliographic data, images of complete specifications
ESPACE-CH	CH-A3, -A5, -B5 from 1990	Bibliographic data, images of complete specifications
ESPACE-DK	DK-B from 1990	Bibliographic data, images of complete specifications
ESPACE-ES	ES-A1, -A2, -A6, -T1, -T2 from 1990	Bibliographic data, images of complete specifications
ESPACE-FI	FI-C (old law), FI-B (new law) from 1976	Bibliographic data, images of complete specifications
ESPACE-IT	IT-A1, -U1 from 1993–1995	Bibliographic data, images of complete specifications
ESPACE-PT	PT-A, -U, -T from 1980	Bibliographic data, images of complete specifications
ESPACE-ACCESS-ASEAN	Brunei, Indonesia, Malaysia, Philippines, Singapore, Thailand, Vietnam (start date ranging from early 1980's)	Bibliographic data, some English abstracts

(*) note – this product is being replaced during 2005/2006 by a new disk series ESPACE-ACCESS-EPC which will cover bibliographic data on national documentation from all the member states of the EPC.

Table 36: Test disks / discontinued series

Name	Country coverage
ESPACE-AU	Australia
ESPACE-BR	Brazil
ESPACE-CA	Canada
ESPACE-CIS	Commonwealth of Independent States (USSR less the Baltic States)
ESPACE-CL	Chile
ESPACE-DOPALES	Central and South America
ESPACE-GR	Greece
ESPACE-IE	Ireland
ESPACE-Malaysia	Malaysia
ESPACE-MC	Monaco
ESPACE-MX	Mexico
ESPACE-Philippines	Philippines
ESPACE-Thailand	Thailand
ESPACE-Vietnam	Vietnam

Table 37: A selection of non-EPO disk-based products

Product	Coverage	Producer/distributor
DEPAROM	DE-A, DE-C, DE-U, DE-T	Bundesdruckerei, Germany
COSMOS / BREV	FR	INPI, France
ESPACE-PRECES	BG, CZ, HU, PL, RO, SK	Hungarian Patent Office
ESPACE-SI	SI-B	Slovenian Intellectual Property Office
ESPACE-UK	GB-A from 1976	Patent Office, United Kingdom
Patent Abstracts of Japan	English language abstracts of JP-A documents from 1976	JAPIO, EPO
US PatentImages	Facsimile images of US patents. Discontinued?	MicroPatent
EAPO	EA-A, EA-B (separate series)	EAPO, Moscow
Korean Patent Abstracts	KR-A	Korean Intellectual Property Office
PIPACS	HU-A, -B, -U	Hungarian Patent Office
PCT Gazette	WO front page data from 1997	Bundesdruckerei, Germany
Deutsches Patentblatt	German national patent gazette; weekly	Bundesdruckerei, Germany
USAPAT	Facsimile images of US granted patents (current law US-B, old law US-A)	USPTO
USAAPP	Facsimile images of US published applications (US-A)	USPTO
Patents Bib	Bibliographic information, 1969–date	USPTO
Patents Class	Current classification information for all US patent types, including utility patents from 1790–date	USPTO
Patents & Trademarks Assign	Assignment deeds on US patents and trademarks	USPTO
Patents Assist	Variety of support materials, including list of attorneys and agents, Index to the US Patent Classification, IPC – USPC Concordance, Manual of Classification, and Manual of Patent Examining Procedure.	USPTO

► INTEGRATED DISK-INTERNET PRODUCTS VIA MIMOSA

One of the criticisms of any disk-based product in a fast-moving field is the speed – or lack of it – in providing updates to the information. This may be in the form of complementary data or more current data. Since the development of MIMOSA, the EPO has pioneered an effective way of countering this problem.

Records may be viewed after a MIMOSA search in a variety of formats. One such format is shown in Figure 16, which shows a front-page style of display of the bibliographic data from a European Patent in ESPACE-ACCESS. Several fields, including the publication number and International Patent Classification, are formatted as "hot links", meaning that the user is able to retrieve the facsimile images of the entire document, located on the internet esp@acenet server, or the definition of the IPC, located on the WIPO server, by clicking on the record from the DVD search. Of course, this requires that the user has an active internet connection available, but it does illustrate the way in which a powerful, convenient offline search can be complemented by the storage capacity of an online document delivery service.

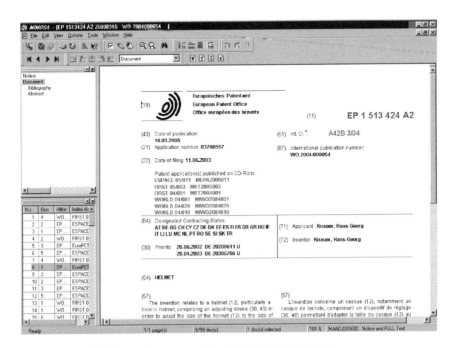

Figure 16: MIMOSA application searching ESPACE-ACCESS disks

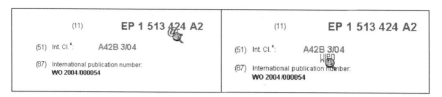

Figure 17: Hot-link to esp@cenet

Figure 18: Hot-link to WIPO classification site

Services such as ESPACE-Bulletin or ESPACE-ACCESS are typically updated on a monthly basis, by means of an update disk. However, this does not mean that the subscriber has to wait a month to get the latest data. In both cases, a subscriber to the disk-based product is additionally supplied with an account to retrieve interim data-sets, for the weeks between disk issue. These downloaded data-sets can be installed on the user's hard drive, and searched by MIMOSA in exactly the same fashion as the disks. Once the new information arrives in DVD form, the update file can be discarded. From the user's viewpoint, the service looks exactly as if it was a fully current disk product.

▶ PROPRIETARY ELECTRONIC DATABASES

By far the largest group of databases in the multi-national arena are proprietary products. Many have been established over many years and form the backbone of the professional patent information industry. They are increasingly distributed by a variety of means, including web-browser based search tools. The following discussions have been aimed at providing a glimpse at the content, rather than the mode of distribution, since it is the former which ultimately determines whether the database is a useable tool for the searcher.

World Patent Index (WPI) (Thomson)

This bibliographic file, widely known simply as "Derwent" amongst the patent-searching community, is probably the oldest multi-national electronic patent database in existence. The earliest product was produced by Mr. Monty Hyams from 1948, and was a manually produced weekly bulletin, "British Chemical Patents Report". This grew during the 1950's into Derwent Publications Ltd. It later became known as Derwent Information Ltd and was purchased by the Thomson Group.

The WPI file is mounted on a number of commercial host systems, including Dialog, Questel-Orbit, STN International, Delphion and Westlaw.

The earliest Derwent products were paper-based bulletins used mainly for the purposes of patent current awareness. Initially, Mr. Hyams and his colleagues travelled regularly from the UK to Belgium, to take advantage of the rapid-publishing system in force for Belgian patents. It was realised early on that the published patent titles were poorly suited to rapid scanning for relevance, and the process of creating a specially-structured rewritten title was started. This is still used in the modern bibliographic database. As technology improved, it became feasible to cumulate the current awareness service into a retrospective search file, which was initially launched publicly on the ORBIT service, in 1976.

The subject coverage of the early Derwent products was limited to the field of pharmaceutical patents only, in the so-called Farmdoc [sic – see footnote [1]] service. Coverage commenced in 1963. Two years later, agricultural chemicals were added (Agdoc), followed in 1966 by polymers (Plasdoc). In 1970, coverage had extended to general chemistry (as the Chemdoc service) and the remainder of the specialist chemical sector. The combined product was initially called the Central Patents Index and latterly Chemical Patents Index, CPI. For the convenience of subscribers, the output was divided into a number of lettered sections. The first three components became the sections A, B and C, whilst the remainder were split into sections D through to M. This categorisation formed the basis of the Derwent Class system, or Derwent sections, which are still used for indexing of database records to the present day.

Table 38: Chemical Patents Index (CPI) sections

Derwent Class (Section)	Definition	Earliest date covered
A	Polymers and plastics	1966
B	Pharmaceuticals	1963
C	Agricultural chemicals	1965
D	Food, Detergents, Water Treatment and Biotechnology	1970
E	General Chemicals	1970
F	Textiles, Paper Making	1970
G	Printing, Coating, Photographic	1970
H	Petroleum	1970
J	Chemical Engineering	1970
K	Nucleonics, Explosives, Protection	1970
L	Refractories, Ceramics, Cement, Electro(in)organics	1970
M	Metallurgy	1970

[1] Popular legend has it that the final decision on the name for the new pharmaceutical service was taken in Italy, and consequently used the Italian form of the word.

Additional countries were also added between 1963 and 1970, and have been progressively added over subsequent years, until today's database covers over 40 publishing authorities.

By 1974, demand for a corresponding abstracting service for the mechanical and electrical arts resulted in the creation of GMPI (General and Mechanical Patents Index – later re-designated the Engineering Patents Index, EngPI) and the EPI (Electrical Patents Index) respectively. These services covered patents from substantially the same countries as CPI, with the major exception of Japan, which was not fully covered in non-chemical fields until after 1995. The two additional areas of subject matter were similarly divided into Derwent Classes, as shown in Table 39.

The combined CPI/EPI/GMPI database was marketed as the Derwent World Patent Index, or WPI.

Table 39: Non chemical sections of WPI

Derwent Class (Section)	Definition	Earliest date covered
P	General (engineering)	1974
Q	Mechanical (engineering)	1974
R	(Electrical) *	1974–1979
S	Instrumentation, measuring and testing	1980
T	Computing and control	1980
U	Semiconductors and electronic circuitry	1980
V	Electronic components	1980
W	Communications	1980
X	Electric power engineering	1980

* used initially for all EPI patents; the classification was subsequently expanded into sections S-X and the database records were retrospectively re-indexed.

The distinctive aspects of the WPI database, as it had become, were clear from the beginning:

- re-written, informative titles and abstracts in English for all records, irrespective of the original language of publication
- logical subject-matter based categorisation into segments, which could be purchased separately, particularly useful for current awareness or provision of full texts
- two enhanced deep-indexing systems (Manual Codes and the chemical Fragmentation/Polymer codes) to improve retrieval
- standardised formats for publication numbers and application numbers
- standardised assignee names, supplemented by a standard Assignee Code system which grouped some subsidiaries and superseded company name changes

- error checking and standardisation in fields derived from primary data, such as the International Patent Classification
- the development of database rules for a patent family system, making a clear distinction between first appearance of a new invention (the basic) and subsequent corresponding applications (equivalents) from other countries. This enabled Derwent to concentrate indexing effort upon a single example from each patent family.

The original Derwent editorial and database production system was constructed in logical stages, which led to an enormous range of different products (on paper, microfiche and microfilm, CD-ROM and electronic formats). Many of these have been phased out in recent years, in favour of electronic products, but the legacy still makes itself felt. Consequently, it is useful to be aware of the ways in which the system has developed.

Patents entering the database production system were channelled into a particular editorial group according to whether the subject matter was covered in the database (as noted above, Japan was only covered for chemistry, so engineering patents were not included at all for many years), and whether the publishing country was so-called 'major' or 'minor' (of which more later). The subject group reflected the Derwent Classes. If appropriate, a patent could be allocated to more than one class, but the 'primary' class was used to determine which printed bulletin the abstracts would appear in.

After preparation of a short abstract and new title, the printed Alerting Abstracts Bulletins were produced for each Derwent Class. All new basics from major countries had their database records enhanced with Manual Codes. The online abstract field contained the text of the Alerting Abstract, which is available to all users of the online file. After release of the Alerting Abstracts, an enhanced version of the abstract was produced and released only to pre-paying Derwent subscribers, according to the sections of the Derwent system covered by their subscription. These so-called Documentation Abstracts were also produced in paper bulletins and subsequently on microfilm and scanned images on CD-ROM (the Documentation Abstracts Journal, or DAJ, on CD-ROM). Later still, paper reproductions and microfilm copies of the full patents were also produced by Derwent section. Neither the Documentation Abstracts nor the full texts was loaded onto the database. In recent years, the new form of the DAJ (now referred to as Enhanced Abstracts) have been made available online, but still only for subscribers, in the form of a separate controlled-access database. The same database also provides access to the subscriber-only portions of the indexing, namely the Chemical Manual Codes and the fragmentation or polymer coding, covering publications issued in sections A, B, C or E.

One of the key benefits for a subscriber company was the use of a common accession number system. This enabled a user to perform a search using subscriber indexing, retrieve an Alerting Abstract for initial relevance screening, and then locate the corresponding Documentation Abstract for detailed study and/or the complete patent text in a single step. With the advent of dynamic linking from within search databases to third-party databases containing the complete documents, much of the value of this system has been superseded, but the products are still produced and have retained some of their user base within industry.

The printed Derwent products, in all technical areas, typically contained a single clipped image to aid comprehension of the text abstract. These images were too large for the available bandwidth to handle until the early 1990's, when the first images were loaded, in the engineering sector back to 1988, followed by images from chemical patents back to 1992.

In the all-electronic environment of today's WPI file, the distinction between major and minor countries has become less significant than before. However, it is still possible that recall may be affected for some searches, so a short explanation is helpful.

Essentially, a publication from a major country is given the full indexing treatment, and the corresponding database record will include any deep indexing appropriate to the subject sections concerned. If this publication is a basic, it follows that the database family record is fully indexed from the point of its creation, and any subsequent equivalent patents are retrievable as if they had also been deep-indexed, since the same 'pool' of indexing applies across the entire family.

In a small percentage of cases, the first appearance of a new invention is from a minor country, and the added indexing is not created immediately. At this point, the document is only retrievable via a restricted range of search fields. Full indexing is only added to the record when (or if) a subsequent member of the same patent family appears from a major country. This later member is fully indexed and the corresponding fields are populated in the updated family record. From this point onwards, the basic minor country publication is retrievable using the full range of retrieval tools. The time interval between the creation of the partially-indexed minor country basic record and the addition of full indexing via a major country equivalent may be only a matter of a few weeks, so to all intents and purposes the minor country publication appears to have carried the full indexing from inception, and no documents are lost in the search.

A more substantial impact upon retrieval occurs in the (relatively rare) circumstances where a new invention only appears in a minor country, and never re-publishes with any major country equivalents at all. In these cases, the database record for this invention will be less fully indexed than if the invention had appeared in a major country.

For reference purposes, the current status of major or minor is included in the list of overall country coverage in Table 40. The same table can be referred to in considering the other multi-country files discussed

Table 40: Country coverage for selected multi-country databases

Country code	Country name	INPA-DOC	CAS	WPI	MPI	WIPS	PlusPat/FamPat	Minesoft/RWS PatBase	Lexis-Nexis Univentio Total Patent	Esp@cenet Worldwide
AP	AFRICAN REGIONAL INDUSTRIAL PROPERTY OFFICE (ARIPO)	1984	2000		1984	1984	1984	Present	1984	1985
AR	ARGENTINA	1973	1959	1974–1976	1973	1973	1973	Present	1973	1973
AT	AUSTRIA	1969	1907	1975	1825	1969	1969	1899	1969	1899
AU	AUSTRALIA	1973	1927	1963–1969, 1982+	1945	1973	1966	1973	1973	1941
BA	BOSNIA AND HERZEGOVINA	1998			1998	1998	1998	Present	1998	1998
BD	BANGLADESH							Pending		
BE	BELGIUM	1964	1928	1963	1923	1964	1926	1926	1964	1923
BG	BULGARIA	1973	2000		1973	1973	1973	Present	1980	1973
BN	BRUNEI							Pending	1980	
BO	BOLIVIA							Pending	1991	
BR	BRAZIL	1973	1957	1975	1973	1973	1973	Present	1973	1974
CA	CANADA	1970	1910	1963	1940	1970	1973	1973	1970	1940
CH	SWITZERLAND	1969	1910	1963	1888	1974	1920	1888	1969	1888
CL	CHILE		1919					Present	1991	
CN	CHINA	1985	1985	1985	1985	1985	1986	1985	1985	1985
CO	COLOMBIA							Pending	1991	
CR	COSTA RICA							Pending	1991	
CS	CZECHOSLOVAKIA	1973	1955	1975	1973	1973	1973	Present	1973	1973
CU	CUBA	1974			1974	1974	1974	Present	1974	1974
CY	CYPRUS	1975			1921	1975	1975	Present	1975	1921
CZ	CZECH REPUBLIC	1993	1993	1993	1993	1993	1993	Present	1993	1993

DD	EAST GERMANY	1973	1954	1963	1952	1973	1951	1973	1952
DE	GERMANY	1967	1899	1963	1879	1966	1877	1967	1877
DK	DENMARK	1968	1909	1974	1901	1968	1895	1968	1895
DO	DOMINICAN REPUBLIC						Pending	1991	
EA	EURASIAN PATENT OFFICE (EAPO)	1996			1996	1996	Present	1996	1996
EC	ECUADOR						Pending	1991	
EE	ESTONIA	1995	2000			1995	1973	1995	1995
EG	EGYPT	1976	2000	1976	1976	1976	Present	1976	1976
EP	EUROPEAN PATENT OFFICE (EPO)	1978	1978	1978	1978	1978	Present	1978	1978
ES	*SPAIN*	1968	1946	1983	1968	1968	Present	1978	1968
FI	FINLAND	1968	1960	1974	1933	1968	1973	1968	1933
FR	FRANCE	1968	1900	1963	1902	1970	1791	1968	1902
GB	UNITED KINGDOM	1969	1901	1963	1863	1971	1617	1969	1863
GE	GEORGIA						Pending	1991	
GR	GREECE	1977	2000		1977	1977	1977	1977	1977
GT	GUATEMALA						Pending	1991	
HK	HONG KONG	1976	2000	1976	1976	1976	1976	1976	1976
HN	HONDURAS						Pending	1991	
HR	CROATIA	1994	2000	2000		1994	Present	1994	1994
HU	*HUNGARY*	1973	1925	1975	1973	1973	Present	1973	1973
ID	INDONESIA	1996				1996	Present	1996	1988
IE	IRELAND	1973		1963–1969, 1995+	1948	1973	1973	1973	1948
IL	*ISRAEL*	1968	1956	1975	1968	1968	1973	1968	1968
IN	INDIA	1975	1935	2004	1975	1975	Present	1975	1998
IT	ITALY	1973	1913	1966–1968, 1977+	1933	1973	1973	1973	1933
JO	JORDAN						Pending		
JP	**JAPAN**	1973	1901	1963	1958	1976	1973	1973	1928
KE	KENYA	1975		1975	1975	1975	Present	1975	1975

Table 40: continued

Country code	Country name	INPA-DOC	CAS	WPI	MPI	WIPS	PlusPat/FamPat	Minesoft/RWS PatBase	Lexis-Nexis Univentio Total Patent	Esp@cenet Worldwide
KR	KOREA, REPUBLIC OF	1978	1995	1985	1978	1979	1978	1978	1978	1978
LT	LITHUANIA	1992	1994		1994	1992	1994	Present	1992	1994
LU	LUXEMBOURG	1945	2001	1984	1945	1945	1946	1973	1945	1945
LV	LATVIA	1994	1994		1993	1994	1994	Present	1994	1993
MA	MOROCCO								1993	
MC	MONACO	1975	2000		1957	1975	1975	1975	1975	1957
MD	MOLDOVA	1994	2000		1994	1994	1994	Present	1994	1994
MN	MONGOLIA	1972			1972	1972	1972	Present	1972	1972
MT	MALTA	1967			1967	1967	1968	Present	1967	1967
MW	MALAWI	1973			1973	1973	1973	Present	1973	1973
MX	MEXICO	1981	1956	1997	1980	1981	1981	Present	1980	1980
MY	MALAYSIA	1953			1953	1953	1971	1988	1953	1953
NI	NICARAGUA							Pending	1991	
NL	NETHERLANDS	1964	1912	1963	1914	1964	1912	1912	1964	1914
NO	NORWAY	1968	1907	1974	1936	1968	1968	1973	1968	1936
NZ	NEW ZEALAND	1978	2000	1992	1978	1978	1979	1978	1978	1978
OA	AFRICAN INTELLECTUAL PROPERTY ORGANISATION (OAPI)	1992			1960	1992	1966	Present	1992	1960
PA	PANAMA							Pending?	1991	
PE	PERU							Pending	1991	
PH	PHILIPPINES	1975		1992	1975	1975	1975	Present	1975	1975
PL	POLAND	1973	1957		1962	1973	1973	Present	1973	1962
PT	PORTUGAL	1976	2000	1974	1971	1976	1976	1976	1976	1971
PY	PARAGUAY							Pending?	1991	

RO	ROMANIA	1973	1952	1975	1973	1973	1973	Present	1973	1970
RU	**RUSSIA**	1993	1908	1993	1993	1993	1994	1993	1993	1993
SE	**SWEDEN**	1968	1908	1974	1905	1968	1968	1973	1968	1904
SG	**SINGAPORE**	1983	2000	1995	1983	1983	1983	1983	1983	1989
SI	SLOVENIA	1996	2000		1992	1996	1992	Present	1996	1992
SK	SLOVAKIA	1993	1994	1993	1993	1993	1993	Present	1993	1993
SM	SAN MARINO							Pending		
SU	**SOVIET UNION**	1972	1940	1963	1940	1972	1972	1972	1972	1940
SV	EL SALVADOR							Pending	1991	
TH	THAILAND							Pending	1991	Present
TJ	TAJIKISTAN	1998			1998	1998	1998	Present	1998	1998
TN	TUNISIA							Pending		
TR	TURKEY	1973	2000		1973	1973	1973	Present	1973	1973
TT	TRINIDAD & TOBAGO				1994		1994	Present	1994	1994
TW	**TAIWAN**	2000	1958	1993	1983	2000	2000	2000	2000	1983
US	**UNITED STATES**	1968	1905	1963	1859	1976	1920	1867	1790	1836
UY	URUGUAY							Pending	1991	
UZ	UZBEKISTAN	1997			1997	1997	1997			1997
VE	VENEZUELA							Pending	1991	
VN	VIET NAM	1984			1984	1984	1984	Present	1984	1984
WO	**WORLD INTELLECTUAL PROPERTY ORGANIZATION (WIPO)**	1978	1978	1978	1978	1978	1978	1978	1978	1978
YU	YUGOSLAVIA	1973			1973	1973	1973	Present	1973	1973
ZA	**SOUTH AFRICA**	1971	1939	1963	1971	1971	1971	1973	1971	1971
ZM	ZAMBIA	1968			1968	1968	1968		1968	1968
ZW	ZIMBABWE	1980			1980	1980	1980		1980	1980

Note:
Country names printed in **bold** received 'major country' indexing treatment in the Derwent WPI file from the start of their coverage.
Country names printed in *italics* received 'minor country' indexing treatment in the Derwent WPI file from the start of their coverage, but were later promoted to 'major country' status and are currently indexed accordingly.
All other countries with an entry in the WPI column are treated as 'minor countries' within the Derwent WPI file

elsewhere in this chapter. It should be remembered, however, that this only shows the earliest year of coverage for the specific Kinds-of-Document contained in the respective files, and that coverage of each Kind-of-Document for a given country may vary; for example, the WPI contains records of AU-A documents from 1963, but did not include AU-B documents until 1993. Also, a starting year indicates the earliest year of any form of coverage; for example, TotalPatent has French bibliographic data from 1968, and full text from 1980, so the earlier date is used in the Table.

As indicated above, the full power of the WPI indexing system is only available to subscribers. It represents a substantial investment in development time and in its maintenance and upkeep. The system is only available in the chemical arts, and has three components:

1. The CPI Manual Codes, consisting of a set of approximately 7,500 hierarchically-grouped indexing terms, represented by a systematic notation. The term listing has been revised a number of times since it was first created in 1963, including several times in the last few years. It appears that, for the future, a more frequent revision will be applied, at approximately annual intervals. This will help to ensure that the terms reflect current technology. The notation is designed to allow truncation, permitting the searcher to broaden or narrow their field of search. Although Manual Codes are rarely adequate on their own to define a complete search, they are extremely valuable in excluding unwanted subject matter or refining a search with too many answers. Each database record in the chemical area will have at least one Manual Code applied; the range covers is approximately 1 to 8 Codes per record. The corresponding Manual Code system in the electrical area (EPI) is open to all users, but the vocabulary is structured in a very similar manner. The EPI Manual Code system contains approximately 9,500 codes. There are currently no Manual Codes for the mechanical area, although it is understood that Thomson are considering introducing them. An example of the Manual Code hierarchy is shown in Table 41.

2. The chemical fragmentation codes, consisting of approximately 2,200 alphanumeric codes. Each code represents a small chemically-significant fragment, such as the presence of a specific element or functional group. If a chemical patent discloses a single compound, all the corresponding fragment codes appropriate to that compound are attached to the database record. For generic ("Markush") disclosures, chemical fragment indexing is generated which corresponds to the range of compounds encompassed by the disclosure; for example, if a wide range of esters are disclosed, the code for

Table 41: Example CPI Manual Code hierarchy

Manual Code	Definition	Date of introduction
K	Nucleonics, Explosives, Protection	1970
K07	Health Physics	1970
K07-A	Protective measures, monitoring, shielding, clothing etc.	1970
K07-A01	Personal dosimeters	1972
K07-A02	Shielding	1994
K07-A02A	Transport/storage containers	1994
K07-A02B	Fall-out shelters	1994
K07-A03	Decontamination	1986

'ester' will be added. By linking together the individual codes, the searcher is able to retrieve all records which specifically *or generically* disclose the compound(s) of interest to the search. The system is extremely complex to use to its full potential, but remains one of the few ways in which a true generic patentability search can be conducted. Competing topographical-based systems such as Marpat and MMS (discussed later in this chapter) operate on a different search model, and currently only permit retrieval back to 1978 at the earliest, whereas Derwent fragmentation codes allow searching back to 1963 for some subject areas. Work is under way at Thomson to back-index document records from the period 1963–1980 with the most precise set of codes, introduced in 1981; this will enhance the precision of searchability in the older part of the file. A few example codes are given in Table 42.

3.   The polymer coding (Plasdoc) system was introduced in 1966, and has undergone a number of revisions since. It operates in essentially the same manner as the chemical fragment codes, but instead of indexing small portions of an organic or inorganic molecule, the polymer codes characterise the monomer and repeat units of polymeric materials. There are additional codes enabling the functionality and method of manufacture of the polymer to be indexed. As with the chemical fragment codes, it takes a lot of skill to be able to use the system to best advantage. In recent years, some software tools have been developed to assist the novice in devising a suitable search strategy using the polymer codes.

Table 42: Example Chemical fragmentation code hierarchy

Series	Code	Definition
A2:		Alkaline earths
	A200	General (present but not fully defined)
	A204	Beryllium
	A212	Magnesium
	A220	Calcium
	A238	Strontium
	A256	Barium
D6:		1-N only; 2 rings (heterocyclic ring systems containing two rings and only 1 nitrogen atom as heteroatom)
	D601	Indole (excluding D602)
	D602	Di (or poly)hydroindole
	D611	Isoindole (including 1,2-dihydroindole)
	D612	Isoindole (excluding D611)
	D621	Quinoline (excluding D622)
	D622	Di (or poly)hydroquinoline
	D631	Isoquinoline (excluding D632)
	D632	Di (or poly)hydroisoquinoline
	D640	Benzazepine
	D650	Benzazocine
	D660	Indolizine and quinolizine
	D670	Tropane
	D680	Quinuclidine
	D690	Other 1-N,two-ring systems, not specified above
	D699	More than one ring systems from D6 coded.

Patent Citation Index (PCI) (Thomson)

The PCI is a companion product to WPI. It uses the same family structure to group inventions into larger records, but the emphasis of this file is to facilitate the use of search reports in citation searching. The file is available on STN International and Dialog, and as part of the web-based Derwent Innovations Index (DII).

The assumption behind PCI is that the items cited in a patent application's official search report (or, in the case of a US granted patent, the 'References Cited' list) can be treated in the same way as the bibliography in a conventional journal article or review. The challenge in the patents field is to recognise that family groupings can affect both the citing patent and the cited patent. In respect of the citing patent, it is quite possible that equivalent family members may both cite the same patent; following the citation link may suggest that a new document exists which co-cites known prior art, but in fact the new document is none other than an equivalent of a known case. In respect of the cited patent, it is quite possible (indeed likely) that two examiners in different countries, each intending to cite the same invention, will do so by means of citing their own local family member. This gives the impression that the two search reports do not have any items in common, when in fact they do. Both of these problems can be circumvented if both citing and cited patents are grouped into their respective patent families. The PCI achieves this by using the same family structure as WPI.

The original PCI used the cumulated search reports from Austria, Australia, Belgium, Canada, European Patent Office, France, Germany, Japan, the Netherlands, New Zealand, PCT international applications, South Africa, Sweden, Switzerland, the United Kingdom and the United States, compiled into the standard family structure of the WPI record. Documents which co-cite an item from a known search report can be retrieved, irrespective of whether they cited the same family member or another one.

The launch of PCI included both examiner citations (from formal search reports) and applicant citations (additional references from the body of the text, provided by the applicant and not present in the formal search report). It proved very labour-intensive to extract the latter, so the product was soon relaunched as a record of examiner citations only, and the country coverage reduced to only 6 countries: the EPO, Germany, Japan, PCT international applications, the United Kingdom and the United States.

The PCI is the only database which systematically collates search reports in this fashion. Once the searcher is aware of the pitfalls and caveats surrounding the use of the citation technique, it can prove a valuable additional resource. Its major use is probably during patentability searches, when it can be applied to either retrieve older literature (beyond the formal start date of most bibliographic files) or contemporaneous literature citing items in common.

PlusPat and FamPat (Questel-Orbit)

The PlusPat file is derived from a core based upon the EPO's internal search file, called EPODOC. This employed a strict family structure more suited to the needs of a patent office search examiner, resulting in smaller families. The number of countries covered was originally around 20 national authorities, but following the takeover of the INPADOC organisation by the EPO in the early 1990's, the INPADOC family file and the EPODOC file were gradually merged, effectively increasing the EPODOC coverage to around 70 countries. The major strengths of EPODOC were

- the inclusion of some document types not covered in INPADOC (for example, the old Act JP-C certificates)

- enhanced time coverage for some countries; for example, British patents are included from 1909 and German from 1877
- provision of ECLA classification for a substantial proportion of the file.

The EPODOC file was loaded on the Questel system for many years as the EDOC file. In the late 1990's, this was relaunched as PlusPat. It is exclusively available via the Questel-Orbit system. The PlusPat development has included the addition of more English-language abstracts, further classification systems (including current US classes for US records), search reports including relevancy indicators, and clipped images. The file is currently standing at some 50 million records, and is updated weekly. Despite not having the detailed proprietary indexing provided by WPI, PlusPat's combination of abstracts and multiple classification systems make it a powerful search tool across many fields of technology.

The principal weakness of PlusPat lies in the record structure. Records contain either a single publication stage, if that is all that has been released, or the corresponding multiple stages for the same application (e.g. a modern US-A and US-B or an EP-A and EP-B will be grouped together). For international families, it is necessary to use the Questel command to create the family dynamically. Since some family members may contain fields not found in others, it becomes necessary to run this command repeatedly throughout the session. For example, a search using an ECLA term (present in some 50% of the file) combined with a title word or phrase may yield a zero result, but a search consisting of the steps of searching by ECLA, retrieving the family structure and then adding the same title word or phrase may well produce a hit, where the classification has been applied to one family member and the title word used by another family member.

This shortcoming in the PlusPat search procedure has been addressed by the release of the FamPat file. The individual bibliographic sources are identical to PlusPat, but the records are now grouped into international families. The rules for family selection are unique to FamPat, and will generally yield families with more members than the strict EPODOC algorithm, but fewer than the INPADOC system. The unique feature of the FamPat family is that it can be retrospectively re-structured, eliminating the need for cross-referencing family records which is sometimes found in WPI. The effect is to bring additional family members in, such as non-Convention filings, multiple US applications derived from US provisional filings (often not cited in a format which permits their capture algorithmically), and cognated cases.

The detailed country coverage for FamPat can be found in Table 40.

API Encompass and WPAM (Questel-Orbit)

Any searcher involved in patent searching for more than a trivial period of time will soon discover that most patent databases have some unique feature which makes them more or less suitable for a specific kind of search. The question is often asked as to whether it would be possible to create a 'super-database', containing not only a merged set of bibliographic records (years, countries) but also a merger of the value-added indexing providing by one or more commercial database producer. One prominent proponent of the creation of such 'super-databases' – or at least 'super-records' – was Stuart Kaback, who expressed the idea at least as far back as 1983[1]. The WPAM database is a rare example of just such co-operation. It has successfully combined the indexing of the WPI file with that created by the American Petroleum Institute (API), specifically aimed at the oil and gas industries.

For many years, the API obtained Derwent data under licence, in their particular subject field, and added a very powerful, text-based system of controlled indexing to these records. The enhanced records were released as the APIPAT file. The coverage was heavily dependent upon the WPI file, but some additional material was also present – this included coverage of India and Poland (drawing upon CAS records) and possibly some limited content from countries with significant oil production such as Venezuela, not covered by any other file.

The Central Abstracting & Indexing Services of the API were spun off during the early 1990's as EnCompass, which was acquired in 1999 by Engineering Information, Inc., a subsidiary of Reed-Elsevier <http://www.ei.org>. The new owners have promoted web-based implementation of their databases, but the original forms are still available on the commercial hosts as well. Prior to the acquisition, Questel-Orbit had already created the merged WPI/API file, which retains the subscriber access restrictions from both suppliers.

The particular strength of WPAM is in patentability searching in the oil and gas industries, but the indexing system makes it useful for a wider range of general process chemistry and chemical engineering, not just limited to small carbon-count molecules. As indicated above, the country coverage is virtually identical to WPI, but with earliest content dating from 1964 and hence pre-dating Derwent's own coverage of the industry sector, which did not commence until 1970. A more detailed breakdown of the variation is given by Simmons[2].

INPADOC PFS and Open Patent Services

The INPADOC file family started life during the early 1970's as a product of INPADOC GmbH, or the International Patent Documentation Centre, established by agreement between WIPO and the Republic of Austria and based in Vienna. In contrast to Derwent WPI, which focuses on creating a quality retrospective file for patentability and other subject-based searching, the principal focus of INPADOC is to establish a comprehensive family database. Each record is comparatively brief (main bibliographic details only) but the range of countries covered quickly exceeded those in WPI. At the present time, coverage is available for over 70 countries, compared with fewer than 50 for WPI.

The initial range of INPADOC products was distributed on microfilm, or made available via direct network access to a computer centre in Vienna. Subsequently, the file was made available on a number of commercial hosts, including Dialog, STN International, Questel-Orbit, Lexis-Nexis, MicroPatent and Patolis.

INPADOC products have traditionally been divided into distinct 'modules' or 'services' and some are still referred to by these names:

- PFS   Patent Family Service
- PCS   Patent Classification Service
- PAS   Patent Applicant Service (sorted by IPC)
- PAP   Patent Applicant Service (sorted by priorities)
- PIS   Patent Inventor Service
- PRS   Patent Register Service

Of these products, the PFS is the main source for the commercial products as far as bibliographic details are concerned. The PRS relates to legal status information, and will be considered in more detail in chapter 10. The implementation of INPADOC on STN and Dialog keeps the bibliographic data (PFS) and legal status data (PRS) in the same file, whereas the Questel-Orbit version separates the legal status service as a separate searchable file, called LEGSTAT.

Since little value-added data is being including in the compilation of PFS, it is possible to include new information very rapidly. The INPADOC centre receives its data directly from national patent offices, or in a few cases keyboards data from paper gazettes where electronic supply was not possible. All subject areas are covered, providing an electronic record of the complete patent publication record for each country. In some cases (such as Germany, Austria and Japan), INPADOC has branched out beyond the coverage of other bibliographic files, to include utility models and short-term patents.

The INPADOC organisation was incorporated into the European Patent Office in 1991, and established as the Vienna sub-office of the EPO, dedicated to patent information products and services. The principal strength of the INPADOC database today is the breadth of country coverage and the comprehensive family algorithm, enabling a searcher to gain a rapid overview of the patent situation for an invention, on the basis of a single known case. The database is updated weekly, although time lag between formal publication date and actual entry into the database will vary from zero to many weeks, depending upon the patent office supplying the data. Most major countries have their bibliographic data added with 4–6 weeks at maximum, with many being available within days.

A typical bibliographic record in INPADOC will include basic data such as title, inventors, applicant, application and priority data, classification (usually IPC) and sometimes an applicant's abstract. No further abstracting or indexing takes place before the record enters the file.

Table 40 includes the basic range of countries and years in the file. For more detailed coverage tables, the user should refer to the INPADOC part of the EPO website, at <http://www.european-patent-office.org/inpadoc/index.htm>, which includes detailed manuals on content, numbering conventions and Kind-of-Document codes, FAQ sections, downloadable spreadsheets on currency, and a regular newsletter.

Following the INPADOC incorporation into the EPO, a project was undertaken to merge the bibliographic data in the existing EPO multi-country search file DocDB with the content of INPADOC. The resulting merged data set forms the core data for a new XML service from the EPO, called the Open Patent Services, or OPS. Details of this are available at a sub-domain of the esp@cenet site, address <http://ops.espacenet.com/>. Instead of providing a fully-functional search system, with its own command language, the EPO has provided an XML-format data warehouse. Each user – either individual company or commercial information provider – is able to create their own interface and command system to access the same data, providing it to their customers in a format and structure which accords with their particular usage. This can include configuring the system to filter out records or fields which are not appropriate for that user. This could mean that in the future, there will be many different services providing access to "OPS data", but not all of them will display the same level of data content, which will be controlled by the interface design. More information on the service can be found in an article in EPIDOS News[3]. One example of a search service developed around the OPS data is the GetPat@Web product from INCOM IPS GmbH, at <http://incom-ips.de>. The PatBase service from Minesoft draws upon OPS data, but instead of simply creating an interface, the data are physically downloaded for incorporation into a larger search tool. Both forms of using the OPS data are likely to be seen in a range of new products within the next few years.

Pharm (Questel-Orbit)

The Pharm (formerly Pharmsearch) file is multi-national in coverage, but restricted to a specific technology field, namely pharmaceuticals. The file producer is the French national patent office, INPI. As with PlusPat, it is exclusively available on the Questel-Orbit host system. It contains bibliographic details for pharmaceutical patents and patent applications from Germany, the EPO, France (including the closed BSM series from 1961–1978), the United Kingdom, the United States and PCT international patent applications.

The original Pharmsearch file was designed to work in tandem with a database of generic chemical structures, called MPharm. This file had indexed records of chemical structures starting from the mid-1980's for the above countries, and the Pharm file had the corresponding bibliographic records. However, in the early 1990's, the MPharm file was merged with the corresponding Derwent file WPIM to form the MMS (Merged Markush Service), which is discussed in more detail later in this section. At the time of the merger, it was decided to back-index all the records for the six authorities in the Pharm file to 1978. At the time of writing, this has been completed for four out of the six, and work continues on the German and UK content.

It should be noted that since the merger of the structure files, the bibliographic file has not been indexed to the same depth as the original Pharm file. For the initial period from launch until the MMS merger, the Pharm file contained added indexing fields enabling a subject search on aspects such as therapeutic use, extraction, biological or chemical processes, formulations, therapeutic effects and toxicity. These fields were added to both ongoing records and older records for a short period after the merger, but ceased around 2000. This means that only the middle time period and a small part of the older and newer records have this available for searching (the approximate content is summarised in Table 43). This unfortunately means that the added keywords are un-useable as a systematic search tool.

The principal value of Pharm is still by way of its linkage with corresponding structure records. Patentability searching in the MMS file by means of sub-structures creates a list of candidate answers, which are crossed over to the corresponding bibliographic records for further processing or screening for relevance.

Table 43: Pharm country coverage

Publishing authority	Bibliographic details and abstracts only	Fully-indexed coverage including added keywords
DE	1981–1992, 2000–date	1992–2000
EP	1978–1985, 2000–date	1985–2000
FR	1978–1985, 2000–date	1985–2000
FR-M		1961–1978
GB	1981–1992, 2000–date	1992–2000
US	1978–1985, 2000–date	1985–2000
WO	1978–1991, 2000–date	1991–2000

Other Thomson bibliographic products

Over the last decade, the Thomson corporation has purchased a number of other patent information suppliers, specialising in either alerting services or cumulated databases. The process of integrating some of the product range is still not completed, and will probably take a course dictated as much by the customers of the former products as by economies of scale. At the present time, it is difficult to obtain clear information on the content or future of some of the range.

With the purchase of Current Drugs Ltd, Thomson acquired their flagship product IDdb (Investigational Drugs Database), which covers not only patents information, but also company profiles and drug pipeline reports, technical meeting reports, news and journal literature. On the patents front, content is derived from the Patents Fast-Alert range of bulletins, covering patents from WO, EP, US, JP and GB in the pharmaceutical field. A minor product is the Agro Patent Fast Alert, which does the same thing for the agrochemical and plant biotechnology sector.

A second acquisition, the confusingly named Current Patents Ltd., brought with it the Current Patents Gazette, again dedicated to the pharmaceutical industry. Their informed comment on weekly new publications forms the basis for the added-value patent content of DOLPHIN. The coverage of the Gazette is principally limited to WO, EP, GB and US, although additional countries may be included if they form the first publication of a new invention. DOLPHIN (the Database Of alL PHarmacuetical INventions) itself is based on INPADOC data, covering some 70 countries and including both bibliographic and legal status information.

Patents Preview is a sister product to the main WPI file, but again concentrating on the pharmaceutical sector and limiting coverage to a small number of significant authorities, WO, EP, JP, US, GB, DE and FR. The aim is to provide an alerting service covering current research developments and competitor intelligence within 8 days of publication. The abstracts are written separately from those of the WPI editorial system, and focus on research leads in the form of specific compound disclosures and therapeutic activity.

Drug Patents International (DPI)

The Drug Patents International database is produced by IMSWorld Publications, part of the IMS Health group based in London. The database is hosted on Questel-Orbit, Dialog and STN. It is structured in a manner which is quite distinct from most multi-national patent databases, in that each record in the file is dedicated to a single pharmaceutical compound, including its chemical structure, synonyms and CAS Registry Numbers. In essence, this forms a directory of marketed drugs. Each record is then supplemented by patent coverage, including bibliographic data for the patents protecting the drug and its formulations and processes. It also includes data on patent extensions and anticipated expiry dates. Information on the country coverage of DPI is difficult to establish; publicity claims a "worldwide" coverage, but anecdotal evidence suggests that information can vary substantially in its quality and quantity for different countries.

The format of the DPI file does not make it very suitable for patentability searches, but it is an ideal source to establish questions such as the size and form of a given drug company's therapeutic portfolio, or to estimate the time before a given known product will come off patent and be open to generic competition.

At the time of writing, it was announced that IMS Health had been taken over by the Dutch media group VNU. There are a number of market research companies in the VNU stable, and it is expected that the IMS takeover seeks to complement these with the statistical marketing reports on the pharmaceutical industry produced by IMS. The future of the specialist databases such as DPI is not known at this time.

GeneSeq

GeneSeq is a searchable database of nucleic acid and amino acid sequences disclosed in patents. It is produced by the Thomson Derwent company, and draws upon the same basic coverage as the WPI file. It provides a means of directly searching the sequences using a variety of commercial algorithms, to assist in establishing questions of patentability.

The file is available on the STN International system. Searchers in industry often use a specialist software application, STN Express, to assist in the process of constructing a search strategy and viewing results. Once a record has been retrieved by structure, the corresponding Derwent family data can be viewed directly or crossed into the companion WPI file for further searching.

The coverage of GeneSeq is identical with the WPI file (some 40 countries) and it is claimed that more the half of the sequence data do not appear in any other publicly available sequence database.

Chemical Abstracts / Marpat

The Chemical Abstracts Service (CAS) is a part of the American Chemical Society, and since 1907 has been responsible for producing the secondary publication, "Chemical Abstracts." This service, now in the form of the electronic database, provides access to the world literature of chemistry, in the form of abstracts and indexing to the journals, reports, conference, thesis and patent literature. Although in the early days, journals formed its principal coverage, some patents have been included from the beginning, and today more than half of the abstracts produced each year are from the patent literature.

The coverage of CAS was based upon editorial decisions of the publishers, and developed independently of the other major bibliographic files such as WPI. However, for the period from approximately 1975–1995, INPADOC provided a major data feed, and no country would be covered unless it was also in the INPADOC file. In recent years, CAS has been making content decisions independently, and so the coverage has diverged from that of INPADOC. More detail is found on their website at <http://www.cas.org/EO/caspat.html>, and in older printed versions[4].

As with many of the Thomson niche products, the CAS file is not a complete collection of all the patent documents from each country covered. A sub-set in the field of chemistry is chosen, which is defined on the basis of a range of groups from the International Patent Classification and/or the United States Patent Classification. Some groups are defined as 'core', that is, all patents bearing a class from that list will be abstracted and indexed; other groups are 'non-core', which means that patents will be screened and only selected for inclusion if the document analyst considers that there is enough chemical content to warrant the inclusion.

The country coverage list for the CAS file is given at Table 40. Apart from the caveat that general and mechanical inventions are not covered at all, there is a further restriction on the actual content, based on the so-called 'national' criterion. This selection policy, typically applied to a number of Eastern European countries, dictates that only patents from a corporation or individual resident in the country of publication will be included in the file. This is a form of family selection, since it tends to exclude the bulk of patent applications filed under the Paris Convention by applicants from abroad, and allows indexing effort to be concentrated upon patents from local inventors and inventing companies.

The CAS bibliographic file exists in a number of different electronic versions. The most comprehensive, which includes abstracts and patent family data, is loaded on the STN International host. This includes data back to the beginning of CAS in 1907, and even selected articles from the beginning of the century. It also provides enhanced classification information. The corresponding loads of the file on Dialog and Questel-Orbit only covers the time period of 1967 to date, and contain no abstracts or patent family data.

Many patent searchers will approach the CAS bibliographic file via the corresponding Registry file, which is a database of specific chemical structures disclosed in each record. This is only available via the STN International host. Any disclosed chemical compound – from any source – is checked against the master database at the time of input. If it is not known prior to this time, a structure identity record is created, and a unique identifier is allocated to the compound, in the form of the CAS Registry

Number ®. These numbers have a characteristic format NNNNNN-NN-N, and can be used as a crossover key from the structure database to the corresponding bibliographic records. There are well over 25 million individual compounds registered in the CAS Registry file. These can be searched on the basis of structure or sub-structure, using a specialist command language to create a search enquiry in the form of a connection table. The computer matching of the query connection tables with the database connection tables produces an answer set in the form of the Registry Numbers of the matching compound(s). These numbers can then be linked to the originating article(s) which disclosed the compound(s). The ability to query by sub-structure, combined with the wide country coverage of the bibliographic file, makes the CAS Registry file on STN a primary source for the searcher undertaking chemical patentability searches.

One of the drawbacks of the Registry file is that a new compound is only included in the file if there is evidence in the corresponding article that the compound was actually made or isolated – typically, this evidence might be in the form of a piece of physical property data or a spectral record. As a result of this criteria for inclusion, many of the chemical compounds discussed in patent specifications have no corresponding CAS Registry record. This is because a substantial proportion of chemical patents disclose some fully-characterised compounds and so-called "Markush structures". The name is derived from the inventor of US 1506316 (granted 1924), Eugene Markush, who achieved passage of his claim 1 on alternative processes for dyestuff production by the simple linguistic expedient of a closed list of alternatives (*"selected from the group consisting of aniline, homologues of aniline and halogen substitution products of aniline"*), thus avoiding the use of the word 'or', which was anathema to the patent office of the time. Markush structures are generic disclosures based around a core substructure with many optional chemical substituents, and can encompass many thousands, or millions, of discrete chemical compounds. Very few of these alternative forms (which some commentators refer to as 'prophetic' or 'paper' chemistry) have actually been made, so cannot fulfil the CAS criteria for inclusion in the Registry file. An example Markush structure, from German patent application DE 103 60 370 A1, is shown in Figure 19.

In order to address the issue of these missing compounds, the Marpat file was created in the late 1980's. New search software algorithms had to be developed in order to provide the functionality required, and the American Chemical Society holds a patent on the method of searching generic chemical structures which has been implemented in the Marpat system[5]. The country coverage of the Marpat file is identical to the main bibliographic file, with the exception of patents from the former Soviet Union (although Russian Federation patents are included only from the year 2000). However, the time range is limited to the period from 1988 to the present. The main area in which Markush structures are used is for

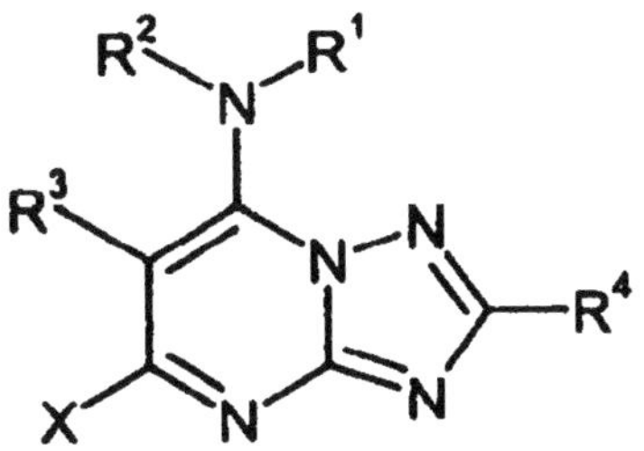

Figure 19: An example of a Markush (generic) chemical structure

organic chemistry, which is fully covered in the file, but alloys, metal oxides, inorganic salts, intermetallics and polymers are not included.

As with the original CAS Registry structure search, the searcher frames their request using specialist software applications, which convert a drawn generic structure into a form of connection table which is able to match against the database records. Marpat search results can take a considerable time to interpret, in order to understand where the generic enquiry has caused a hit in the structure. However, it is clear from anecdotal evidence that both the CAS Registry and Marpat files have their part to play in overall chemical patentability searches, as it frequently happens that each file yields unique answers to the same basic enquiry.

MMS (Questel-Orbit)

The history of the MMS file runs closely in parallel with that of the Marpat file. Both systems seek to address the same need – to retrieve chemical patents from the prior art which generically disclose a specific compound, without characterising it fully.

At the same time as CAS was developing Marpat as a way of accessing the CAS bibliographic file, Derwent Information and the French Patent Office, INPI, were seeking to use alternative methods to access their WPI and Pharm files respectively. The Derwent generic chemical file was known as WPIM (WPI Markush) and the French as MPharm. Coverage for each dated from the late 1980's at launch, on Questel-Orbit. Both systems used the DARC software as the basis for the query construction and retrieval. DARC was originally developed to search the CAS Registry file of specific compounds, and the extension of the original DARC system to include generic structures has been discussed by Benichou et al.[6] and references therein.

After a number of years of working independently, Derwent and INPI joined forces to create the Merged Markush Service, or MMS. This consists of a single file of generic chemical structures, providing a key into the Pharm and WPI files. Since the WPI file includes pharmaceuticals, there is some overlap between the bibliographic content – a given chemical structure may link to a Pharm record for which there is also a WPI record, or vice versa.

As discussed above, work has been undertaken to extend the bibliographic portion of the Pharm file back to 1978 for 6 major patent authorities in the field of pharmaceuticals (corresponding in large part to Derwent section B). This has included not only the bibliographic data for Pharm, but also the corresponding Markush structures for MMS. There is also work to provide Markush structures for additional Derwent sections on agrochemicals (section C) and general chemistry (section E), for the same 6 authorities. From 1987 forwards, the full range of Derwent major countries is covered, in all of sections B, C and E.

The MMS file has recently been reformatted to operate on a Unix platform, and this requires the searcher to make use of the Imagination software to prepare and run a search. This is provided free of charge by Questel-Orbit.

A search in the MMS file will usually yield a mixture of structure results, with answers coming from either of the two bibliographic files. As with the CAS Registry system, the crossover key is in the form of a single unique compound number, but this time the number represents not one compound but one Markush structure, enveloping many individual compounds. The compound number may cross into the Pharm file to retrieve a single patent bibliographic record , or into the WPI file to retrieve a Derwent family record. In either case, once the crossover has been achieved, further searching using the other fields in the database is possible.

ChinaPats

This bibliographic file is available on the Questel-Orbit (file CPAT) and Dialog (file 344) systems. It is produced by the EPO in co-operation with the Patent Documentation Service Center in China. The content comprises English-language abstracts and bibliographic details of all unexamined Chinese applications since the beginning of their modern patent law in 1985. The basic Chinese bibliographic data is supplemented by INPADOC family information of all equivalent cases which had been published at the time of publication of the Chinese family member.

A similar restriction on coverage applies to this file as was used for the early days of the Patent Abstracts of Japan content; namely, that abstracts are assumed to exist in an alternative language for cases claiming non-Chinese priority. These abstracts can be located via the family data. Abstracts are only included in the file where the applicant (individual or corporate) is resident in China.

The ChinaPats file does not include data on Chinese utility models or granted Chinese patents. The current Chinese law is based heavily on the EPC model, and publication occurs twice, once at 18 months unexamined and a second time at grant. Users should be aware that the format of Chinese patent publication numbers has changed at least twice since 1985. To improve awareness of Chinese patent documentation, a new FAQ site has been created as part of the EPO Asian patent information support programme; this can be found at < http://patentinfo.european-patent-office. org/prod_serv/far_east/index.en.php>

Korean Patents

The KoreaPat file is produced by the Korean Institute of Patent Information (KIPI) on behalf of the Korean Intellectual Property Office (KIPO), and is currently available exclusively on STN International. Much of the same data is available in the form of disk-based products from KIPO.

Due to the changes in law during the coverage of the database, two distinct document types are covered. The earliest content dates from 1979, during which period South Korean patent law was similar to that of the US, publishing only once at grant. Documents from this period were allocated the KD code of B (KR-B). The last applications granted under this old law were published in 2001. During the late 1990's, Korean law changed to a form of deferred examination with early publication. The coverage of the database therefore switched to the new 18 month publications, with code KR-A, from the earliest published in the year 2000, and continues to the present day.

KoreaPat records contain standard bibliographic information, including inventor and assignee data, IPC and title and abstract in English. Clipped images of a representative drawing is also included where available. The file is updated monthly.

▶ PUBLIC INTERNET SOURCES

The internet has become the medium of choice for patent offices and many commercial producers to distribute their products. This section will consider some of the free-of-charge websites and portals available. It should be noted that few of these services offer encrypted or secure access, and in common with most internet search sites have little active support for the user. However, the unique information content makes it impossible to ignore these sites as useful complements to established commercial offerings.

National patent office websites

This section cannot purport to be a full listing of all patent office websites, not least because it will be out of date as soon as it is completed. Users wishing to review the latest situation are referred to one of the many directory sites available, noted in chapter 6.

Due to their increasing commercial importance, and availability of data, two specific country websites will be considered, in addition to a number of portal sites.

Chinese Patent Office

The official homepage of the Chinese Patent Office (SIPO) is at <http://www.sipo.gov.cn>, which has a link to English-language pages (an alternative URL is <http://www.cpo.cn.net>). This site provides access to bibliographic data and abstracts for unexamined patent applications from 1985 to date, and bibliographic data only for utility models for the same period.

In addition, for the searcher, there is a further site at <http://www.cnpat.com.cn>, produced by the China Patent Information Center. This site provides an English search mask giving you access to English abstracts and the full texts of Chinese patent documents. Bibliographic data and full texts of Chinese utility models are also available. Since most of the site is in Chinese, it is difficult to gauge the content accurately, but it appears to cover the same range of years as the official patent office site.

Korean Patent Office

The information activities of the Korean Intellectual Property Office (KIPO) are managed by an affiliated organisation, the Korea Institute of Patent Information (KIPI), founded in 1995. The English pages of their website at <http://eng.kipris.or.kr> offer access to the KIPRIS system (Korea Industrial Property Rights Information Services). This has loaded a large volume of non-Korean data, including Japanese, US and the EPO. Basic bibliographic coverage of Korean patents and utility models goes back to 1947. It also provides access to the Korean Patent Abstracts (KPA) service, which provides English abstracts of Korean patent documents and forms the basis of the KoreaPats file on STN. On the website, some legal status information is available in English and full texts of Korean patent documents can be retrieved in facsimile mode (TIFF format files). Registration is required, but the site is free-of-charge to search.

Patent Office portal sites

Surf-IP (Singapore Patent Office)

The Surf-IP site at <http://www.surfip.gov.sg> is a portal site produced by the Singapore Patent Office. It provides a single search window through which to interrogate the free search files at the Singapore, Japanese, Chinese, and Taiwanese patent offices, plus the USPTO, esp@cenet, United Kingdom and Canadian systems. It also provides simultaneous searching in AltaVista and Google on the same subject, which can be useful to retrieve non-patent literature. The system is optimised for Microsoft Internet Explorer and does not work well under other browsers. Certain features of the site require pre-registration and/or membership, which may be Associate (non-paying) or Premium (paying). Detailed content of the search files is difficult to establish at present; in particular, it is not clear how many years' worth of Singapore data are included. Some information on data coverage for the other offices is available via their national web-pages.

esp@cenet (European Patent Office)

The esp@cenet ® search service was launched by the EPO in 1999, and has quickly become a very popular search service.

It consists of two layers, or levels, of server. Each national patent office of the member states of the EPO has undertaken to provide a minimum of a rolling two-years' worth of bibliographic data for its own patents. Some offices have taken this further, and loaded many more documents; some are experimenting with provision of full text, or at least abstracts. All data on these so-called Level 1 servers are in the national language of the office concerned, and typically only provide titles and application, publication and classification information. In addition to these national Level 1 servers, two small files with two-years' worth of EPO and PCT data are provided by the EPO itself.

The largest file on the system is the so-called Worldwide file, which is sometimes referred to as the Level 2 server. This provides access to multi-country bibliographic data, including titles and abstracts, all in English. The file structure is based upon the EPODOC internal search files at the EPO. Country coverage for this file is shown in Table 40. The earliest coverage date for any given country is usually for bibliographic data only; more recent years provide viewable (not searchable) character-coded text for some documents, and facsimile images in PDF format. Results are grouped in patent families using the EPO definition, and at least one member of each patent family is available in facsimile mode. At the time of writing, these images are available only in one-file-per-page display, but the EPO has undertaken that one-file-per-document retrieval will be available on completion of the technical requirements, possibly as early as the end of 2005.

In the level 2 server, the bibliographic results from an individual search can be linked to the INPADOC legal status, or the rest of the INPADOC family. Patents cited in search reports are available as direct links to the documents; these can also be reached by clicking on the links in an epoline Register record. Although searching is not possible in full texts, it is possible to gain a useful insight into the state of the art by employing the ECLA classification tool. This is a search engine designed to assist non-specialist users to select suitable terms from ECLA, to use in their search. A large percentage of the documents loaded in the Worldwide file will have a search field for ECLA; the main exceptions are Japanese and Russian/ Soviet Union documents.

The esp@cenet service is available under a number of different interfaces, which can be accessed by substituting the appropriate country code for xx in the general URL <http://xx.espacenet.com>. For example, access to <http://nl.espacenet.com> provides a Dutch interface for searchers who prefer to use this. This does not provide any form of translation of the data, which must be still searched in the language as supplied – the only change provided by the address is the language of the interface, including the search mask.

In recent months, more detailed help files have been loaded which provide more information on the content of the Level 1 servers. Full tabular files giving the Level 2 content are already in place. A help forum at <http://www.espacenet.com> is also available, giving access to the staff at the EPO who designed the system.

DEPATISnet (German Patent and Trade Mark Office)

DEPATISnet is a multi-country portal providing search access to a range of countries via the DPMA (German Patent and Trade Mark Office). It is available at <http://depatisnet.dpma.de>, with either a German or English search interface. The characteristics of this site are somewhat different from other free-of-charge portals, in that it offers the option of secure (https) access and a much more sophisticated command language, based upon the IKOFAX system used within the DPMA. The data available remains in the national language, with the exception of Japanese content which is based upon the PAJ file and is in English. Most documents, as with esp@cenet, are available in PDF format, although DEPATISnet offers different resolutions up to 300 d.p.i. for screen viewing or printing.

The content of the system is expanding all the time; Table 44 provides a summary of the main coverage. This has been enhanced with basic bibliographic information from DocDB, which brings in equivalents from many more countries for the family search. Searching is possible in the usual fields, such as title, abstract and classification, but not in the full texts except for German documents from 1987. One added-value aspect, similar to the availability of ECLA in esp@cenet, is the provision of two IPC classification

Table 44: Main DEPATISnet country coverage

Country code	Country name	Earliest year coverage
AT	Austria	1900
CH	Switzerland	1900
DD	East Germany	1951
DE	Germany	1877
EP	European Patent Office (EPO)	1978
FR	France	1900
GB	United Kingdom	1900
JP	Japan	1976
US	United States	1900
WO	World Intellectual Property Organization (WIPO)	1978

fields – one reflects the IPC as published by the patent authority concerned, and the second (a so-called 'search file IPC') is allocated by the German examiners on receipt of the document, and may differ from the original.

▶ CONTROLLED-ACCESS INTERNET

The majority of the familiar internet sites in the patent field are free-of-charge. However, as web technologies have developed, a number of specialist database production companies have started to reconfigure their data to work within a browser, providing a more familiar interface for the novice user. Since the data being provided is commercially-produced, such systems provide access only on a password or account-based system. Pricing models vary, from daily purchase of a password to a flat fee for annual unlimited access or a pay-as-you-go model. This section will not consider commercial browser-based forms of traditional host systems (such as DialogWeb or STN on the Web), since the data content offered does not differ from that described elsewhere in this book.

Password- or account-based systems

Patent Warehouse/Total Patent (Lexis-Nexis Univentio)

The Univentio corporation, based in the Netherlands, has been well-known since the 1950's as a supplier of alerting services, full-document delivery and latterly as a producer of full-text databases which it licenced to other database vendors, such as STN. In 2004, the company started on a new direction, by developing a search system to distribute its own content directly. This was launched as Patent Warehouse. Shortly afterwards, Univentio was taken over by the Lexis-Nexis group, and the product was re-christened Total Patent. It is currently still available at <http://www.patentwarehouse.com> although this is likely to change.

The distinctive aspect of TotalPatent's offering is the large proportion of full-text files. These are produced by advanced OCR technology by Univentio themselves, and in a number of cases corresponding machine translations into English are produced at the same time. The TotalPatent interface permits the searcher to specify which file(s) they use, and runs a simultaneous search across the selection. The overall country coverage is provided in Table 40, but the content of full-text available at the time of writing is provided in Table 45.

Table 45: Univentio full-text sources

Country/ Kind code	Country Name	Full-text available (start year)
AT-B	Austria	1980
AU-B	Australia	1983
BE-A	Belgium	1980
CA-A/C	Canada	1973
CH-A	Switzerland	1980
DE-A	Germany	1980
DE-C/B	Germany	1980
DE-U	Germany	1980
DK-B	Denmark	1980
EP-A	European Patent Office (EPO)	1978
EP-B	European Patent Office (EPO)	1980
ES-A	Spain	1980
FR-A	France	1980
FR-B	France	1980
GB-A	United Kingdom	1979
GB-B	United Kingdom	1980
JP-A	Japan	1980
LU-A	Luxembourg	1980
MC-A	Monaco	1980
NL-A	Netherlands	1980
NL-C	Netherlands	1980
NO-A	Norway	1980
NO-B	Norway	1980
PT-A	Portugal	1980
SE-B	Sweden	1980
US-A/B	United States	1836
US-A	United States	2001
WO-A	World Intellectual Property Organization (WIPO)	1978

In addition to the full text files, the TotalPatent product has incorporated a wider range of bibliographic-only countries, and INPADOC legal status information. Document delivery in a number of formats is available. At the time of writing, the product is very new and is likely to develop over time, with the financial and resource backing of Lexis-Nexis.

PatBase (Minesoft/RWS)

The PatBase product <http://www.patbase.com> is a co-operative effort between Minesoft Ltd., an information services supplier based in London and RWS Ltd, one of the UK's largest patent information brokers and translation agencies.

The product draws heavily upon public-domain sources, but is increasingly being supplemented by proprietary data. A principal bibliographic source is the OPS server of the EPO, supplemented by additional data from national patent office publication servers. The cumulated data are downloaded to a Minesoft server and reformatted into families, essentially based upon the INPADOC algorithm but with further corrections applied. The resultant database is available from the PatBase server, and covers some 75 patent-issuing authorities. Version 2 of PatBase has expanded the content by adding over 10 million full-text patent documents from the US, EPO, PCT and the United Kingdom. These full texts have been integrated into the existing patent families.

The PatBase system also has built-in links to take advantage of external suppliers where appropriate. For example, requests for legal status can be fulfilled either from the OPS server, the epoline Register or corresponding national registers, without a separate account being needed by the user. Display of facsimile documents is provided by links to existing sources such as esp@cenet. Drawing pages can be reformatted into a proprietary 'mosaic' showing all drawing pages on a single screen. The definitions of the various classification schemes available in the file are reached from services such as the WIPO classification listings.

The system is based upon a conventional browser, and provides an number of viewing aids, including keyword-in-context features and multi-colour highlighting of hit terms, which can be presented in the form of a document map, showing where hits on search terms have occurred. Country coverage is summarised in Table 40.

Delphion (Thomson)

The Delphion service <http://www.delphion.com> started life as an offshoot of IBM, the Intellectual Property Network in 1997. It was spun off as a separate corporation in 2000, at which time a substantial proportion of its content had grown beyond the original free US patent service, and commercial terms were starting to be applied. The following year, Delphion became one of the first services (outside of the Thomson group) to offer the WPI file on a browser-based platform. Further paid-for services were launched, including access to analytical tools for viewing search results.

At the end of 2002, Delphion was acquired by Thomson. During 2003, further full-text collections were added to the service, and synergies with the (Thomson-owned) Westlaw service were introduced. The overall content is shown in Table 46.

Table 46: Delphion file content

File	Content	Full-text availability	Bibliographic data
US Patents – applications	US-A, 2001–date	2001–date	2001–date
US Patents – granted	US-A/B, 1790–date (*)	1974–date	1971–date
Derwent WPI	Full range of WPI countries	None	1963–date
European Patents – applications	EP-A	1987–date	1979–date
European Patents – granted	EP-B	1991–date	1980–date
German Patents – applications	DE-A	1987–date	1968–date
German Patents – granted	DE-C/B	1987–date	1968–date
	DE-U	1987–date	1968–date
INPADOC	Full range of INPADOC countries	None	Various – typically early 1970's; legal status included
Patent Abstracts of Japan	JP-A	None	1976–date
Switzerland	CH-A	1990–date (#)	1969–date (##)
PCT international applications	WO-A	1978–date	1978–date

(*) images only 1790–1971 – no searchable text
(#) images only – no searchable text
(##) via INPADOC data

Since the Thomson takeover, the service has added a number of different pricing plans, affecting the search files available to different classes of user. There has also been an emphasis on analytical and visualisation tools, including citation linking and the Excel-based PatentLab II. 'Corporate tree' data to assist portfolio searching has been loaded under licence from CHI Research (now part of ipIQ).

WIPS Global

The WIPS Global tool <http://www.wipsglobal.com> is an English-language launch of a product developed in South Korea <http://www.wips.

co.kr>. It is a compilation and reformatting into a web-based format of a number of existing products, including the GlobalPat CD-ROM range, PAJ, KPA, Chinapats, INPADOC and US data. Some Japanese data are provided in full-text, but the majority consists of basic bibliographic data plus abstracts in English. The applicant name data in a number of the files has been standardised to facilitate cross-over between the files.

One specific claim to distinction is that the service is able to include Korean data (KR-A and KR-B publications) into the INPADOC core families faster than the INPADOC file itself, producing enhanced family information. This is particularly useful at the grant stage, given the short opposition period available in Korea.

One concern with the Korean data translated into English is the timeliness of delivery, which can be quite slow in comparison with industry expectations.

The WIPS organisation has also developed a range of visualisation and linking tools surrounding this data set, marketed as the PM Manager.

Table 47: Country coverage of WIPS service

Country/ Kind code	Country name	Content	Earliest year coverage
US-A	United States	Abstracts, claims	2001–date
US-A/B	United States	Abstracts, claims	1976–date
EP-A	EPO	Abstracts, claims	1978–date
EP-B	EPO	Claims	1980–date
WO-A	PCT	Abstracts	1978–date
CH-A	Switzerland	Abstracts	1974–2003
DE-A	Germany	Abstracts	1966–2003
FR-A	France	Abstracts	1970–2003
GB-A	United Kingdom	Abstracts	1971–2003
JP-A	Japan	Abstracts	1976–1988
JP-A	Japan	Full-page images	1989–date
JP-A	Japan	Full text (Japanese)	1983–date
JP-B, JP-U	Japan	Full text (Japanese)	1996–date
KR-A	South Korea	Abstracts (English)	2000–2003
KR-B	South Korea	Abstracts (English)	1979–2003
KR-A, KR-U	South Korea	Abstracts, claims (Korean)	1983–date
KR-B, KR-Y	South Korea	Abstracts, claims (Korean)	1979–date
KR-A	South Korea	Family data	1983–date
KR-B	South Korea	Family data	1979–date
KR-U	South Korea	Family data	1983–date
KR-Y	South Korea	Family data	1979–date
CN-A	China	Abstracts (English)	1985–2001
INPADOC	Multiple	Some abstracts	1968–date

Since all the fields within each file loaded on the WIPS system have been standardised, it provides opportunities for meaningful analysis without some of the large clean-up operations necessary when merging information from several sources.

MicroPatent Patent Index (MPI) (MicroPatent)

MicroPatent, as the name suggests, were best known throughout the 1970's and 1980's as suppliers of microfilm and CD-ROM copies of documents, particularly of US patents. There were quick to adapt their product to the internet, and in 1996 created two distinct search tools, one comprising bibliographic information only and a second dedicated to full text. The website, at <http://www.micropat.com> was well used as a patent document delivery service, and still offers a patent copy and file history service.

The original MicroPatent company was purchased by Information Holdings Inc. (IHI) in 1997, and began to pursue a specialism in patent and other intellectual property information on the web. When the Aurigin company's analysis and visualisation tool became available on the market, it was purchased by MicroPatent in 2002, which began to compete directly with Delphion's search and analytical service. However, IHI was itself acquired by Thomson (owners of Delphion since 2002) in late 2004. Shortly prior to the acquisition, MicroPatent had been engaged in considerable expansion of the service, developing its own multiple-country family database (MicroPatent Patent Index, or MPI), as well as loading INPADOC data and creating a command-line professional version of its web-based search system. The MPI-INPADOC Plus system is now promoted for 'front page' searching, and the PatSearch FullText solution for full-text retrieval.

One novel aspect of the information load in full text is the integrated EP-WO file. This helps to circumvent the problem caused by substantial

Table 48: MicroPatent full text availability

File	Content	Full-text availability
European Patents – applications	EP-A	1978–date
European Patents – granted	EP-B	1991–date
France – applications	FR-A	1971–date
German Patents – applications	DE-A	1989–date
German Patents – granted	DE-C/B	1989–date
German utility models – granted	DE-U	1989–date
Japan – Patent Abstracts of Japan	JP-A	None
United Kingdom	GB-A	1916–date
US Patents – applications	US-A	2001–date
US Patents – granted	US-A/B	1836–date

numbers of missing full-texts in the EPO-generated file, representing transfer of PCT cases into the European regional phase without corresponding re-publication (Euro-PCT transfer cases).

Country coverage of the MPI file is listed in Table 40; the availability of full text is shown in Table 48.

QPAT (Questel-Orbit)

The QPAT platform is a web-based account with secure access, providing access to a range of Questel-Orbit's patent databases in a browser environment. Much of the content is identical to the files loaded on the 'native', command language-based, Questel system, which have been described under the country chapters earlier in this book. A useful comparison between Delphion, MicroPatent and QPAT was presented at the International Chemical Information Conference in 2004[7]. The essential content of the QPAT system is virtually identical to that of Delphion, with the exception of WPI which is not available on QPAT. The nearest corresponding file is the PlusPat/FamPat multi-country collection, described earlier. The visualisation tool corresponding to Delphion's PatentLab II was anacubis – however, this company went into liquidation during 2005 and it is unclear at present whether QPAT will be able to implement a replacement.

Encrypted systems

As observed elsewhere in this book, the bulk of internet, browser-based search tools provide information over the public networks, and offer limited security by way of encryption or secure connections. A few, such as DEPATISnet, at least offer an optional access method using SSL, but this is the exception with free-of-charge systems. It is usually only once one starts to pay real money for access that the data provider enhances their system to include secure encryption.

There are two aspects to data security which the patent searcher needs to consider:

1. Searcher-to-server communications – that is, can my search strategy be read by a third party, who might then be able to infer my research interests?, or
2. Server-to-searcher communications – that is, can the information which I wish to access be read by other users who have no right to access it?

The second aspect is particularly important when considering paperless-office developments at various patent offices. If such processes are to work at all, it is important that the appointed representative of an inventor (such as a patent agent or attorney) is able to monitor the stages of progress of an application before it is laid open to public inspection. The examination process might be fatally compromised if a third party was able to gain access to a priority document.

The principal encrypted systems available at the time of writing are those available under the major Tripartite patent offices (EPO, USPTO, JPO) and for the PCT. Each of these offices provides a means of submitting a patent application electronically, and monitoring the progress of the application through all its stages up until grant. The EPO's epoline ® system and the USPTO's PAIR system are discussed in chapter 10 in the context of access to legal status information. Both exist in two forms, a public and private system. The public versions enable any third party to view, in electronic form, the same documents which have hitherto been made available in paper, such as the early unexamined publication and the contents of the file wrapper. These records are unencrypted and only made available after the publication of the unexamined case (or, in the case of old Act US documents, after the grant). The private versions of these two systems extend the availability of such information back to the first submissions. This enables a restricted user base to submit official forms and documents, pay fees and respond to correspondence from the patent office in a fully electronic environment. One advantage for the patent agent is that there are fewer delays and uncertainties; they can immediately check that a fee has been received, or that their letter arrived within the deadline for action required by the patent office.

Several of the major authorities are moving towards a system of full electronic filing. The EPO have handled this under the overall epoline umbrella. The EPO developed a suite of online filing software, which initially enabled the applicant to file an EP application electronically. The user is issued with a smart card reader and smart card with PIN code to control access to the system.

In 2002, WIPO modified the Administrative Instructions under the PCT to establish the legal framework and technical standards for electronic filing and processing of PCT applications. Subsequently, the EPO expanded the epoline service to enable PCT electronic filing for European applicants who wished to use the EPO as receiving Office. The corresponding PCT software, called PCT-SAFE (Secure Applications Filed Electronically), was launched for all users February 2004. The established technical standards ensured that the EPO and PCT filing software was compatible. At the present time, there are three ways in which a user could lodge an application under the PCT:

I.   A PCT-EASY filing (in the form of paper specification plus diskette containing the official forms and abstract) which is prepared using the PCT-SAFE software, but submitted by conventional fax and by mail

2. A totally paper filing, sent by fax and by mail
3. A totally electronic PCT-SAFE filing, prepared using PCT-SAFE software and submitted by either secure online transmission or using physical media such as CD-R.

The EPO has been a major player in moving towards totally electronic filing, and has released a number of user tools, including PatXML software, which enables a user to create EP and PCT patent applications in XML using a standard word-processor. This enables the electronic document to be easily integrated with epoline submissions, and also speeds up the process of preparing the document for official publication at a later stage in its life.

▶ REFERENCES

1. "Online patent searching: the realities". S. Kaback, Online **7**(4), 22–31 (1983).
2. "Patents" E.S. Simmons. Chapter 3, pp.23–140 in Manual of Online Search Strategies, volume II: Business, Law, News and Patents. (eds.) C.J. Armstrong; A. Large. Aldershot: Gower Press, 2001. ISBN 0–566–08304–3.
3. "Open Patent Services – or how raw data can be served pre-cooked." EPIDOS News No.3/2003. pp.1–2.
4. "Patent information from CAS: coverage and content." Columbus: ACS, 1996.
5. "Storage and retrieval of generic chemical structure representations." W. Fisanick / American Chemical Society, US 4642762, granted Feb 10, 1987. US application number 06/614219, filed May 25, 1984.
6. "Handling genericity in chemical structures using the Markush DARC software." P. Benichou, C. Klimczak; P. Borne. J. Chem. Inf. Comput. Sci **37**(1), 43–53 (1997).
7. "Internet Patent Information in the 21st Century: A Comparison of Delphion, Micropatent, and QPAT". N. Lambert :inProc. International Chemical Information Conference & Exhibition, Annecy, France, 17–20 October, 2004. Due to be reprinted in World Patent Information in 2005.

8 Common search types (I) – Alerting searches

The patent information industry has a long history of conducting what, in the wider context, are currently referred to as 'alerts', or in older terminology, 'selective dissemination of information' (SDI) services. Within the patent community, these procedures are commonly referred to as 'watch services'. A number of companies around the world, which are today best-known as database producers or distributors, began life as a nationally-based watch service; examples include Univentio in Holland, and Research Publications in the USA (later subsumed into the Thomson group). Even the Derwent organisation, producer of the World Patent Index file, began life producing current awareness bulletins in the late 1950's. Watch services as understood by the legal community often relate to a legal status monitoring process, although the same term can also equally be applied to bibliographic monitoring e.g. by assignee or subject.

Watch services may be obtained in a variety of ways:

- Purchase of standard bulletins created by database producers, using prefabricated strategies
- Using standard bibliographic databases, selecting by time segment (update), and customised strategies; these may be run in-house or sub-contracted
- Sub-contracted to specialist database producers focussed on provision of watch services only.

▶ STANDARD BULLETINS

The advantage of standard bulletins is that all the hard work of constructing a search strategy and running it against document updates each week or month, is taken out of the hands of the customer, and given to the actual database producers. Since these organisations know their own products very well, they are able to construct search profiles which are optimised for use within their database. Historically, such bulletins were delivered in paper form, but increasingly they may be sent out in electronic facsimile forms (such as PDF files) or electronic updates to an in-house database (such as Lotus Notes or Domino files).

Thomson Derwent have for many years had a range of standard bulletins, using their Alerting Abstracts sorted according to broad subject areas defined by the Derwent Class system. These are supplemented by a series of subject-specific bulletins, called the *Engineering Industry Patents Profiles* (EITP) and the *Industry and Technology Patents Profiles* (ITP). The EITP series are available as Folio Infobases, whereas the ITP series can be obtained as either PDF or Folio products. The Alerting Abstracts can be obtained in a variety of formats, including paper.

In addition to the series of profiles listed, Thomson Derwent also produce the Patents Previews series. This is a product dedicated to the pharmaceutical industry, published in print and on diskette, or by FTP delivery for loading into in-house databases. The country coverage is more limited than the profiles, concentrating on only seven major authorities (WO, EP, JP, US, GB, DE, FR). The aim is to offer a dedicated competitor intelligence service within 8 days of publication over the whole range of pharmaceutical R&D. This service was founded at a time when the main Derwent WPI database was taking longer to update than this, and was focussed upon the very time-sensitive needs of the pharmaceutical industry.

It remains to be seen whether the Patents Preview products will continue to have a place in the future, as the WPI First View file is designed to address the issues of timeliness across the whole subject range; some customers may find that running their own profile against WPIFV may meet their needs as well as – or better than – the dedicated service. In the same way, the GeneSeq FASTAlert companion file to the main GeneSeq database of genetic sequences was intended to provide a rapid access to newly published information, ahead of the full database which is more suited more retrospective searching.

Some level of patent current awareness can be achieved by a selection of other tools or products. These range from simple periodical listings in academic journals like "Nature", through websites of lobby groups or special-interest groups (Worldwide RFID Patent Watch, Nanotech Bulletin), through news releases by university research foundations or similar, to IP consultancies. The selection policy may be obvious (such as the simple IPC-based classification of pharmaceutical patents used in the Current Patents Gazette), through somewhat more subjective (intellectual selection of new food science patents in Leatherhead Food Research Association's "Food Industry Updates" series), to the obscure (many 'patent of the week' columns).

Table 49: The Thomson Derwent range of current awareness products

Alerting Abstracts by Class

Section A	Polymers and Plastics
Section B	Pharmaceuticals
Section C	Agrochemicals
Section D	Food, Detergents, Water Treatment and Biotechnology
Section E	General Chemicals
Section F	Textiles and Paper-making
Section G	Printing, Coating and Photographic
Section H	Petroleum
Section J	Chemical Engineering
Section K	Nucleonics, Explosives and Protection
Section L	Refractories, Ceramics, Cement and Electro (in)organics
Section M	Metallurgy
Section P	General Engineering
Section Q	Mechanical Engineering
Section S	Instrumentation, Measuring and Testing
Section T	Computing and Control
Section U	Semiconductors and Electronic Circuitry
Section V	Electronic Components
Section W	Communications
Section X	Electric Power Engineering

Engineering Industry Patents Profiles

Aerospace
Automotive
Computer Technology
Electrical Power Engineering
Electronics & Semiconductors
Telecommunications &
   Broadcasting

Industry & Technology Patents Profiles

Aerospace	(7 titles)
Automotive	(25 titles)
Communications	(22 titles)
Computing and e-business	(15 titles)
Discrete Electronic Devices	(14 titles)
Domestic and Leisure Equipment	(10 titles)
Electric Power	(10 titles)
Electronic Circuits	(10 titles)
Food Technology	(5 titles)
Image and Audio Recording and Reproduction	(16 titles)
Instrumentation and Testing	(2 titles)
Machining and Manufacturing	(9 titles)
Mechanical and civil engineering	(14 titles)
Medical Devices	(5 titles)
Miniaturised Technologies	(3 titles)
Packaging and Packing	(6 titles)
Paper Technology	(4 titles)
Semiconductor Technology	(7 titles)

▶ IN-HOUSE STRATEGIES

Any of the commercial databases mounted on the major hosts (STN, Dialog, Questel-Orbit, MicroPatent, Delphion) can be used to run current awareness profiles. The user is able to construct a strategy in much the same way as if they were running a retrospective state-of-the-art or patentability search, but store it at the host end for automatic repeat running. Depending upon the host service, it may be possible to vary the frequency of running the search; for example, on a weekly-updated database, it may be more cost-effective to run a profile each month, effectively cumulating 4 runs of the search.

The responsibility for defining the search strategy under these circumstances rests entirely with the customer, although most database producers should be able to provide advice and support on the process. The main danger with this type of current-awareness technique is that it is easy to forget the need for periodic revisions of the strategy. The temptation is to create the strategy once, and let it run thereafter unmodified. It may indeed continue to generate useful information, but many such strategies will contain search terms which may get modified over time (for example, a patent assignee name which disappears as a result of merger, or a US classification code which is replaced by a new sub-division). It is vital to ensure that the contents of each strategy are systematically reviewed for continued accuracy, and modified if required.

A further skill in the process of creating a current-awareness strategy is in the use of very broad search terms. There is a temptation to use precisely the same search terms as would be applied for a full retrospective search, but merely run it against a smaller section of the file, such as the weekly or monthly update. However, it is often true that a search term which would be difficult or impossible to use in a retrospective search because of ambiguity or excessively high retrieval can be a useful term in the mini-database created for each run of the profile. It is always worth examining a search strategy intended for a current awareness profile, to see whether it uses the most appropriate search terms for the size of database against which it will be run.

One of the advantages of developing your own strategies for alerting purposes is that they can be highly focussed or tailored to specific needs, perhaps a single research project or department. However, the process is labour-intensive, and some companies prefer to sub-contract the process of actually running the profile to an external supplier. If taking this approach, it is crucial to establish good lines of communication, both for the initial definition of the profile and to allow for a rapid, effective means of updating it. The responsibility of each part must be clearly defined, otherwise there is a risk that the process will develop a momentum of its own, and not be revised to reflect either changing research interests or modifications in databases. After a while, such a process will generate fewer and fewer relevant answers, and become effectively worthless to the customer.

► SPECIALIST SUPPLIERS

The advantage of the Derwent series of products is that individual patent records are added to each profile or section on the basis of an intellectual assignment, using the proprietary subject classification which is also applied across the retrospective file. Most other current awareness bulletins allocate records to a profile or group on the basis of a public subject classification such as the IPC. Users may find either approach helpful, depending upon their sector of industry and whether the subject is broken down in a helpful manner. A typical example of an awareness service based upon IPC are Univentio's PatentSummaries product, with some 350 different technical areas covered. Their corresponding PatentSummary Plus and PatentNavigator products make use of additional keyword search tools, for cases where the industry is difficult to define accurately by classification alone.

Specialist suppliers of patent current awareness may deliver in paper format or electronic. In the United States, due to the free availability of US patent data, an entire cottage industry of 'alert providers' has grown up in recent years. In many cases, they are linked to provision of complete documents, sometimes providing the actual alerts free of charge but recouping costs by document delivery fees. In Europe, fewer established options exist, although companies do exist. Examples include Infoco Systemet A/S of Denmark, Centredoc of Switzerland, Polyresearch NV from the Netherlands and Europatent (part of World Patent Services) in Germany.

Options for delivery mechanism include paper, e-mail alerting, images of pages or complete searchable texts. Some suppliers use the output from alerting services as the source material for an entire workflow system, allowing for distribution of documents, annotation and in-house indexing, and archiving. One such system is provided by Patent Café <http://www.patentcafe.com>.

9 Common search types (II) – Patentability and freedom-to-operate searches

This chapter will discuss two types of search, which have some techniques in common. These are the patentability search and the infringement (or freedom-to-operate, FTO) search.

The starting requirement for both types is a good mechanism to search by subject. In the case of the patentability search, our focus is a specific invention – perhaps still at the very early stages of development in a promising research project, or maybe reached the stage of an early proto-type product. The inventor, working in collaboration with their patent agent or attorney, is aiming to establish whether an application for patent grant is likely to succeed. If this can be clarified before the patent applica-tion is filed, it may be possible to save substantial amounts of time and money. The searcher therefore comes to the project at a point when the inventor can describe in some detail the salient features of their invention, and it is these features which form the primary search concepts.

▶ THE PATENTABILITY SEARCH

Although a patentability search can be conducted after the patent applica-tion has been filed, it is generally more cost-effective if the results are already at hand when the application is at the drafting stage. This is because it is easier to draft a patent application to avoid the known prior art from the beginning, than it is to file an initial application and then have to amend it in order to avoid a later-located document.

Some industries or companies have a policy of not conducting full patentability searches themselves, but relying upon the official search from the patent office. Whilst this undoubtedly saves cost in the short run, the effectiveness of this strategy varies according to the nature of the industry. If a company is able to put a project on the shelf for the period between filing and receiving the official report, then this approach will enable the applicant to respond in a very focussed manner to the prior art which the patent office itself has located. However, it is common for the applicant to want to continue developing and optimising the invention after the application is filed. Under these circumstances, it is in their interests to know the general technical environment surrounding their invention as early as possible. This will help to guide the further research in the 12–15 months between filing and receipt of the official search report. A thorough retrospective search before, or immediately at, the time of filing, preferably followed up by a regular monitoring process until the early publication at 18 months, will help to ensure that there are no nasty surprises when the official search report is received.

As discussed in Chapter 1, most countries require that a patent application satisfies four criteria in order to proceed to grant. It is the role of the inventor and attorney to show that the invention has merit in the area of industrial utility and does not fall into one of the classes of prohibited subject matter. The patentability search aims to address the remaining two aspects, namely novelty and non-obviousness (or inventive step).

The search strategy requirement for novelty and inventive step are related, but subtly different. Both criteria are defined in relation to the "state-of-the-art". Novelty is the requirement that the invention in hand does not already form part of the state-of-the-art. Inventive step is the quality that the invention would not be obvious to a person well versed in the appropriate technical field – in other words, someone who knows the relevant state-of-the-art. Therefore, our starting point for a patentability search has to be that we have access to as much of the legally-defined state-of-the-art as is possible to get. This means that we require one or more databases containing records

- over many years (novelty relates to 'disclosure at any time before the priority date')
- from many document types (novelty does not distinguish between a journal, patent, conference proceeding, report, internet web-site or other 'document type')
- in all languages (novelty is still destroyed even if the disclosure is not in the official language of the examining patent office)

In practical terms, such a starting point requires that our search databases provide the following elements:

a)   they must cover literature from **multiple countries**. This is to ensure that unique disclosures from one particular country are not missed. The nature of patents creates a complication at this point. The non-patent searcher, seeking to retrieve disclosures from the journal literature, might achieve their purpose efficiently by searching a range of different databases, each with its own unique content or geographic range, such as individual publishers' websites or national union catalogues. Due to the lack of overlap, they are unlikely to retrieve the same item twice. However, for the patent searcher, duplication is a potential problem, as it is likely that a given prior invention will have been patented in several countries. This could lead to the retrieval of essentially the same document several times during a search, once for each country where it is patented. Consequently, the searcher must either search a range of single-country sources and reconcile themselves to a post-search processing stage, to de-duplicate the results, or (preferably) conduct their search in a patent family database, where each invention is only counted once.

b)   they must cover **multiple technologies**. Patentability searching is, by its very nature, attempting to locate a reference to something that (we hope) has never been done before. A genuinely new and non-obvious invention is quite likely to include a degree of cross-pollination with other technical disciplines, which may mean that the search has to cross the line between hitherto unrelated subject areas. Whilst prior art to a 'pure' chemical invention is unlikely to be located in a 'pure' engineering database, there may well be certain aspects from remote areas of the prior art which have a bearing upon the case being searched. The experienced patentability searcher soon comes to sympathise with Oscar Wilde's contention that *"the truth is rarely pure and never simple"*. It is a wise precaution to search in a database which covers a wide slice of applicable technology, rather than limit the approach to a highly-focussed database, whose coverage policy may ignore tangential but relevant items.

c)   they must include detailed **subject indexing** and **search features**. This is particularly important if we are to fulfil our task to determine both novelty and inventive step. Establishing novelty appears, on the face of it, to be a straightforward search process – if nothing is found, the invention is new. However, we cannot allow our definition of 'new' to mean merely that 'no document uses the same words'. The drawback of first-level databases is that they capture documents individually, and do little to relate them to the wider corpus of knowledge, either in time or by subject. That is, a full-text record of a patent published last year will use last year's terminology. Throughout technology, the vocabulary and key terms are in a constant state of change. Unless the searcher is also a skilled subject specialist with a remarkable memory, it is quite likely that they will miss relevant literature if they are relying purely upon the words in each isolated specification as their retrieval keys. A better choice would be a database which imposes a common subject classification, indexing or other taxonomy across the full time range of its coverage. The importance of this for the searcher was highlighted by a decision of the European Patent Office's Technical Board of Appeal[1], in which it was stated that :

> "... identical processes yielding identical results constitute anticipation, even if described in terms different from those of the case in suit ..."

This ability to discriminate between a simple co-occurrence of text terms and a genuine degree of 'similarity' is vital if the search is to be able to address the issue of inventive step. It could be argued to some extent that establishing novelty, where we wish ideally to locate one document which discusses all aspects of our case in hand, is a simple one of finding a 'direct hit'. Inventive step, on the other hand, can be compromised if we are able to find one or more documents which, taken together, disclose some or all of the features of the invention. In other words, establishing inventive step requires 'fuzzy searching', in which we aim to locate a 'indirect hit', or one which possesses certain degrees of similarity to our case. It is very hard to achieve this objective in a first-level database, without additional concept analysis or subject indexing tools.

d) they must include both **patent and non-patent literature.** In the majority of Western industrialised countries, the definition of the state-of-the-art is no respecter of document type. If an applicant wishes to obtain a patent within these 'universal novelty' jurisdictions, then searches must be conducted with this definition in mind. This applies even if the applicant is based in another part of the world, and intends to lodge their priority filing locally. Hence, a company based in New Zealand which wants to obtain patent protection in a major trading bloc such as Europe, the United States or Japan needs to conduct their patentability searching to the higher standards of the target country. This is despite the fact that their local patent office examine and grant a New Zealand patent under local novelty rules, which exclude any patent publication older than 50 years. Unfortunately, few databases offer a consistent handling of all literature types in their subject field, which would enable a single search to locate relevant prior art irrespective of the original document type. One of the exceptions is the Chemical Abstracts Service (CAS) bibliographic files, which apply a common indexing scheme to both chemical patents and non-patents. In other subject areas, it is necessary to supplement an initial patent search by a second search in the non-patent literature, merging the results. In recent years, the European Patent Office has substantially increased its efforts to search the non-patent literature (NPL). One of the ways in which it is helping the process is by applying classification marks from its in-house ECLA system, designed to store and retrieve patents, to items of NPL as well. This provides a common retrieval framework, similar in practice to the CAS indexing. However, such systems are still rare.

e)   they must be **rapidly updated**. The final criterion for a good patentability source is that the content is up-to-date. This is a difficult target to achieve with value-added databases, as the processes for refining first-level data inevitably take time, with the result that there can be an appreciable time-lag between the actual publication date of a patent document and its first appearance in the database. Many of the first-level databases can release new documents on the day of publication, and this makes them ideal for a top-up search, to supplement the main body of retrospective literature, and for ongoing monitoring for any competing applications whilst the case is being examined. However, even the value-added suppliers have made substantial strides in recent years, and offer fully-indexed records for new patents within a few days of publication. The main caveat for the searcher is to be aware of any persistent or transient data supply difficulties affecting their chosen database, before relying upon it for the patentability search. Such information, on 'data gaps' and timeliness issues, is only slowly becoming widely available, usually through the medium of the database producer's website or similar communications to the user community.

▶ THE INFRINGEMENT SEARCH

Many of the remarks concerning how to choose a source, or sources, for a patentability search also apply to an infringement search. This search type is also known as a 'freedom-to-operate' or 'freedom-to-practice' search. The objective is to avoid the possibility of infringing someone else's patent. If a company or individual wishes to engage in activities which may fall within the patent rights of another patent holder (for example, making, selling or importing a protected product), they will need to obtain permission – and probably a licence – from the patent holder. Alternatively, they may choose to modify what they intend to do, so that it falls outside the scope of the patent. In either case, the infringement search is an exercise to identify whose patent rights may present a restriction upon future actions. Failure to conduct an infringement search can lead to a costly waste of time at best, if manufacturing or marketing plans have to be modified at the last moment, or legal action for infringement at worst.

The infringement search starts by seeking to identify patents held by third parties which are 'about' the intended product or process – in other words, a subject-based search. However, we can ignore the issue of non-patent literature, since there are no enforceable rights associated with these, and concentrate on patents-only sources. Once a list of candidate patents is obtained, it can be limited by two further criteria.

Firstly, since patents are territorial, the infringement search need only concern itself with patents which confer rights upon the patent holder in the specific country where we plan to operate. Thus, the existence of a United States patent on a product which we hope to manufacture in the United Kingdom is no threat to operations, *provided that* we do not attempt to export the product to the US. Our search results should consider any regional patent systems which protect inventions in the proposed country of operation. For example, if it is our intention to manufacture an item in Spain, it becomes necessary to search both national Spanish patents and any European Patents which have effect in Spain – either would be a bar to operations within that country. In some circumstances, it may be possible to impose this limitation at the beginning of the search, by utilising a database which only contains patents from the countries with which we are concerned.

The second limitation relates to the legal status of any located, relevant patents. The patent holder will only be able to enforce their rights against an alleged infringer if they (the patent holder) have maintained the patent in force, including payment of any required renewal fees. They cannot allow their patent to lapse if they have no interest in working the invention themselves, and then revive it, merely for the purposes of deterring a competitor from entering the market. It is usually necessary to check upon the legal status of a patent in a separate step, by consulting official register data from the patent office concerned. Alternatively, the INPADOC database provides a consolidated source to legal status data from official sources in 40 countries, and is available on a variety of platforms.

A third limitation also applies to freedom-to-operate searches, but generally falls outside the remit of the searcher or patent information specialist. This is the issue of claim interpretation. Patentee rights may only be enforced in relation to the claims portion of a patent document, not the entire disclosure. Once a search has been made to identify relevant documents, it is usually the task of the patent agent or attorney to provide a legal opinion on whether the intended action falls within the exact scope of the patent claims. This stage should not be attempted by anyone unfamiliar with the relevant patent law.

With these search requirements in mind, it becomes clear that for an infringement search, our databases need to comply with the following standards:

a) comprehensive coverage of the **country and/or region** in which operation is planned. This is not always as straightforward as is seems; there are a surprising number of dependent territories and semi-autonomous regions in the modern world, where it is not immediately obvious which country's patents hold force. For example, a United States patent provides rights to the holder in the territory of Puerto Rico, even though that island does not have full statehood. Similarly, should we be contemplating setting up operations in Greenland, it would be necessary to consult some – but not all – Danish patents. Before conducting an infringement search, it is necessary to have a detailed description of exactly *what* is planned and *where*.

b) good access to **multi-technology sources,** for the same reason as for a patentability search. In trying to avoid infringement, it would be foolish to overlook a relevant patent simply because it falls outside of the 'obvious' subject area and hence not covered in the database which we selected for the search.

c) good detailed **subject search** facilities, again for much the same reasons as for patentability. With an infringement search, the oldest relevant patents may be those which are coming to the end of their natural life, having been filed nearly 20 years before. Indeed, it is often the oldest documents which are the most commercially important to the patent holder and would be the most robustly defended if it did come to legal action. Hence the search must ensure that retrieval is comprehensive across many years' worth of variable terminology.

d) ready access to the exact **text of claims**. Although it is the attorney's job to provide opinion on the likelihood of actual infringement, the searcher can assist the process by including the full text of the claims of any candidate answers in their report. It is only the claims which can be infringed, not the body of the disclosure. The internet has made it significantly easier to complete an infringement search, by providing easy access to patent claims. Many countries now publish their specifications by this route, either as static facsimiles (TIFF or PDF page images, with drawings embedded) or as plain text.

e) links to the **legal status** of retrieved records. As with the claims, there will often be aspects of a legal status record which require specialist interpretation, but the searcher can assist by ensuring that the complete information is provided to the attorney, in relation to any specific cases identified in the search. If the located patent has expired, lapsed or been revoked, then it may be possible to proceed with actions which would otherwise have been considered infringement. However, there may be local restoration or appeal procedures which could revive an apparently dead patent, and proper legal advice is needed before commercial decisions are made.

► REFERENCE

1. European Patent Office, Technical Board of Appeal Decision No. T303/86. CPC International. Decision delivered 8 Nov 1988.

10 Common search types (III) – Portfolio and legal status searches

► **THE PORTFOLIO SEARCH**

The portfolio search is based upon an attempt to reconstruct an accurate record of the intellectual property holdings of a particular 'body', usually corporate but sometimes personal as well. In either cases, the principal challenge is identifying those patents which truly belong to a body at the date of search. However, this is not just a simple matter of looking up a name or corporation index, since both individuals and companies can change identity over time (the former principally by way of marriage or divorce and the latter by the corporate equivalents of merger, acquisition or devolution).

At any given point in time, the intellectual property portfolio of a company will almost always consist of a mixture of items:

- Non-patent IP (such as trade marks, designs and domain names) – these need to be borne in mind as setting the context for the patent IP, but will not be considered further here.
- Patents on inventions which were originated by the company ('local technology')
- Patents on inventions originated outside the company, but which have been subsequently acquired ('bought-in' technology)
- Licences to work patents held by a third party, which generate revenues for the licensing company ('leased' technology)

In addition to these, the portfolio search will often locate items which used to belong to the company, but should no longer be counted within their portfolio by reason of sale or re-assignment ('transferred-out' technology). In some circumstances (for example, if the portfolio exercise is intended to identify the innovative capacity of the company), these items should be brought to the attention of the search requester.

It should be clear that one of the primary considerations of a portfolio search is that the searcher needs a thorough understanding of the historical and current structure of the corporation under review. Patent bibliographic databases usually only capture the name of the patentee as at the date of publication of the patent, and do not update this information, no matter how many times the company (and its IP) changes hands in subsequent years. To perform the search, we therefore need to know the present formal company name, common synonyms and abbreviations, common trading identities of subsidiaries and joint-ventures, the ultimate parent or holding company. In addition, we need all of the above for at least the last 20 years, as it is possible that today's company could still holds in-force patents granted up to 20 years before, to any one of the multiple predecessor identities.

A second aspect which needs to be considered with a portfolio search is the question of the maintenance of any identified patents. Many companies hold what appears on the surface to be an impressive inventory of patents, but commonly a substantial proportion of the items on the list will be expired or lapsed patents, and do not contribute to the overall portfolio, at least in the sense of giving an impression of the company's industrial muscle. Once a document listing has been compiled, it is necessary to double-check each item to determine whether post grant actions such as re-assignment or non-payment of annuity fees, revocation or other litigation have occurred, all of which will affect the value of the portfolio as a whole.

To assist the searcher, some database producers have standardised assignee names. This at least helps to remove the problem of missing items due to trivial name variations, and in some cases serves to group together patents from known subsidiaries. The Derwent Patentee Code is the largest commonly available system for doing this; it is by no means perfect, and should be used with caution, but it can serve to help the patent searcher towards the ultimate goal. Documentation on the Patentee Code listing can be obtained from Thomson Scientific. Some attempts have been made (e.g. by CHI Research in the United States) to compile dictionaries of company structure, to assist in patent portfolio searching, but these are generally limited in usefulness and/or very expensive to produce. In all cases, the searcher is best advised to spend some time in the established business information tools (such as Who Owns Whom or similar directories) before attempting a portfolio search.

There are two further aspects of a portfolio search, both of which relate to the timing of the search. Since a portfolio search is often used to try to assess the industrial strength of a particular firm, it is important to bear in mind that patent information – no matter how carefully it is collected – can usually only indicate the performance of a company's R&D programme *as is stood some 18 months before*. This is because of the built-in time lag between patent filing and publication. Clearly, this means that any meaningful search in the patent literature must be supplemented by further work in conventional news, business and financial information sources, to fill this gap. The other 'timing' issue, which relates equally to all searches involving legal status, is to remember that we are observing a fluid situation, or a snap-shot picture, by consulting databases at a specific point. The most accurate legal status databases available can only give us a result which relates *to that day*; by the following day, new information may have been added, which has the potential to re-shape our opinions of the portfolio entirely.

▶ LEGAL STATUS

The legal status search may be an enquiry in its own right, to establish the standing of a specific document, or as an adjunct to another type of search, such as a portfolio assessment.

The basic principle of legal status searching is to establish whether the located document represents an enforceable right. The searcher's motive may be varied. They may be wishing to obtain a licence to work the patent themselves, to know how to guide their research to avoid the possibility of infringement, or to enter the market as soon as the patent expires.

Services from patent offices

The advent of the internet has revolutionised the availability of information from national patent offices. The newsletter of the United Kingdom's Patent & Trade Mark Group (PATMG) has a regular column written by Stephen van Dulken of the British Library, providing details of new resources of this type, and barely an issue passes without some expansion or change in the situation. Suffice to say that many European national offices (UK, Germany, Denmark, Netherlands. ...) and a substantial proportion of offices from other industrialised countries make their official register information available free-of-charge via the internet. Rather than try to provide an inventory of services in this book, the reader is best served by consulting one of the directory services referred to in chapter 6.

Register information provided by patent offices falls into several distinct classes. The simplest register is searchable by patent grant number, and provides a bibliographic record of the ownership of the patent at the date of grant. The next refinement is to include data on post-grant events, which may include such matters as re-assignment data, records of payment (or non-payment) of maintenance fees, licences granted (particularly if under legislative requirement, such as UK compulsory licences), expiry and term extension. The more complete registers can provide a good outline of the prosecution history of a case, with cross-references to divisional or continuation cases deriving from the master record.

The most comprehensive form of patent office service offered so far is to include the ability for a third party to view every item of correspondence passing between the applicant and the patent office in relation to a specific application, from the first official form with the priority documents through to the notice of acceptance and beyond. To date, these so-called 'file inspection'-type registers are relatively rare. Two in place are those from the USPTO, known as IFW (Image File Wrapper) and the EPO's file inspection system, which is bundled under the umbrella of the epoline ® service.

PAIR and Image File Wrapper

The PAIR (Patent Application Information Retrieval) system was the first stage of release by the USPTO of status information. The USPTO has released a tutorial on the use of PAIR, which can be downloaded from <http://www.uspto.gov/ebc/pair/cbt.htm>.

There are two forms, public PAIR and private PAIR. The public PAIR system is open to all, and enables a legal status record to be retrieved for most US cases subsequent to a publication stage. Before 2001, that meant that the PAIR record could only be viewed once the patent had been granted, but following the introduction of early publication by the US, it is now possible to view the PAIR record whilst the patent is still under prosecution, provided the corresponding US A document has been laid open. Private PAIR is an encrypted system only available to registered patent agents or patent attorneys in the United States, and it enables them to monitor all the cases for which they are the appointed representative, including stages of progress prior to publication. This is an extremely useful system, in that with modern electronic filing, it enables them to monitor dispatch and receipt of documents, payments and official actions. Private PAIR access is also possible for the independent inventor, or a person granted limited recognition, who have been allocated a customer number, and have a digital PKI certificate issued to them.

The coverage of the public PAIR system is not yet extended to all in-force US patents, and it is not clear whether it will ever be so. Present-day filings are being included from the first day, but information on the extent of the back-file is not comprehensive.

One of the biggest drawbacks on the public PAIR system is the inability to search on interim filing numbers. There are only three search types available; by application number, by patent number (the modern US-B number) or by publication number (current US-A numbers). The application number field requires both the serial number and the series number to work properly, otherwise an error message is returned. The only application number which returns a record is the one immediately preceding grant. For example (fictitious details), if granted patent US 3456789 was issued from application number 04/567891 which was a continuation of abandoned application 04/098765, then only the first two numbers would retrieve a result; the first filing would yield no results. In the same way, no foreign priorities are searchable in PAIR, only domestic filing numbers.

Public PAIR provides the searcher with a great deal of information on the progress of the case towards grant, and more recently has included cross-references to so-called 'child' information, such as re-issue cases based on the patent being viewed, and maintenance fee payments. However, it does not form a complete prosecution history. For this, the companion Image File Wrapper (IFW) service is required.

The IFW service provides scanned electronic versions of the paper 'file wrappers' available from the USPTO. These documents, which may run to many hundreds of pages for complex cases, provide a complete record of all communications between applicant and patent office during the processing of a patent application. IFW is also in two parts, with users of Private PAIR able to see electronic versions of their non-published cases as well as the public records on all published cases. The US law firm of Oppedahl & Larson LLP were heavily involved in testing the IFW system, and much more detail on the background and content of IFW can be found in the presentation by Oppedahl[1]. The same firm has also set up a discussion list for users of PAIR, details of which can be found at <http://www.patents.com/pair>

The essential operation of IFW is based on a link from the PAIR record. Initially this provides an electronic table of contents for the file wrapper. Users may select part or all of the documents from the available list, which is then sent to the user's e-mail address in the form of a zipped file, containing TIFF format images of the document(s). The IFW system includes all cases filed since mid-2003, and work on back-scanning the paper file wrappers for older cases is continuing. However, as with PAIR, it is unlikely that the entire collection will be loaded.

epoline ® – Web register and file inspection

The epoline service is a portal produced by the European Patent Office. As with PAIR/IFW, it is a rapidly developing service, which has seen many changes since the earliest components were launched in 2001. For a good review of how the system has changed, see the recent paper by Rogier[2] and references therein.

The first component of epoline <http://www.epoline.org> was a replacement for the X.25-based legal status register, using a computer in The Hague to provide stages of progress data on European Patent applications. The Web Register allowed greater flexibility in both search fields and display formats. Unlike PAIR, which only provides three search possibilities, the Online European Patent Register permits searching by 11 criteria (Application number, Application date, Publication number, Publication date, Priority number, Priority date, Applicant, Inventor, Representative, Opponent or Classification (IPC)). In practice, by far the most common fields used are the first ones, allowing a case-by-case inspection of pending or granted applications which the user may be monitoring – either their own or those of a competitor.

As with public PAIR, the free Register only provides access to cases which have reached at least the stage of unexamined application (EP-A). The record includes all the standard bibliographic items (required under Rule 92 of the EPC), plus additional information such as renewal fee payments and documents cited in the search report. The latter are provided in the form of links to the actual documents in the esp@cenet service.

An example record from the Register (for EP 666666-B) is shown in Figure 20. It can be seen that opposite the application number is a small 'folder' icon. This informs the user that the corresponding file inspection is also available electronically. Clicking on this icon provides the table of contents for the dossier, as shown in Figure 21. The operation to download elements from the dossier is essentially identical to the PAIR system, which is not surprising since the USPTO licenses the EPO-developed software for its service.

The Secure File Inspection is epoline's equivalent to the US private PAIR, allowing encrypted access to non-published cases for authorised representatives. It is also integrated with the online electronic filing service, allowing cases to be deposited with the EPO in approved electronic formats.

The EPO is continually developing refinements on the epoline system. These include the ability to request e-mail updates whenever a Register entry is modified. This facility is provided by the WebRegMT (Monitoring Tool) software. It is expected that soon the epoline service will be able to deliver more targeted alerting, to provide announcements on specific actions rather than any new action taking place. At the moment, such precision is only possible using commercial host systems (such as using the INPADOC legal status codes).

It is worth commenting that, just as the OPS service has opened the door to developers to produce their own front-ends to patent bibliographic information, at least one organisation has created a new front-end to legal status information. This is marketed as EP Tracker, from Minesoft <http://www.eptracker.com>. As the name suggests, the earliest versions provided access only to the EPO Register, but later extensions have permitted user-friendly tracking of events on the UK and German registers as well.

Multi-country coverage (INPADOC-PRS)

For many years, the legal status module of INPADOC, the PRS, formed the principal electronic search tool for legal status. It remains very

Online European Patent Register - Results

Status of the database as of 21-07-2005 (dd-mm-yyyy)

Choose your View: All data mentioned in Rule 92 and EPIDOS

Return to Search Screen

Most recent event	
Grant	
Date of publication	27-04-2005 [2005/17]
Publication numbers, publication type and publication dates	EP0666666 A2 09-08-1995 [1995/32] EP0666666 A3 02-01-2003 [2003/01] EP0666666 B1 27-04-2005 [2005/17]
Date of grant	27-04-2005 [2005/17]
Application numbers and filing date	EP19950480005 (95480005.8)
Date of filing	24-01-1995 [1995/32]
Date of publication of search report	
Date of publication of search report	02-01-2003 [2003/01]
Priority number, priority date	US19940192884 07-02-1994 [1995/32]
Classification (IPC) and bulletin number	H04L12/24, H04L12/42, H04L29/00 [1995/32]
Designated states	DE , FR , GB [1995/32]
English title	Method and apparatus for improved throughput in a multi-node communication system with a shared resource [1995/32]
French title	Méthode et dispositif pour débit amélioré dans un système de communication à plusieurs noeuds avec une ressource partagée [1995/32]
German title	Verfahren und Vorrichtung für verbesserten Durchfluss in einem Vielfachknoten-Kommunikationssystem mit einem gemeinsamen Betriebsmittel *[1995/32]*
Designated states, applicant name, address	FOR ALL DESIGNATED STATES International Business Machines Corporation New Orchard Road Armonk, N.Y. 10504/US [2005/17]
Inventor name, address	01 / Cidon, Israel / 2600 Netherland Avenue, Apt. 2507 / Bronx, New York 10463 / US 02 / Georgiadis, Leonidas / 36 Old Mill Road / Chappaqua, New York 10514 / US 03 / Guerin, Roch Andre / Scenic View No.4H, Rochambeau Drive / Yorktown Heights, New York 10598 / US 04 / Shavitt, Yuval Yitzchak / Harofe 29 / Haifa / IL 05 / Slater, Andrew Emlyn / 2262 Parker Lane / Yorktown Heights, N.Y. 10598 / US [1995/44]
Representative name, address	Therias, Philippe

Figure 20: Example record from epoline Register

important today, since it offers a facility to search across patent families and/or large numbers of documents which is simply not available in the patent office systems. Where INPADOC-PRS has been loaded on a commercial host, it is possible for a searcher to run a subject or assignee search, and to cross the large numbers of documents found into the legal status file in one operation, to check on validity, lapse and so on.

The legal status information in INPADOC is sourced from national patent office gazettes, and codified into standard 'events'. These event codes and the corresponding explanatory text are then entered as discrete subfields linked to the bibliographic record of the patent to which they belong. For example, the INPADOC PRS data for GB2200000-B includes the following event:

PRS Date :	1993/09/15
PRS Code :	PCNP
Code Expl.:	PATENT CEASED THROUGH NON-PAYMENT OF RENEWAL FEE
EFFECTIVE DATE:	19930116

The PRS date is the date on which the information entered the database, whilst the effective date is the date on which the action became effective.

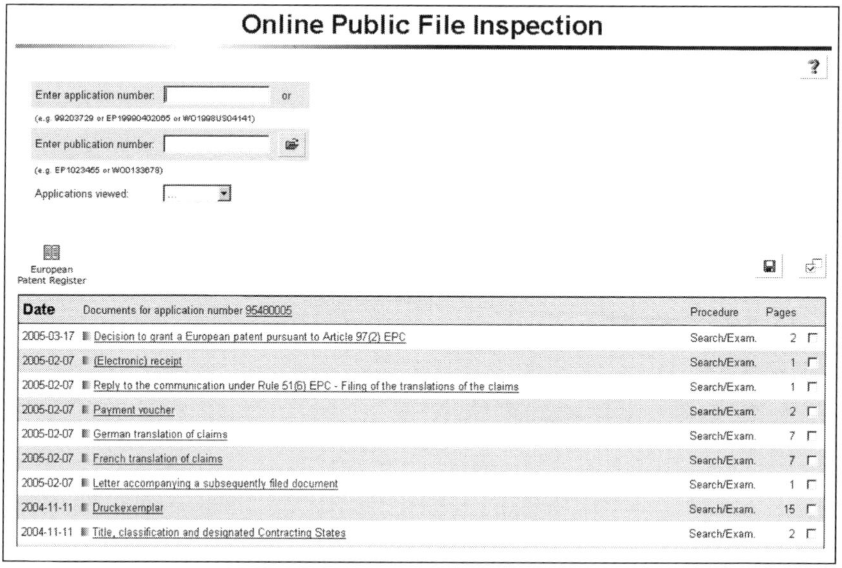

Figure 21: EPO file inspection – table of contents

In this instance, announcements about expiry do not appear in the UK gazette until after the time interval for restoration has passed – hence an announcement in a gazette in September 1993 that a patent has been ceased since the preceding January. It is not unusual for legal status information to be retro-active in this way, and it is important that users should be familiar with local legislation and practices before interpreting the output from any legal status database. Some of the factors concerned have been described by Adams[3].

The PRS code in the example above enables the searcher to pinpoint specific actions and to search for them in their own right, rather than checking case-by-case using patent number as the search key. In a commercial host, it would be possible, for example, to construct a strategy to retrieve all GB cases which had ceased through non-payment of renewal fee during a given year.

The coverage of the PRS service in INPADOC has expanded substantially in recent years, due to the importance of PCT information. As this system has become a more popular method for both small and large applicants to enter the patent processing stream, it has become more important to be able to monitor the fate of such applications. Specifically, it is useful to be able to monitor whether an applicant has in fact entered the national (or regional) phase, especially since the recent reduction in usefulness of the list of designated states. It is arguable that it is even more important to be aware of *non-entry* to the national phase; in other words, when the applicant has made a conscious decision not to use their PCT application as a route to pursuing national patent protection in a given country. During the 1990's, the EPO was charged by WIPO to initiate a project to collect PCT entry and non-entry data for as many countries as possible, and to include this in the INPADOC-PRS data set.

A further expansion of PRS data has taken place with the inclusion of SPC (or equivalent pharmaceutical term extension) information from a number of countries. The following table (Table 50) contains a summary of the country coverage as of mid-2005. Note that this does not distinguish those countries for which both patent and utility model legal status is provided, and that in some cases the only legal status information on patents is in the form of the registration of European Patents designating that country, not for the national patent system.

Commercial sources for United States legal status

In addition to the legal status provided by PAIR and INPADOC, the searcher wishing to obtain data on US granted patents is well-provided for, with a range of additional commercial search files. The best known of these are Litalert and PAST (both produced by Thomson) and CLAIMS/CPLS (a sister file to the CLAIMS bibliographic files, from WoltersKluwer).

Litalert is available from Dialog, STN, Questel-Orbit and Westlaw. It contains records of patent lawsuits filed in the US District Courts since 1973. The record structure is usually fairly brief, but searching by patent number is allowed, and this can provide sufficient court data (such as a docket number) to allow retrieval of more information via the US court system.

The PAST (Patent Status) file overlapped substantially with Litalert, and has now been withdrawn as a separate product from the commercial hosts. Its coverage was more concentrated on non-court post-grant actions, such as the issue of certificates of correction, requests for re-examination and so on. As such, much of the information is now available in PAIR, or by direct browsing of the electronic Official Gazette (eOG) on the USPTO website.

The CLAIMS/CPLS (Current Patent Legal Status) file also concentrates on post-grant actions. The information is sourced from the USPTO Official Gazette and includes certificates of correction, reassignment, re-examination requests and certificates, extensions (including those under the AIPA and for pharmaceuticals), expiry due to non-payment of fees, reinstatements, reissue requests, adverse decisions on interference actions, and disclaimer/ dedication data. Most coverage dates from the early to mid-19080's. The file can be used in tandem with the corresponding bibliographic file, for example to retrieve the text of any claims modified by re-issue or re-examination. The CLAIMS/CPLS file is available on Dialog and Questel-Orbit (known as CRXX).

Table 50: INPADOC PRS coverage as of 2005

Country code	Country	First(-last) year of national or EP legal status	PCT entry data	PCT non-entry data	SPC or equiva-lent
AT	Austria	1975	Yes	No	Yes
AU	Australia	2000	Yes	Yes	No
BE	Belgium	1984	No	No	Yes
BG	Bulgaria	No	Yes	No	No
BR	Brazil	1995	No	No	No
CA	Canada	1992	Yes	Yes	No
CH	Switzerland	1958	No	No	Yes
CL	Chile	1990–1998	No	No	No
CN	China	2001	No	No	No
CZ	Czech Republic	2000	No	No	No
DD	East Germany	1992–2004	No	No	No
DE	Germany	1978	Yes	Yes	Yes
DK	Denmark	1982	No	No	Yes
EE	Estonia	2004	No	No	No
EP	EPO	1978	No	No	No
ES	Spain	1992	Yes	No	Yes
FI	Finland	1993	No	No	No
FR	France	1969	No	No	Yes
GB	United Kingdom	1968	Yes	No	Yes
GE	Georgia	No	Yes	No	No
GR	Greece	1989	No	No	No
HU	Hungary	1990	No	No	No
HK	Hong Kong	2004	No	No	No
IE	Ireland	1993	No	No	Yes
IL	Israel	1996	No	No	Yes
IT	Italy	1989	No	No	Yes
JP	Japan	No	Yes	Yes	No
KE	Kenya	No	Yes	No	No
KR	South Korea	No	Yes	Yes	No
LT	Lithuania	1995	Yes	No	Yes
LU	Luxembourg	No	No	No	Yes
LV	Latvia	No	Yes	No	No
MC	Monaco	1972–1992	No	No	No
MD	Moldova	1994–1999	No	No	No
NL	Netherlands	1993	No	No	Yes
NO	Norway	2001	No	No	Yes
PH	Philippines	1990–1997	No	No	No
PT	Portugal	1991	No	No	No
RO	Romania	No	Yes	No	No
RU	Russian Federation	No	Yes	No	No
SE	Sweden	1995	No	No	Yes
SI	Slovenia	1994	Yes	No	No
SK	Slovakia	No	Yes	No	No
TW	Taiwan	2000	No	No	No
US	United States	1968	Yes	No	Yes
UZ	Uzbekistan	No	Yes	No	No
WO	PCT	1978	No	No	No

The questions surrounding the actual status of a US patent have been considerably confused due to the law changes on term introduced in 1995 and the subsequent modifications in later legislation such as the AIPA, not to mention pharmaceutical extensions. A good review of the complexity of the situation appears in the paper by Clark *et al.*[4]. A recent presentation by Matula[5] also graphically illustrated the hazards of reliance upon a single source for patent litigation information in the US courts. A much earlier paper by Snow[6] is still a useful reminder of some non-patent databases which yield useful information in this area.

Japanese legal status – Patolis

One of the key areas – for the Western searcher – which is still largely missing in the field of legal status information is that from Japan. With the introduction of the free web service, IPDL, on the Japanese Patent Office website, a limited amount of legal status actions started to become available in the English language, but only for patents and then only from 1995 onwards. No legal status information at the national level is released into the INPADOC file. The principal English service which provides any depth of legal status for Japan is the Patolis service, a commercial web-based tool which was discussed in Chapter 4 in respect of its bibliographic content. The same service provides a much greater depth of legal information, both in terms of the types of documents (both patent and utility model actions are recorded) and range of years covered (from 1955 for patents and 1960 for utility models, depending upon the legal action concerned). The Patolis Corporation has also recently launched a printed directory, "Extended Pharmaceutical Patents", with extensive listings of Japanese patent term extensions[7].

▶ VALIDITY AND OPPOSITION SEARCHING

These types of search are similar in scope to a novelty or patentability search, in that it must address many document types and periods. However, they are addressed in this chapter because they have an additional – and essential – legal aspect to them.

The aim of a validity or opposition search is to gather material for legal proceedings, questioning the validity of an opponent's patent. The objective is to raise questions as to whether a specific granted patent in fact complies with the requirements for patentability; to put it another way, to support an argument for revocation. In a validity search, the searcher's clients may have been accused of infringing the patent in suit, and are attempting to nullify the effect of that accusation by finding grounds to invalidate the patent. The simple argument is to "kill the patent, before it kills you." If a party accused of infringement is able successfully to show that the plaintiff's patent is not valid, they have no case to answer. This form of search can take place at any point during the life of the patent.

An opposition search is designed to raise questions of patentability early in the life of a patent. Opposition proceedings – where they exist – tend to be handled by a special division of the granting patent office, rather than by the courts. In the case of the European Patent system, opposing a patent immediately after grant is an effective way of removing its effect in all the designated states simultaneously. Failure to take advantage on this procedure means that any later opponent has to mount parallel proceedings before the national courts in each state where nullity is sought.

In both cases, the aim of the searcher is to identify subject matter which was published before the priority date of our known patent, and hence raise objects on grounds of lack of novelty or inventive step. It is therefore an essential step for the searcher to liaise with the legal specialists involved, to ensure that the priority date(s) are well understood. In complex cases, different parts of a patent application may have distinct priority dates attached to them (for example, if several cases were cognated into a single Convention filing), and the searcher must understand the cut-off date for each part of the search.

As with a patentability search, the primary sources must cover multiple countries and multiple technologies sources. As well as extensive subject indexing, a validity search is one area where full-text can be a powerful support. Damaging prior disclosures may have happened through the examples or discussion part of a patent document, just as much as in the claims, and such items may not be highlighted by the use of abstracts in the search. Again, the type of literature providing the disclosure is not relevant, and all available patent and non-patent literature must be searched. Frequently, 'grey' literature such as theses and reports can yield valuable material in support of the invalidity argument. Specialists in some search types (e.g. opposing software patents, see <http://www.bustpatents.com/>) maintain that more prior art is found in the non-patent literature than in patents, and the searcher must certainly cast the net very widely in conducting these types of search.

One useful aspect for search engines used in opposition searching is if the user is allowed to restrict their results by date. However, it is important to bear in mind that not all records in a database will populate the publication field to the same degree of accuracy. For example, a record for an article from a quarterly periodical will only list the publication date by month, not by day. The searcher should understand the command syntax thoroughly before applying date limitations, as this may run the risk of eliminating relevant material by accident.

A related issue on publication dates is that of citing the internet. Being the fluid medium that it is, material which could potentially invalidate a patent may appear one day and disappear the next. Searchers using internet sources should ensure that they maintain some form of tangible record as to exactly when and where the prior art located; if need be, this can include taking a printout of the relevant web pages and adding a date stamp. Formalised disclosure databases such as the Research Disclosure journal and the web-based IP.com <http://www.ip.com> provide an accurate audit trail for the contents of their files. For the viewpoint of the EPO on using and citing internet-based references, see the article by Archontopoulos[8].

▶ REFERENCES

1.   "Getting the most out of free databases at the USPTO". C. Oppedahl :in Proc. PIUG Annual Conference, Baltimore, Maryland, 22–27 May 2004.

2.   "epoline ® : Register Plus and Online Filing update." V. Rogier, World Patent Information, **27**(3), 251–256 (2005).

3.   "A short examination of the timeliness and accuracy of United Kingdom patent legal status data sources". S. Adams, World Patent Information **24**(3), 203–209 (2002).

4.   "The face of the patent is not the whole story: determining effective patent life of a pharmaceutical patent in the United States." A. M. Clark; H. Berven. World Patent Information **26**(4), 283–295 (2004).

5.   "Shepardize a patent: a post-processing example". R.A. Matula :in Proc. PIUG Annual Conference, Crystal City, Alexandria, Virginia, 21–26 May 2005.

6.   "Drug patent extension information online: monitoring post-approval regulatory developments." B. Snow. Online **18**(4), 95–100 (1994).

7.   Details for purchasing copies are available from the Patolis website, <http://www.patolis.co.jp/en/products/pharmaceutical>.

8.   "Prior art search tools on the Internet and legal status of the results: a European Patent Office perspective." E. Archontopoulos, World Patent Information **26**(2), 113–121 (2004).

11 ▎ Commercial intelligence

▶ STATE-OF-THE-ART SEARCHES

The function of a state-of-the-art search is to provide a broad overview of a defined field of technology. A principal purpose behind such a search is to enable a company which may be contemplating entry to a new technical field to understand who are the major competitors or manufacturers, and what are the key technologies in the field. For this reason, this search type may also be referred to as a 'technology overview' search. The results of such a search may assist a company in identifying gaps in the field which it may be able to exploit. At the other extreme, the search may show that the sector is already very crowded or competitive, or the technology is far removed from the company's existing skill base, which may deter the putative entrant from making the investment at all. An intermediate result would perhaps be to show that some gaps still exist, which can be exploited with a judicious combination of new research and joint ventures with identified experts in the sector. Whatever the outcome, the state-of-the-art search is a prime example of where patent information can be used to prevent wasteful duplication of research.

The fundamental requirements for a good state-of-the-art search have much in common with a patentability search. However, whereas the latter is conducted when one has a specific invention already in mind, the searcher conducting the state-of-the-art search is more concerned with the larger picture, at the industry level rather than the invention level. For example, instead of searching for references which might anticipate our new intermittent windscreen wiper mechanism, we wish now to review the whole field of automobile controls and actuators. As a consequence of this approach, we can complete a state-of-the-art search by using a broad-based subject indexing system, such as Derwent Class Codes, Chemical Abstracts section codes or even IPC to the sub-class level. Databases with proprietary indexing are particularly useful here, as they are often designed with up-posting (collation of detailed marks into broader groups) in mind; the public classifications can, paradoxically, be more difficult to use when generating a broad search, since the concept behind such systems is usually to apply the most detailed mark available, and up-posting may be more labour-intensive.

A second aspect of the state-of-the-art search is the decision concerning multi-country coverage. If the company conducting the search has already made decisions as to where it plans to manufacture and/or sell any products arising out of its new venture, then added care should be taken to ensure that the intellectual property in force in those specific territories is identified. At the extreme, if the company is content to operate entirely within one country, a good initial view of the technological landscape can be obtained by searching in single-country databases. However, it should always be borne in mind that, once a research programme has started to generate potentially patentable new inventions, any patentability searches will need to be done in the light of the local definition of prior art – which may be universal.

The state-of-the-art search conducted in patent databases should ideally be supplemented by a range of business sector assessments derived from other sources. Non-patent literature such as market reports, company annual reports, press releases from individual companies, sector analysts or trade associations, financial returns and so on, can add further details, especially late-breaking technical developments which may be buried in the 18-month 'black hole' between patent filing and early publication. The searcher should never forget that patents can only indicate one aspect of the overall shape of a market sector. It is not unknown for market leaders to hold relatively few, or no, patents in their own name, but to exert their influence through patents licenced from other companies, or by effective use of trade secrets and other non-patented know-how. At the very least, the conduct of corresponding searches in the non-patent literature should be able to provide a degree of confirmation of the picture revealed by the patents. If the findings of the two searches appear to contradict one another, then further review of the situation is indicated.

Traditionally, the state-of-the-art search has been limited by the amount of information which the customer can absorb and make sense of. It was often recommended that the search should include good access to the complete texts of any patents identified, to enable a judgement to be made on their importance. This is particularly true if the search appears to have identified one or more seminal texts – the preamble to such patents can often be in the form of mini-reviews, and help the competitor company to gain a good overall picture relatively rapidly.

▶ PATENT ANALYSIS TOOLS AND TECHNIQUES

In recent years it has become more accepted that a state-of-the-art search can be reviewed without having actually to read all the patents. An entirely new field of data visualisation techniques has grown up, ranging from simple frequency rankings to sophisticated mapping and linking software. Whilst is it not recommended that the sales pitch that *"You will never have to read another patent"* is taken at face value, these aids can certainly accelerate the understanding of a large set of data.

One of the motivations behind the development of software to "post-process" patent search results has been simply the ever-increasing numbers of results obtained from even the most tightly constrained search strategy. If a prior art search listing succeeds only in overwhelming the customer with a mass of indigestible data, it serves no real purpose, and cannot assist in the decision-making process. As a result, many software packages have been developed which seek to assist the user to make sense of the mass of information. This can sometimes be achieved by a simple spreadsheet-style ranking of assignee or inventor data, display of time-based graphs of numbers of applications against year of filing, or similar. Some tools are being built into the retrieval suite itself, such as the colour maps of hit-term highlighting found in PatBase and similar products.

Analysis tools can be broken down into a number of types. The simplest are capable of handling answer sets of several hundred at most, and rely upon pre-formatted or fielded information which is imported into a display application. One such example is the SmartCharts product from Biz-Int Solutions (see <http://www.bizcharts.com>), which provides an Excel-like output for rapid screening of search results. Similar visualisation tools are now built into the STN Express software package, from STN International. Other producers include Invention Navigator from SIP GmbH <http://www.patentfamily.de>, PatCite, IPDiscover and MatheoPatent.

The use of more complex tools – referred to by some as "patinformatics" – takes the user beyond the need to handle the output from a restricted search, and are much more focussed on analysing an industry-wide survey, using tens or hundreds of thousands of documents. There is a tendency at this scale to move away from analysing fielded data, and more towards mining of the raw text of the patent specifications.

With either type of tool – small or large scale, fielded or unfielded data – the validity of the results depends in equal part upon the accuracy of the initial search and the application of the analysis stage. For this reason, it is good practice to ensure that the source(s) of data underlying the analysis are thoroughly understood before offering an interpretation of the output. Some tools are designed to operate only with their own integrated search files, whilst others offer the user the chance to select the data themselves. Some of the tools which can import from one or more external sources are produced by companies such as ClearForest, CoBrain/Invention Machine, Wisdomain, Semio Corporation (Entrieva), OmniViz, InfoSleuth, Delphion (PatentLab II), TechTracker, InXight, Search Technology (marketing Vantage Point software, marketed in conjunction with Thomson as Derwent Analytics), Synthesis Partners, M-CAM, CHI Research (now part of ipIQ), and IBM/Synthema.

Space does not permit for a survey of these tools, but a number of reviews have been published in recent years. Recommended reading is the two foundational papers by Trippe[1,2] and the ACS symposium which he organised, which contained a range of useful papers[3]. One of the problems of dealing with these topics is that very few companies have realistic case studies available to show the efficacy of the tools, and the few who have tend to regard the output as conferring commercial advantage, so are reluctant to go into print concerning how useful the tools have been. The result is a large supply of anecdotal evidence with little objective assessment, either of the tool in isolation or of its performance opposite equivalent tools. To a large extent, we still do not know whether the maps, diagrams or spreadsheets produced by these packages are an accurate reflection of commercial life or an artefact of the process of their creation. However, it is clear that the ability to bring some semblance of order to a mass of information has attractions for hard-pressed industry information departments, and development of these and many more tools will continue.

▶ REFERENCES

1. "Patinformatics: identifying haystacks from space." A. J. Trippe. Searcher **10**(9), 28–41 (Oct 2002).
2. "Patinformatics: tasks to tools." A.J. Trippe. World Patent Information **25**(3), 211–221 (2003) and refs. therein.
3. "Technical Intelligence". Proc. Symposium of the Chemical Information (CINF) Division of the American Chemical Society, held at the ACS 221st National Meeting, San Diego, CA, April 3–4, 2001. Paper Nos. CINF 34–37, 45–48, 57–62, 71–74.

12 Specialist techniques

▶ **SEARCHING OF CITATIONS**

One of the earliest products to tackle patent citation searching was from the IFI Claims stable, the CLAIMS/Citation suite of files, available on Dialog. These provided the means to follow references from US patent search reports from 1947 to date, in either direction. The later development of internet websites, with their built-in facility for relating documents by means of a hyper-link, have accelerated the use of citations (both forward and back) in document searching generally, and patent searching is no exception.

The principles of citation searching in the scientific literature were formalised[1] by Eugene Garfield of the Institute of Scientific Information (ISI) , although the technique had been well recognised in legal circles for many years. The background has been described by Weinstock[2]. Garfield's work led to the development of the Science Citation Index and similar products in the social sciences and arts & humanities. The basic tenet of this form of search is that the references cited by an article of known relevance can be re-used as search terms, to locate further literature which also cites at least one of the items from the known article's bibliography. The more items from their common bibliographies that the two articles have in common, the stronger the supposed link between them.

Garfield's early work also included some application of the technique to patents[3]. However, in applying this principle to patent documents, there are two additional challenges. The first is a subjective assessment of the validity of the citation principle. When applied to journal literature, it is established practice for authors systematically to cite the earlier foundational articles from which their work has grown. In other words, the bibliography of a journal article is taken to be reasonably complete and thorough in its content, without bias for or against other works which pre-date the current one. However, the problem of applying this principle to patents is that patent search reports are not intended to be systematic bibliographies of all relevant preceding work. In the case of a search report appended to an unexamined patent application, it contains items which the examiner feels present the most significant barriers to patentability – in other words, the list may contain one or more items of 'knock-out' prior art which will, in due course, prevent the application reaching the status of a patent. There is no attempt to compile a systematic review of all previous work, only those items which damage the chances of the current application. Consequently, a patent search report may well fail to cite one or more pieces of significant earlier work, simply because they do not bear directly upon whether the current application is patentable. The citation principle is further distorted if the search report is from a US granted patent. Under these circumstances, the items in the list, used as search terms to locate further art, are *by definition* pieces of prior art which *failed to prevent patentability* of the current item. It is arguable, then, that the citations of a US listing are more likely to take the searcher away from the subject matter contained in the current invention, rather than closer towards it.

The second challenge is the issue of patent families and citation practice. The paper by Michel *et al.*[4] shows clearly that each national patent office tends to favour citing documents from its own national collections i.e. the USPTO will preferentially cite US documents, the JPO will cite JP and so on. This is probably a reflection of the order in which document collections are searched, plus other factors. Whatever the exact reason, the implication for citation searching is that two patent documents may well cite the same *invention* but in the form of different family members. It is precisely this issue which PCI was established to solve, by utilising the family structure of WPI.

▶ PATENT CLASSIFICATION

New entrants to patent searching will typically try to apply whatever rules and techniques they have learnt from other search experiences, be that Google or some more sophisticated tool or database. At their most fundamental, these experiences promote the idea that word-based searching will serve to retrieve sufficient numbers of documents, sufficiently precisely, to fulfil the information need. Unfortunately, in patent searching, the legal requirements do not allow this flexibility. To ensure that a greater proportion of the prior art is found, the great majority of searchers will eventually move to supplement their word searching by other means, which often includes classification[5]. There are a number of extant classification schemes applied to patent documents.

The International Patent Classification and its derivatives

The International Patent Classification, or IPC, has been in force since 1968, and is currently employed by approximately 100 patent offices worldwide. The scheme is administered by WIPO, through the Strasbourg Agreement[6], which allows the signatory states a seat on the revision process.

The IPC has gone through 7 periodic revisions since its inception, at approximately five-year intervals. In its present form, the seventh edition, it consists of a hierarchical classification of technology, divided into some 67,300 sub-divisions. One or more classification marks, corresponding to the sub-divisions which best represent the subject matter of the patent, are applied to the front page of the document. The same data are transferred to the electronic search files, and can be used to create a subject-based strategy for information retrieval.

The notation of the IPC reflects the hierarchical structure to some extent, in that it is divided into 8 sections (A-H), followed by numeric classes (two digits) and a further single letter for the sub-class. Beyond this, the notation represents main groups (one or two digits) followed by an oblique slash and a numeric sub-group of up to 5 digits, although most are two to three in length. Hence a typical mark may be made up in the following manner:

Level	Notation	Definition
Section	B	Performing operations, transporting
Class	B65	Conveying; Packing; Storing; Handling thin or filamentary material
Sub-class	B65D	Containers for storage or transport of articles or materials, e.g. bags, barrels, bottles, boxes, cans, cartons, crates, drums, jars, tanks, hoppers, forwarding containers; accessories, closures, or fittings therefor; Packaging elements; Packages
Main Group (*)	B65D 1/00	Containers having bodies formed in one piece, e.g. by casting metallic material, by moulding plastics, by blowing vitreous material, by throwing ceramic material, by moulding pulped fibrous material, by deep-drawing operations performed on sheet material
Sub-group	B65D 1/10	Jars, e.g. for preserving foodstuffs

(*) the main group is always indicated by a /00 notation, whereas the sub-groups are represented by further digits.

A listing of the main classes of the IPC can be found at Annex C.

With practice, it is possible to utilise the IPC to greatly improve the retrieval of relevant prior art, without relying upon word-based search terms. A variety of tools exist to help the user, including the loading of the seventh edition text of the IPC on the WIPO website, and a CD-ROM based tool, IPC:CLASS, which stores all seven editions and the Revision Concordance Lists between them[7].

One of the key problems with the IPC has been that it is essentially frozen for a five year period between revisions (see Table 51). This means that if the technical field of an invention is particularly fast-moving, it becomes progressively less easy to classify with any degree of precision, until such time as that part of the scheme is revised to incorporate aspects of the subject matter. This would in itself create significant problems for the searcher, but is exacerbated by the fact that, once bibliographic records including an IPC mark are created (at the time of publication), they also remain frozen in time. Even if newer or more precise marks are introduced by later revisions of the scheme, the document front pages and the corresponding database records remain as under the old version. As a result, the searcher wishing to use the IPC to search back to the theoretical maximum (1968) will have to locate all the relevant marks across each revision period and cumulate them into a single strategy. Although this can be achieved by means of the Revision Concordance Lists, which maintain a permanent record of the changes between editions, it is a time-consuming process.

As a consequence of these shortcomings, the IPC will be radically revised effective 1 Jan 2006, when the eighth edition will be launched. The new IPC will split into two distinct schemes. The core scheme will retain many of the features of the existing IPC, with a three-year revision period, and will be used by smaller patent offices wishing to classify a paper-based collection of documents. The other part will be the advanced IPC. This will be revised on a much more frequent basis, probably 3 or 6-monthly, to reflect changing technology. In addition, the back-file problem will be addressed, in that the bibliographic records of all patent documents affected by a classification revision will be amended to the current standard. At the

Table 51: IPC revision periods

Edition	Dates in force
First	1 Sep 1968 – 30 Jun 1974
Second	1 Jul 1974 – 31 Dec 1979
Third	1 Jan 1980 – 31 Dec 1984
Fourth	1 Jan 1985 – 31 Dec 1989
Fifth	1 Jan 1990 – 31 Dec 1994
Sixth	1 Jan 1995 – 31 Dec 1999
Seventh	1 Jan 2000 – 31 Dec 2005

time of writing, it is not yet clear how commercial database producers will handle this new fluid situation. A great deal of information on the reform of the IPC has been loaded on the WIPO website, at <http://www.wipo.int/classifications/ipc/en/>, including a new version of WIPO standard ST.8, showing how the new marks will appear on patent front pages.

Despite the size and widespread application of the IPC, some large patent offices progressively found that it was not sufficient for their needs. Both the EPO and the JPO have enhanced the IPC for in-house use. Their schemes are called ECLA (European Classification) and the FI (File Index) system, and increase the number of available sub-divisions to around 130,000 and 190,000 respectively.

The ECLA system already has many of the features which will adopted in the reformed IPC, including the accelerated revision process and back-indexing of the search files. Marks from the scheme do not appear on the printed documents, as they are allocated after publication by search examiners at the EPO. ECLA classification is applied to patent documents from a range of countries, including those defined in the PCT Regulations as the minimum documentation set required for international searches. This includes patents from the EPO and PCT from 1978, plus Germany, the United States, France, United Kingdom and Switzerland from 1920. The main exception to the rule is that Japanese documents do not usually have ECLA applied to them, as alternative retrieval mean exist.

The application of ECLA across documents from many countries means that it is a powerful search tool for patentability searching, and indeed is widely used within the EPO itself for such purposes. ECLA is increasingly available to the external searcher, via tools such as esp@cenet and several of the databases on the Questel-Orbit system. It has recently been loaded onto one version of the Chemical Abstracts file, on STN. As well as being applied to patent documents, ECLA is also used to classify some parts of the non-patent literature. As before, marks are applied by the EPO examiners, and permit retrieval of journal articles in the same search as the patent prior art. Questel-Orbit has loaded the EPO's search file of non-patent literature, called NPL, on its system. Users may sometimes observe that an EPO search report may cite journal literature with a dummy form of "patent number"; these are records from the NPL file, which carry an XP prefix to identify them, and are often classified by ECLA.

The FI system is the Japanese extension of the IPC, but unlike ECLA is only applied to the national documents (note- this is not to be confused with the now-defunct Japanese national classification system, described in chapter 4). Since approximately 2000, unexamined Japanese applications have had FI classes printed on the front page. It is available as a search tool via the JPO website, and also from Patolis. Various help files exist, but at this point in time, there is less information available to help the non-Japanese user to learn about the system. Some of the most comprehensive files are part of the Patolis user-guide, available to non-subscribers from their website. The patent translation company, Paterra Inc. has produced a number of concordances between the different systems, plus some user-training material. <http://cxp.paterra.com/>. An article by Schellner[8] also provides useful background.

It is important at this point to distinguish between the FI system, a classification based upon the IPC, and the F-terms, a separate indexing system devised by the JPO. The F-term (File Forming Terms) system is a unique Japanese indexing approach, applied only to Japanese documents. Although devised by the JPO, the F-terms are actually assigned by a quasi-autonomous agency, the Intellectual Property Cooperation Center (IPCC), established in 1985. The same organisation acts an external resource for the JPO in the conduct of its patentability searches, through their Center of Search Affairs. As with FI, the F-term system has grown out of demand from patent office search examiners to overcome the deficiencies of the IPC as a search tool, when faced with large volumes of prior art. It is a complex multi-dimensional scheme, allowing for very precise retrieval by the skilled user, but a detailed description is outside of the scope of these pages. The paper by Schellner also includes some background on the F-term system. They are available as a search tool via the JPO website and also on the Patolis system. It is believed that some commercial information providers are contemplating loading them onto third-party databases, but none has appeared to date.

The notation of both ECLA and FI are based upon the IPC, but the example in Table 52 illustrates how the systems can diverge: the example refers to equivalent patent documents on the same invention. Typically, ECLA marks include additional letter-number extensions to a conventional IPC mark, whereas FI notations may include either a numerical sub-division, a file discrimination symbol (single letter) or both.

A final variant on the IPC theme is the in-house system used by the German Patent Office, which is called DEKLA. As with ECLA, this is not seen on published documents, and little public information has been released on how to use the system. It is not applied to any commercial search files, but is available only within the German Patent Office.

Table 52: Variations in classification for members of the same patent family

Family member	Classification scheme	Class mark
EP 257752-A2	ECLA	A61F 13/58
EP 257752-A2	IPC	A41B 13/02
JP 63–50502 A2	FI	A41B 13/02J
US 4726971-A	US (issue)	428/40
US 4726971-A	US (current)	428/41.9

The US Patent Classification

The United States is one of very few national patent offices to retain its own classification scheme in active use. Although the USPTO does apply IPC marks to its documents, the US system is very much favoured, and from the searcher's point of view IPC marks on US documents should not be relied upon as an accurate guide to the content of the documents. This is because they are applied algorithmically by concordance, and differ appreciably from the marks applied intellectually by other authorities to the same subject matter[9].

Some further detail about the US system has been included in chapter 3, to which the reader is referred. It consists of some 130,000 sub-divisions with a largely numeric notation. As with ECLA, the system is revised rapidly and the older documents are re-classified under the new system. For this reason, it is important for any searcher to be aware of the source of suggested marks for search terms (they may have come from an older document which is no longer classified by that mark), and of whether their selected search tool contains only marks as at issue or reloaded on revision. The USPTO website contains a mass of instructional material in the use of the US system, much of it under the address <http://www.uspto.gov/go/classification>. For comparison purposes, the issue class and the current class of the US equivalent of EP 257752 are included in Table 52.

► ADDITIONAL NON-WORD ELEMENTS

Classification is probably the most familiar manner in which a searcher may retrieve information without having to resort to word-based searching. However, depending upon the technical discipline of the search, there are other techniques which may be equally effective.

The discussions on the WPI, CAS and Marpat files in chapter 7 referred to the use of specialist coding or drawing software to permit direct searching of chemical structures. This is widespread in industry, and even the patent offices are tending to move away from text or classification-based searches in favour of sub-structure techniques in many areas of chemistry.

In the specialist field of biotechnology, tools like GeneSeq utilise sophisticated matching algorithms to directly locate equivalent sections of a genetic sequence. A very large proportion of the information content of a genetic sequence patent is not in the form of descriptive text at all, but only present as primary sequence data. The EPO and WIPO have created separate databases retaining this information in totally electronic form, to assist searchers. A few 'mega-documents' consisting of many thousands of printed pages of sequence data, have appeared. Fortunately, several patent offices have adopted the pragmatic policy of only releasing these cases in CD-ROM form, not on paper. In most cases, the applicant is also able to submit their priority documents entirely electronically, using standard software to validate the data input of the sequence. This considerably reduces the chances of error when releasing the data to third-party information providers.

A related area to sequence searching is that of microbiological inventions. There is provision, under the Budapest Treaty, for an applicant to deposit a sample of a microorganism with a neutral agency, when such an organism cannot be described in writing and forms an integral part of the patent application. Strict rules apply concerning who may have access to sub-samples of the deposit at various stages in the patent application. Specific INID codes exist to enable the applicant to record the information about the deposit agency as part of the front-page data. Unfortunately, this does not always get reliably transmitted to the commercial database providers, even when they have created corresponding database fields within their products. This is unfortunate, since it dilutes the value of having the field present at all if it is not accurately or systematically populated. However, under some circumstances, searching in the appropriate field may enable the searcher to locate patent documents utilising the same or similar microorganisms, without having to resort to full text searching.

The final 'non-text' parameter for a search is that of images. The technical drawings available in patent documents are particularly important for electrical or mechanical searchers, providing a rapid – and sometimes, the only – way of screening results in a list which has been retrieved by a conventional word or class search. Despite much research, developments in the ability to directly search image data have been slow. Some research has been successful in trademarks[10] but not to an extent that holds out much immediate hope for direct image searching in patents. The nearest approach to a practical solution is the various tools (e.g. in esp@cenet, PatBase and WIPS) provide a set of thumbnail images of drawing pages, as a mosaic, which facilitates rapid scanning of an answer set. In the case of registered designs (or US Design Patents), classification schemes exist to enable a search on the graphic elements, and these may be of some assistance in the US, where classes from the US Design classification may be applied to US utility patents where the invention has a particular aesthetic aspect.

▶ **REFERENCES**

1. "Science Citation Index: a new dimension in indexing." E. Garfield. Science **144**(3619), 649–654 (1964).
2. "Citation indexes." M. Weinstock :in Encyclopaedia of Library and Information Science, Volume 5. New York: Marcel Dekker Inc., 1971, pp.16–40.

3. "Breaking the subject index barrier – a citation index for chemical patents."
    E. Garfield. J. Patent Office Society **39**(8) 583–595 (1957).

4. "Patent citation analysis: a closer look at the basic input data from patent search
    reports." J. Michel; B. Bettels. Scientometrics, **51**(1), 185–201 (2001).

5. "Patent searching without words – why do it, how to do it?" S. Adams. Freepint
    Newsletter No. 130, pp.7–8 (6th February 2003). Available at
    <http://www.freepint.com/issues/060203.htm>.

6. "Strasbourg Agreement concerning the International Patent Classification of
    March 24, 1971" WIPO Publication No. 275(E). Geneva: WIPO, 1993. ISBN
    92–805–0444–4.

7. "IPC:CLASS (Cumulative and Linguistic Advanced Search System)". Version 4.1
    for Windows. Geneva: WIPO, 2000. ISBN 92–805–0859–8.

8. "Japanese File Index classification and F-terms." I. Schellner, World Patent
    Information, **24**(3), 197–201 (2002).

9. "Comparing the IPC and the US classification systems for the patent searcher."
    S. Adams. World Patent Information, **23**(1), 15–23 (2001).

10. "Content-based Image Retrieval: A report to the JISC Technology Applications
    Programme". J.P. Eakins ; M.E. Graham. Newcastle, UK: Institute for Image Data
    Research, University of Northumbria at Newcastle, January 1999. Available at
    <http://www.unn.ac.uk/iidr/research/cbir/report.html>.

13 Future developments

▶ THE IMPACT OF THE WORLD TRADE ORGANISATION AND WIPO

The World Trade Organisation was founded in 1995, and currently has some 148 member states, many of them from the developing world. Member states are required to ratify the Agreement on Trade-Related Aspects of Intellectual Property Rights (TRIPS).

The TRIPS Agreement

This Agreement outlines certain minimum standards of patent protection. Member states must offer protection for all inventions, in all fields of technology, provided that they fulfil the normal patentability criteria. Patent protection must also be available for a minimum term of 20 years. A substantial number of developing countries had non-compliant legislation at the time they were admitted to WTO membership, and efforts to ratify TRIPS have resulted in many countries amending their patent laws in recent years. Particularly complex transitional provisions are found in those countries which have hitherto not allowed protection for certain inventions, notably new chemical products or new pharmaceutical drugs *per se*. It was originally intended that most states would have completed this harmonisation by 2005, but the Fourth Ministerial Conference of the WTO held in Doha, Qatar, in November 2001 extended the deadline for least-developed countries to apply provisions on pharmaceutical patenting up to 1st January 2016.

The effect for the information specialist is that the last decade of the 20th century, and probably most of the first decade of the 21st, has produced patent documents under a wide range of transitional laws and regulations, which makes the task of determining patent term and legal effect more than normally complex.

The Patent Law Treaty (PLT)

This treaty, administered by WIPO, is a first step towards framing the legal backbone to a true world patent system. As it stands, it seeks to harmonise the national patent laws of the signatory states, to ensure that they adopt a standard set of administrative processes at the early stages of patent application. This includes regulations recognising the means to obtain a valid filing date, which is the foundation of international patent law, and certain requirements relating to form or contents of international applications under the PCT. These are designed to ensure that an application proceeds smoothly from the PCT international phase to the corresponding national or regional phase. A set of Model International Forms are accepted by the patent offices of the contracting states. A further important step is the implementation of electronic filing. The treaty can be regarded as seeking to define, at the national level, many of the same parameters as are defined by the PCT at an international level, and entered into force on April 28, 2005, with Croatia, Denmark, Estonia, Kyrgyzstan, Nigeria, Moldova, Romania, Slovakia, Slovenia and the Ukraine as contracting states. A further 46 states have signed, but not yet ratified, the Treaty.

The significance of the PLT is that it is seen as the first step towards a corresponding Substantive Patent Law Treaty (SPLT), which would regulate the details of patent examination and grant on an international basis. Negotiations for this have proceeded very slowly, despite the optimism expressed at the Conference on the International Patent System in 2002[1]. Details of progress on the SPLT can be followed at the WIPO website <http://www.wipo.int/patent/law/en/harmonization.htm>.

► THE FUTURE OF PATENT SEARCHING?

It is clear that the science – or art – of patent searching has taken great strides in recent decades. This is not only because of improved access to the information contained in patents, but improved techniques in how to search them. However, there are still challenges ahead. Industrial development has meant that companies are increasingly developing their inventions inside a computer, be it by the use of a CAD-CAM design system for mechanical products or so-called *in silico* developments of drugs or plant varieties. One of the challenges for the future is whether patent offices will accept the deposit of an invention description in the same format as it was first created. If they did, it would certainly speed up comprehension of the application by the examiner, and probably create a more secure basis for determining infringement of the granted patent. Unfortunately, much of the experimental data created during an invention's development currently has to be discarded, and the invention reduced to text and two-dimensional drawings, to fit into current patent office requirements. This is under-standable, in that we do not have the search tools to retrieve the prior art if it did exist in any other format, but as a long-term solution I believe it could be untenable. Much work remains to be done, to develop the search and retrieval tools which will truly fulfil the requirements of universal novelty searching.

If developments such as the SPLT do gain ground, there will be increasing pressure to harmonise search activities, and possibly to move towards a single search which is accepted as definitive by all national patent offices. At the present time, searches done on the same invention by different searchers using different search tools still yield differing prior art. However, in a rush towards harmonisation, there is always a risk of throwing out the baby with the bathwater. A great deal of the research on the current vari-ability in search results has been performed by the legal community – who understandably are concerned at the outcomes – but without being informed by the expertise and contribution of the patent information specialist. It is ultimately in the interests of all parties – inventor, attorney and searcher – to understand the optimum search techniques and move toward a genuinely global search system. But the range and complexity of today's search tools – never mind those of the future – makes the assessment of what is the 'optimum' a far from trivial exercise.

▶ REFERENCE

1. "Conference on the International Patent System, held in Geneva, March 25–27, 2002." WIPO Publication CD777. Geneva: WIPO, 2002. ISBN 92–805–1122–4.

ANNEX A:
USPTO classification

Class Number	Class Title
2	Apparel
4	Baths, closets, sinks, and spittoons
5	Beds
7	Compound tools
8	Bleaching and dyeing; fluid treatment and chemical modification of textiles and fibers
12	Boot and shoe making
14	Bridges
15	Brushing, scrubbing, and general cleaning
16	Miscellaneous hardware
19	Textiles: fiber preparation
23	Chemistry: physical processes
24	Buckles, buttons, clasps, etc.
26	Textiles: cloth finishing
27	Undertaking
28	Textiles: manufacturing
29	Metal working
30	Cutlery
33	Geometrical instruments
34	Drying and gas or vapor contact with solids
36	Boots, shoes, and leggings
37	Excavating
38	Textiles: ironing or smoothing

Class Number	Class Title
40	Card, picture, or sign exhibiting
42	Firearms
43	Fishing, trapping, and vermin destroying
44	Fuel and related compositions
47	Plant husbandry
48	Gas: heating and illuminating
49	Movable or removable closures
51	Abrasive tool making process, material, or composition
52	Static structures (e.g., buildings)
53	Package making
54	Harness
55	Gas separation
56	Harvesters
57	Textiles: spinning, twisting, and twining
59	Chain, staple, and horseshoe making
60	Power plants
62	Refrigeration
63	Jewelry
65	Glass manufacturing
66	Textiles: knitting
68	Textiles: fluid treating apparatus
69	Leather manufactures
70	Locks
71	Chemistry: fertilizers

Class Number	Class Title	Class Number	Class Title
72	Metal deforming	119	Animal husbandry
73	Measuring and testing	122	Liquid heaters and vaporizers
74	Machine element or mechanism	123	Internal-combustion engines
75	Specialized metallurgical processes, compositions for use therein, consolidated metal powder compositions, and loose metal particulate mixtures	124	Mechanical guns and projectors
		125	Stone working
		126	Stoves and furnaces
		127	Sugar, starch, and carbohydrates
		128	Surgery
76	Metal tools and implements, making	131	Tobacco
		132	Toilet
79	Button making	134	Cleaning and liquid contact with solids
81	Tools		
82	Turning	135	Tent, canopy, umbrella, or cane
83	Cutting		
84	Music	136	Batteries: thermoelectric and photoelectric
86	Ammunition and explosive-charge making		
		137	Fluid handling
87	Textiles: braiding, netting, and lace making	138	Pipes and tubular conduits
		139	Textiles: weaving
89	Ordnance	140	Wireworking
91	Motors: expansible chamber type	141	Fluent material handling, with receiver or receiver coacting means
92	Expansible chamber devices		
95	Gas separation: processes	142	Wood turning
96	Gas separation: apparatus	144	Woodworking
99	Foods and beverages: apparatus	147	Coopering
100	Presses	148	Metal treatment
101	Printing	149	Explosive and thermic compositions or charges
102	Ammunition and explosives		
104	Railways	150	Purses, wallets, and protective covers
105	Railway rolling stock		
106	Compositions: coating or plastic	152	Resilient tires and wheels
108	Horizontally supported planar surfaces	156	Adhesive bonding and miscellaneous chemical manufacture
109	Safes, bank protection, or a related device		
		157	Wheelwright machines
110	Furnaces	159	Concentrating evaporators
111	Planting	160	Flexible or portable closure, partition, or panel
112	Sewing		
114	Ships	162	Paper making and fiber liberation
116	Signals and indicators		
117	Single-crystal, oriented-crystal, and epitaxy growth processes; non-coating apparatus therefor	163	Needle and pin making
		164	Metal founding
		165	Heat exchange
118	Coating apparatus	166	Wells

Class Number	Class Title	Class Number	Class Title
168	Farriery	206	Special receptacle or package
169	Fire extinguishers	208	Mineral oils: processes and products
171	Unearthing plants or buried objects	209	Classifying, separating, and assorting solids
172	Earth working	210	Liquid purification or separation
173	Tool driving or impacting	211	Supports: racks
174	Electricity: conductors and insulators	212	Traversing hoists
175	Boring or penetrating the earth	213	Railway draft appliances
177	Weighing scales	215	Bottles and jars
178	Telegraphy	216	Etching a substrate: processes
180	Motor vehicles	217	Wooden receptacles
181	Acoustics	218	High-voltage switches with arc preventing or extinguishing devices
182	Fire escape, ladder, or scaffold		
184	Lubrication	219	Electric heating
185	Motors: spring, weight, or animal powered	220	Receptacles
186	Merchandising	221	Article dispensing
187	Elevator, industrial lift truck, or stationary lift for vehicle	222	Dispensing
		223	Apparel apparatus
188	Brakes	224	Package and article carriers
190	Trunks and hand-carried luggage	225	Severing by tearing or breaking
191	Electricity: transmission to vehicles	226	Advancing material of indeterminate length
192	Clutches and power-stop control	227	Elongated-member-driving apparatus
193	Conveyors, chutes, skids, guides, and ways	228	Metal fusion bonding
194	Check-actuated control mechanisms	229	Envelopes, wrappers, and paperboard boxes
		231	Whips and whip apparatus
196	Mineral oils: apparatus	232	Deposit and collection receptacles
198	Conveyors: power-driven		
199	Type casting	234	Selective cutting (e.g., punching)
200	Electricity: circuit makers and breakers	235	Registers
201	Distillation: processes, thermolytic	236	Automatic temperature and humidity regulation
202	Distillation: apparatus	237	Heating systems
203	Distillation: processes, separatory	238	Railways: surface track
		239	Fluid sprinkling, spraying, and diffusing
204	Chemistry: electrical and wave energy	241	Solid material comminution or disintegration
205	Electrolysis: processes, compositions used therein, and methods of preparing the compositions	242	Winding, tensioning, or guiding
		244	Aeronautics
		245	Wire fabrics and structure

Class Number	Class Title	Class Number	Class Title
246	Railway switches and signals	299	Mining or in situ disintegration of hard material
248	Supports		
249	Static molds	300	Brush, broom, and mop making
250	Radiant energy	301	Land vehicles: wheels and axles
251	Valves and valve actuation	303	Fluid-pressure and analogous brake systems
252	Compositions		
254	Implements or apparatus for applying pushing or pulling force	305	Wheel substitutes for land vehicles
256	Fences	307	Electrical transmission or interconnection systems
257	Active solid-state devices (e.g., transistors, solid-state diodes)	310	Electrical generator or motor structure
258	Railway mail delivery	312	Supports: cabinet structure
260	Chemistry of carbon compounds	313	Electric lamp and discharge devices
261	Gas and liquid contact apparatus	314	Electric lamp and discharge devices: consumable electrodes
264	Plastic and nonmetallic article shaping or treating: processes	315	Electric lamp and discharge devices: systems
266	Metallurgical apparatus	318	Electricity: motive power systems
267	Spring devices		
269	Work holders	320	Electricity: battery or capacitor charging or discharging
270	Sheet-material associating		
271	Sheet feeding or delivering	322	Electricity: single generator systems
273	Amusement devices: games		
276	Typesetting	323	Electricity: power supply or regulation systems
277	Seal for a joint or juncture		
278	Land vehicles: animal draft appliances	324	Electricity: measuring and testing
279	Chucks or sockets	326	Electronic digital logic circuitry
280	Land vehicles	327	Miscellaneous active electrical nonlinear devices, circuits, and systems
281	Books, strips, and leaves		
283	Printed matter		
285	Pipe joints or couplings	329	Demodulators
289	Knots and knot tying	330	Amplifiers
290	Prime-mover dynamo plants	331	Oscillators
291	Track sanders	332	Modulators
292	Closure fasteners	333	Wave transmission lines and networks
293	Vehicle fenders		
294	Handling: hand and hoist-line implements	334	Tuners
		335	Electricity: magnetically operated switches, magnets, and electromagnets
295	Railway wheels and axles		
296	Land vehicles: bodies and tops	336	Inductor devices
297	Chairs and seats	337	Electricity: electrothermally or thermally actuated switches
298	Land vehicles: dumping		

Class Number	Class Title
338	Electrical resistors
340	Communications: electrical
341	Coded data generation or conversion
342	Communications: directive radio wave systems and devices (e.g., radar, radio navigation)
343	Communications: radio wave antennas
345	Computer graphics processing and selective visual display systems
346	Recorders
347	Incremental printing of symbolic information
348	Television
349	Liquid crystal cells, elements and systems
351	Optics: eye examining, vision testing and correcting
352	Optics: motion pictures
353	Optics: image projectors
355	Photocopying
356	Optics: measuring and testing
358	Facsimile and static presentation processing
359	Optical: systems and elements
360	Dynamic magnetic information storage or retrieval
361	Electricity: electrical systems and devices
362	Illumination
363	Electric power conversion systems
365	Static information storage and retrieval
366	Agitating
367	Communications, electrical: acoustic wave systems and devices
368	Horology: time measuring systems or devices
369	Dynamic information storage or retrieval
370	Multiplex communications
372	Coherent light generators

Class Number	Class Title
373	Industrial electric heating furnaces
374	Thermal measuring and testing
375	Pulse or digital communications
376	Induced nuclear reactions: processes, systems, and elements
377	Electrical pulse counters, pulse dividers, or shift registers: circuits and systems
378	X-ray or gamma ray systems or devices
379	Telephonic communications
380	Cryptography
381	Electrical audio signal processing systems and devices
382	Image analysis
383	Flexible bags
384	Bearings
385	Optical waveguides
386	Television signal processing for dynamic recording or reproducing
388	Electricity: motor control systems
392	Electric resistance heating devices
396	Photography
398	Optical communications
399	Electrophotography
400	Typewriting machines
401	Coating implements with material supply
402	Binder device releasably engaging aperture or notch of sheet
403	Joints and connections
404	Road structure, process, or apparatus
405	Hydraulic and earth engineering
406	Conveyors: fluid current
407	Cutters, for shaping
408	Cutting by use of rotating axially moving tool
409	Gear cutting, milling, or planing
410	Freight accommodation on freight carrier

Class Number	Class Title	Class Number	Class Title
411	Expanded, threaded, driven, headed, tool-deformed, or locked-threaded fastener	439	Electrical connectors
		440	Marine propulsion
412	Bookbinding: process and apparatus	441	Buoys, rafts, and aquatic devices
413	Sheet metal container making	442	Fabric (woven, knitted, or nonwoven textile or cloth, etc.)
414	Material or article handling	445	Electric lamp or space discharge component or device manufacturing
415	Rotary kinetic fluid motors or pumps		
416	Fluid reaction surfaces (i.e., impellers)	446	Amusement devices: toys
		449	Bee culture
417	Pumps	450	Foundation garments
418	Rotary expansible chamber devices	451	Abrading
		452	Butchering
419	Powder metallurgy processes	453	Coin handling
420	Alloys or metallic compositions	454	Ventilation
422	Chemical apparatus and process disinfecting, deodorizing, preserving, or sterilizing	455	Telecommunications
		460	Crop threshing or separating
		462	Books, strips, and leaves for manifolding
423	Chemistry of inorganic compounds	463	Amusement devices: games
424	Drug, bio-affecting and body treating compositions	464	Rotary shafts, gudgeons, housings, and flexible couplings for rotary shafts
425	Plastic article or earthenware shaping or treating: apparatus		
426	Food or edible material: processes, compositions, and products	470	Threaded, headed fastener, or washer making: process and apparatus
		472	Amusement devices
427	Coating processes	473	Games using tangible projectile
428	Stock material or miscellaneous articles	474	Endless belt power transmission systems or components
429	Chemistry: electrical current producing apparatus, product, and process	475	Planetary gear transmission systems or components
		476	Friction gear transmission systems or components
430	Radiation imagery chemistry: process, composition, or product thereof	477	Interrelated power delivery controls, including engine control
431	Combustion		
432	Heating	482	Exercise devices
433	Dentistry	483	Tool changing
434	Education and demonstration	492	Roll or roller
435	Chemistry: molecular biology and microbiology	493	Manufacturing container or tube from paper; or other manufacturing from a sheet or web
436	Chemistry: analytical and immunological testing		
438	Semiconductor device manufacturing: process	494	Imperforate bowl: centrifugal separators

Class Number	Class Title
501	Compositions: ceramic
502	Catalyst, solid sorbent, or support therefor: product or process of making
503	Record receiver having plural interactive leaves or a colorless color former, method of use, or developer therefor
504	Plant protecting and regulating compositions
505	Superconductor technology: apparatus, material, process
507	Earth boring, well treating, and oil field chemistry
508	Solid anti-friction devices, materials therefor, lubricant or separant compositions for moving solid surfaces, and miscellaneous mineral oil compositions
510	Cleaning compositions for solid surfaces, auxiliary compositions therefor, or processes of preparing the compositions
512	Perfume compositions
514	Drug, bio-affecting and body treating compositions
516	Colloid systems and wetting agents; subcombinations thereof; processes of
518	Chemistry: fischer-tropsch processes; or purification or recovery of products thereof
520	Synthetic resins or natural rubbers – part of the class 520 series
521	Synthetic resins or natural rubbers – part of the class 520 series
522	Synthetic resins or natural rubbers – part of the class 520 series
523	Synthetic resins or natural rubbers – part of the class 520 series
524	Synthetic resins or natural rubbers – part of the class 520 series

Class Number	Class Title
525	Synthetic resins or natural rubbers – part of the class 520 series
526	Synthetic resins or natural rubbers – part of the class 520 series
527	Synthetic resins or natural rubbers – part of the class 520 series
528	Synthetic resins or natural rubbers – part of the class 520 series
530	Chemistry: natural resins or derivatives; peptides or proteins; lignins or reaction products thereof
532	Organic compounds – part of the class 532–570 series
534	Organic compounds – part of the class 532–570 series
536	Organic compounds – part of the class 532–570 series
540	Organic compounds – part of the class 532–570 series
544	Organic compounds – part of the class 532–570 series
546	Organic compounds – part of the class 532–570 series
548	Organic compounds – part of the class 532–570 series
549	Organic compounds – part of the class 532–570 series
552	Organic compounds – part of the class 532–570 series
554	Organic compounds – part of the class 532–570 series
556	Organic compounds – part of the class 532–570 series
558	Organic compounds – part of the class 532–570 series
560	Organic compounds – part of the class 532–570 series
562	Organic compounds – part of the class 532–570 series
564	Organic compounds – part of the class 532–570 series
568	Organic compounds – part of the class 532–570 series

Class Number	Class Title
570	Organic compounds – part of the class 532–570 series
585	Chemistry of hydrocarbon compounds
588	Hazardous or toxic waste destruction or containment
600	Surgery
601	Surgery: kinesitherapy
602	Surgery: splint, brace, or bandage
604	Surgery
606	Surgery
607	Surgery: light, thermal, and electrical application
623	Prosthesis (i.e., artificial body members), parts thereof, or aids and accessories therefor
700	Data processing: generic control systems or specific applications
701	Data processing: vehicles, navigation, and relative location
702	Data processing: measuring, calibrating, or testing
703	Data processing: structural design, modeling, simulation, and emulation
704	Data processing: speech signal processing, linguistics, language translation, and audio compression/decompression
705	Data processing: financial, business practice, management, or cost/price determination
706	Data processing: artificial intelligence
707	Data processing: database and file management or data structures
708	Electrical computers: arithmetic processing and calculating
709	Electrical computers and digital processing systems: multicomputer data transferring
710	Electrical computers and digital data processing systems: input/output
711	Electrical computers and digital processing systems: memory

Class Number	Class Title
712	Electrical computers and digital processing systems: processing architectures and instruction processing (e.g., processors)
713	Electrical computers and digital processing systems: support
714	Error detection/correction and fault detection/recovery
715	Data processing: presentation processing of document, operator interface processing, and screen saver display processing
716	Data processing: design and analysis of circuit or semiconductor mask
717	Data processing: software development, installation, and management
718	Electrical computers and digital processing systems: virtual machine task or process management or task management/control
719	Electrical computers and digital processing systems: interprogram communication or interprocess communication (ipc)
720	Dynamic optical information storage or retrieval
725	Interactive video distribution systems
800	Multicellular living organisms and unmodified parts thereof and related processes
901	Robots
902	Electronic funds transfer
930	Peptide or protein sequence
968	Horology
976	Nuclear technology
977	Nanotechnology
984	Musical instruments
987	Organic compounds containing a Bi, Sb, As, or P atom or containing a metal atom of the 6th to 8th group of the periodic system

ANNEX B:
Historical JPO classification

Main class	Title
1	Agriculture
2	Forestry and Horticulture
3	Processing Grain
4	Fertilisers
5	Animal Capture
6	Breeding of Animals
7	Sericulture
8	Fishing
9	Prospecting, Mining and Ore Dressing
10	Metallurgy, Alloys, Heat Treatment of Metals
11	Castings
12	Metal Processing
13	General Chemistry
14	Non-Metallic Elements
15	Inorganic Compounds
16	Organic Compounds
17	Solid and Gaseous Fuels
18	Mineral Oils and Liquid Fuels
19	Oils, Fats, Waxes,. Soaps and Detergents
20	Ceramics and Refractories
21	Glass and Enamel
22	Cement, Artificial Stone, Bituminous Material
23	Dyestuffs
24	Pigments, Paints, Coatings and Adhesives

Main class	Title
25	Rubber and Plastics
26	High Polymers
27	Leather
28	Treatment of Wood, Bamboo, etc.
29	Matches and Gunpowder
30	Medicines and Poisons
31	Cosmetics and Perfumes
32	Sugars, Starches and Carbohydrates
33	Salt Manufacture
34	Food, Drink and Nutriments
35	Food and Drink Manufacture
36	Fermentation
37	Tea Manufacture
38	Tobacco
39	Pulps and Paper
40	Silk Yarns
41	Gathering and Manufacturing of Natural Fibres
42	Artificial Fibres
43	Cotton Spinning, Throwing and Yarn Treatment
44	Yarn, Rope, String
45	Braiding
46	Weaving
47	Cloth, Net
48	Bleaching, Dyeing, Cloth Treatment

Main class	Title	Main class	Title
49	Steam Boilers	89	Building
50	Steam Prime Movers	90	Heating, Air Conditioning, Ventilation and Humidity Control
51	Internal Combustion Engines		
52	Hydraulics and Wind-Operated Prime Movers	91	Water Supply and Sewerage
53	Machine Elements	92	Cleaning, Laundering and Scouring
54	Mechanisms and Power Transmissions	93	Illumination
		94	Medical, Surgical and Hygiene Appliances
55	Generation of Electric Power, Electric Driving	95	Protection and Weapons
56	Transformation of Electric Power	96	Telegraphy and Telephony
57	Batteries	97	Telephotography and Television
58	Electric Power Transmission and Distribution	98	Telecommunications
		99	Electron Tubes
59	General Electric Parts	100	Electrical Apparatus
60	Electric Wires and Cables	101	Signals and Indicators
61	Electric Insulation	102	Acoustic Apparatus
62	Electric Materials	103	Photography and Cinematography
63	Pumps		
64	Pumping, Spraying and Tanks	104	Optical Apparatus
65	Pipes and Conduits	105	General Measuring and Testing
66	Valves and Cocks	106	Measurement of Length, Angle and Shape
67	Heating		
68	Cooling and Ice-Manufacture	107	Measurement of Distance, Direction and Location
69	Heat Exchange		
70	Temperature Control	108	Measurement of Volume, Liquid Level, Weight and Specific Gravity
71	Drying		
72	Grinding, Mixing and Separating		
73	Hammering and Compression	109	Time Measurement
74	Cutting, Grinding and Polishing	110	Measurement of Electric and Magnetic Values
75	Wood Cutting		
76	Hand Tools	111	Measurement of Speed, Force, Heat, Light, Atmospheric Pressure, etc.
77	Vehicles in General		
78	Railways		
79	Railway Rolling Stock	112	Strength Testing of Materials
80	Motor Vehicles	113	Analysis and Testing of Materials
81	Bicycles	114	Calculations
82	Miscellaneous Conveyances	115	Handling and Control of Coins and Bank Notes
83	Transportation and Hoisting		
84	Ships, Boats and Diving	116	Printing, Copying, Typewriters and Stamps
85	Aviation		
86	Constructions in General	117	Book Binding, Filing and Paper Articles
87	Roads, Tunnels and Bridges		
88	Water Works	118	Stationery
		119	Training and Educational Equipment

Main class	Title	Main class	Title
120	Sporting and Amusement Equipment	128	Fire-Tools, Kitchen Ranges, etc.
121	Clothes	129	Eating Implements and Tableware
122	Footwear	130	Smoking Implements
123	Sewing and Handicraft	131	Ceremonial and Ornamental Supplies
124	Umbrellas	132	Containers
125	Beauty Culture, Hairdressing and Body Cleaning	133	Bottles, Cans and Barrels
126	Furniture and Household Articles	134	Packing
127	Cooking Utensils	135	Clocks, Keys and Seals
		136	Atomic Energy

ANNEX C:
Classes of the IPC
(Seventh edition)

IPC class	Subject
A01	Agriculture; forestry; animal husbandry; hunting; trapping; fishing
A21	Baking; edible doughs
A22	Butchery; meat treatment; processing poultry or fish
A23	Food or foodstuffs; their treatment, not covered by other classes
A24	Tobacco; cigars; cigarettes; smokers' requisites
A41	Wearing apparel
A42	Headwear
A43	Footwear
A44	Haberdashery; jewellery
A45	Hand or travelling articles
A46	Brushware
A47	Furniture; domestic articles or appliances; coffee mills; spice mills; suction cleaners in general
A61	Medical or veterinary science; hygiene
A62	Life-saving; fire-fighting
A63	Sports; games; amusements
B01	Physical or chemical processes or apparatus in general
B02	Crushing, pulverising or disintegrating; preparatory treatment of grain for milling

IPC class	Subject
B03	Separation of solid materials using liquids or using pneumatic tables or jigs; magnetic or electrostatic separation
B04	Centrifugal apparatus or machines for carrying out physical or chemical processes
B05	Spraying or atomising in general; applying liquids or other fluent materials to surfaces, in general.
B06	Generating or transmitting mechanical vibrations in general
B07	Separating solids from solids; sorting
B08	Cleaning
B09	Disposal of solid waste
B21	Mechanical metal-working without essentially removing material; punching metal
B22	Casting; powder metallurgy
B23	Machine tools; metal-working not otherwise provided for
B24	Grinding; polishing
B25	Hand tools; portable power-driven tools; handles for hand implements; workshop equipment; manipulators
B26	Hand cutting tools; cutting; severing

IPC class	Subject
B27	Working or preserving wood or similar material; nailing or stapling machines in general
B28	Working cement, clay or stone
B29	Working of plastics; working of substances in a plastic state in general
B30	Presses
B31	Making paper articles; working paper
B32	Layered products
B41	Printing; lining machines; typewriters; stamps
B42	Bookbinding; albums; files; special printed matter
B43	Writing or drawing appliances; bureau accessories
B44	Decorative arts
B60	Vehicles in general
B61	Railways
B62	Land vehicles travelling otherwise than on rails
B63	Ships or other waterborne vessels; related equipment
B64	Aircraft; aviation; cosmonautics
B65	Conveying; packing; storing; handling thin or filamentary material
B66	Hoisting; lifting; hauling
B67	Liquid handling
B68	Saddlery; upholstery
C01	Inorganic chemistry
C02	Treatment of water, waste water, sewage or sludge
C03	Glass; mineral or slag wool
C04	Cements; concrete; artificial stone; ceramics; refractories
C05	Fertilisers; manufacture thereof
C06	Explosives; matches
C07	Organic chemistry
C08	Organic macromolecular compounds; their preparation or chemical working-up; compositions based thereon

IPC class	Subject
C09	Dyes; paints; polishes; natural resins; adhesives; miscellaneous compositions; miscellaneous applications of materials
C10	Petroleum, gas or coke industries; technical gases containing carbon monoxide; fuels; lubricants; peat
C11	Animal or vegetable oils, fats, fatty substances or waxes; fatty acids therefrom; detergents; candles
C12	Biochemistry; beer; spirits; wine; vinegar; microbiology; enzymology; mutation or genetic engineering
C13	Sugar industry
C14	Skins; hides; pelts; leather
C21	Metallurgy of iron
C22	Metallurgy; ferrous or non-ferrous alloys; treatment of alloys or non-ferrous metals
C23	Coating metallic material; coating material with metallic material; chemical surface treatment; diffusion treatment of metallic material; coating by vacuum evaporation, by sputtering, by ion implantation or by chemical vapour deposition, in general; inhibiting corrosion of metallic material or incrustation in general
C25	Electrolytic or electrophoretic processes; apparatus therefor
C30	Crystal growth
D01	Natural or artificial threads or fibres; spinning;
D02	Yarns; mechanical finishing of yarns or ropes
D03	Weaving
D04	Braiding; lace-making; knitting; trimmings; non-woven fabrics
D05	Sewing; embroidering; tufting
D06	Treatment of textiles or the like; laundering; flexible materials not otherwise provided for
D07	Ropes; cables other than electric
D21	Paper-making; production of cellulose

IPC class	Subject	IPC class	Subject
E01	Construction of roads, railways or bridges	F23	Combustion apparatus; combustion processes
E02	Hydraulic engineering; foundations; soil-shifting	F24	Heating; ranges; ventilating
E03	Water supply; sewerage	F25	Refrigeration or cooling; manufacture or storage of ice; liquefaction or solidification of gases
E04	Building		
E05	Locks; keys; window or door fittings; safes	F26	Drying
E06	Doors, windows, shutters or roller blinds, in general; ladders	F27	Furnaces; kilns; ovens; retorts
		F28	Heat exchange in general
E21	Earth drilling; mining	F41	Weapons
F01	Machines or engines in general; engine plants in general; steam engines	F42	Ammunition; blasting
		G01	Measuring; testing
		G02	Optics
F02	Combustion engines; hot-gas or combustion-product engine plants	G03	Photography; cinematography; analogous techniques using waves other than optical waves; electrography; holography
F03	Machines or engines for liquids; wind, spring, weight or miscellaneous motors; producing mechanical power or a reactive propulsive thrust, not otherwise provided for		
		G04	Horology
		G05	Controlling; regulating
		G06	Computing; calculating; counting
F04	Positive-displacement machines for liquids; pumps for liquids or elastic fluids	G07	Checking-devices
		G08	Signalling
		G09	Educating; cryptography; display; advertising; seals
F15	Fluid-pressure actuators; hydraulics or pneumatics in general	G10	Musical instruments; acoustics
		G11	Information storage
		G12	Instrument details
F16	Engineering elements or units; general measures for producing and maintaining effective functioning of machines or installations; thermal insulation in general	G21	Nuclear physics; nuclear engineering
		H01	Basic electric elements
		H02	Generation, conversion or distribution of electric power
F17	Storing or distributing gases or liquids	H03	Basic electronic circuitry
		H04	Electric communication technique
F21	Lighting	H05	Electric techniques not otherwise provided for
F22	Steam generation		

APPENDIX 1:
Glossary of patenting terms

Anticipation	If a search reveals **prior art** which is sufficiently close to challenge the **patentability** of an **application**, the application is said to have been 'anticipated'.
Applicant	Person applying for the **patent**. May be an individual or a corporate body (usually the inventor's employer)
Application	Document lodged at a patent office, describing the invention for which the **applicant** seeks protection. Also used to indicate the published document laid **open to public inspection**, typically 18 months after the **priority date**.
Assignee	Strictly, the US corporate body or person in whom the rights to utilise a US-patented invention are invested. Loosely used in relation to non-US patents, to indicate the owner of a granted **patent** (also termed the **proprietor**).
Basic	The first-published member of a patent **family**.
Claims	Sequence of paragraphs at the end of a patent **application** defining the scope of monopoly sought. After **substantive examination**, the same section of the granted **patent** defines the legal rights of the **proprietor.**
Cognating	Procedure for combining two or more patent **applications** into a single case, to be examined as a unit.
Convention date	A later-filed **application** which claims **priority** from an earlier one is required to cite the date (and usually filing details) of the earlier case. Commonality in the Convention details are the basis for grouping patents into a **family**.
Deemed withdrawn	Declaration by a patent office that an **applicant** has failed to complete the necessary actions to ensure continuing examination of their **application**. The case is treated as if the applicant had taken positive steps to withdraw their case.
Designated state	A member country of a regional patent system, in which the **applicant** has indicated they wish to obtain patent protection via the regional route.
Disclosure	Public description or use which usually has the effect of destroying the **novelty** of an application (but see also **Grace Period**)

Division / Dividing out	Procedure for splitting one original **application** into two or more cases, each of which is examined separately.
Equivalent	Second- or subsequently-published member(s) of a patent **family.**
Expiry	Termination of patent rights at the end of the patent **term.**
Family	Cluster of patent documents linked by one or more common **priority date** details. Comprises the **basic, equivalents** and (in some definitions) any **non-Convention** cases.
Gazette	Periodical publication of a national patent office, describing newly-published data on granted **patent** cases within their jurisdiction.
Grace period	An interval (typically 12 months) prior to the earliest patent application, during which time a **disclosure** of the invention will not destroy its **novelty**, provided that the disclosure is by, or authorised by, the inventor.
Grant	Statement by patent office that an **application** has fulfilled the **patentability** criteria and that the **proprietor** will be entitled to enforce their **claims.**
Infringement	Act of carrying out one or more activities which fall within the scope of the **claims** of a granted **patent.**
International Preliminary Examination	A non-binding opinion on the likely patentability of an invention filed under the **Patent Cooperation Treaty**. Conducted by an **International Preliminary Examination Authority** prior to transfer of the application to the **national phase.**
International Preliminary Examination Authority (IPEA)	One of a group of patent offices authorised to complete an **International Preliminary Examination** report on a **Patent Cooperation Treaty** international application.
International Search Authority (ISA)	One of a group of patent offices authorised to complete a **search report** on a **Patent Cooperation Treaty** international application.
Inventive step	One of the common criteria for patentability ; a demonstrable improvement over known technologies, requiring inventive capacity to be discovered.
Lapse	Termination of patent rights before maximum theoretical **term,** frequently due to failure to pay **renewal fees.**
Legal status	Generic term for data concerning the point in the patenting procedure which an **application** has reached, or concerning post-grant events in the life of a granted **patent.**
Maintenance fees	See **Renewal fees**
National phase	Process of **substantive examination** of a **Patent Cooperation Treaty** application, carried out by the national patent offices of the **designated states.**
Non-Convention	An **application** which refers to the same invention as a known **basic**, but which does not claim the same **priority date**.
Novelty	One of the common criteria for patentability ; a demonstration that the invention was not known (in the **public domain**) prior to the **priority date** of the **application**.
Obviousness	One of the common grounds for **opposition** ; objection to a **patent** on the grounds that it lacks **inventive step**.
Open to Public Inspection (OPI)	Action of making available to the public certain details about a patent **application** or a granted **patent**. Details vary widely in content, from short **gazette** entries to the entire **specification.**

Opposition	Legal process carried out before an internal patent office tribunal, in which a third party raises objections to the grant of a **patent.**
Paris Convention	Convention for the Protection of Industrial Property, 1883, which governs reciprocal rights of patent **applicants** and **proprietors** in signatory states. One of the most important aspects is the mutual recognition of **priority date**.
Patent	Certificate recognising the rights of a **proprietor** to enforce their **claims** within a specified jurisdiction.
Patent Cooperation Treaty (PCT)	International treaty concluded at Washington DC in 1970, governing a system of common international **applications.**
Patentability	Set of criteria in local patent law which are used to determine whether an **application** should be granted as a **patent**.
Preliminary examination	Short formal examination of an **application**, to ensure that local minimum standards and legal requirements for filing have been met.
Prior art	Subject matter in the **public domain** before the **priority date** of an **application**, which may be used to demonstrate lack of **novelty** or **inventive step**.
Priority date	The date of first filing of a patent **application**, which defines the cut-off point of the **prior art** to be considered during **substantive examination**.
Proprietor	The owner of a **patent**. The rights may undergo **re-assignment** subsequently.
Public domain	Subject matter which is made available to the general public.
Re-assignment	The process of permanently transferring **patent** rights to a third party.
Rejection	Statement by a patent office that an **application** has failed to demonstrate that it fulfils one or more of the **patentability** criteria, and that no **patent** will be granted based on the application as it stands.
Renewal fees	Periodic fees payable by the **proprietor** to a patent office, required to maintain the rights in the **patent**.
Restoration	Legal procedure to allow a **patent** to return to granted status, usually after accidental **lapse**.
Revocation	Court or patent office action to withdraw the rights of the **proprietor** to enforce the **claims** of a **patent**.
Search report	Literature search listing which, in the opinion of the patent office, contains one or more items capable of leading to **rejection** of a patent **application**.
Specification	The main body of a patent document, containing the detailed description of an invention, often with examples and/or diagrams. Also used to mean the entire document published after **grant**, as distinct from the **patent**.
Substantive examination	Process carried out by a patent office, comparing the detailed contents of a patent **application** against the **prior art**, to determine **patentability**.
Supplementary Protection Certificate (SPC)	Distinct legal instrument, linked to a **patent**, which confers an additional **term** for a portion of the subject matter in the patent **claims**. Limited to use in the pharmaceutical and agrochemical industries.

Term	The period of time during which the **proprietor** is entitled to enforce their **claims** against a third party. Often calculated from the **application** date, although certain US and other national patents count from the **grant** date.
Term Restoration	Procedure to allow a **proprietor** to continue to enforce their **claims**, beyond the normal **term** of a patent, due to unavoidable loss of rights early in the patent-granting process. May be achieved by a **Supplementary Protection Certificate**, or equivalent mechanisms.
Utility (industrial)	One of the common criteria for patentability ; a demonstration that the invention can be used in industry.
Utility model	Simple form of **patent** with less stringent **patentability** criteria, commonly used for protecting small improvements in (mainly) mechanical devices.
Withdrawal	Action by patent **applicant** to terminate proceedings on their **application.**

APPENDIX 2:
Contact list for major database producers, hosts and libraries

NOTE: this listing preferentially provides the UK contact address, where this is available. Many of the organisations listed have local agents.

Name	Address
British Library	96 Euston Road, London, NW1 2DB, United Kingdom. Tel: (+44) (0)20 7412 7919 E-mail: patents-information@bl.uk Web: www.bl.uk
Chemical Abstracts Service	Represented in the UK by: Science Information International Ltd., 34 Worsall Road, Yarm, Cleveland, TS15 9DF Tel: (+44) (0)1642 785925 Web: www.cas.org
Delphion	901 Warrenville Road, Suite 20, Lisle, IL 60532, USA Tel: (+1) 630 799 0600 E-mail: support@delphion.com Web: www.delphion.com
Dialog	Palace House, 3 Cathedral Street, London SE1 9DE, United Kingdom Tel: (+44) (0)20 7940 6900 Tollfree: 00800 33 34 2564 Web: www.dialog.com
EPIDOS	Postfach 90, Rennweg 12, A-1031 Vienna, Austria Tel.: (+43) 1 52126 0 E-mail: infowien@epo.org Web: www.european-patent-office.org (dedicated micro-site at http://patentinfo.european-patent-office.org)
IFI Claims	IFI CLAIMS® Patent Services, 3202 Kirkwood Highway, Suite 203 Wilmington, DE 19808 USA Tel: (+1) 302 633 7200 Tollfree (within US): 800 331 4955 E-mail: info@ificlaims.com Web: www.ificlaims.com

IMS World	IMS Health, 7 Harewood Avenue, London, NW1 6JB, United Kingdom Tel: (+44) (0)20 7393 5100 Web: www.ims-health.com
JAPIO (*)	NCIPI, Information Dissemination Department, 2nd Floor, Japan Patent Office building, 3–4-3, Kasumigaseki, Chiyoda-ku, Tokyo 100–0013 E-mail: PA0671@ncipi.jpo.go.jp
KIPI	6–8th Floor, KIPS 647–9 Yeoksam-dong, Gangnam-ku, Seoul, Korea 135–980 Tel: (+82) 2 3452 8144 Patent Customer call center: (+82) 2 1544 8080 Web: (English site) http://eng.kipris.or.kr/
Lexis-Nexis	Halsbury House, 35 Chancery Lane, London, WC2A 1EL, United Kingdom Tel: (+44) (0)20 7400 2500 Web: www.lexis-nexis.com
MicroPatent	Same postal address as Thomson Derwent Tel: (+44) (0) 20 7424 2340 E-mail: eu@micropat.com Web: www.micropat.com
PATLIB	Contact c/o EPIDOS
Patolis Corporation	Represented in Europe by EPIDOS *q.v.*
PTDL Program	Patent and Trademark Depository Library Program, United States Patent and Trademark Office, P.O. Box 1450, Alexandria, VA 22313–1450, USA Tel: (+1) 571 272 5750 Web: www.uspto.gov/go/ptdl
Questel-Orbit	4, rue des Colonnes, 75082 Paris Cedex 02, France. Tel: (+33) (0)1 55 04 51 00 Tollfree: 00800 07 83 7835 E-mail: uk@questel.orbit.com Web: www.questel.orbit.com
STN International	Represented in the UK by: STN Agency UK, The Royal Society of Chemistry (RSC), Thomas Graham House, Science Park, Milton Road, Cambridge CB4 4WF, United Kingdom. Tel: (+44) (0)1223 432110 E-mail: stnhlpuk@rsc.org Web: www.rsc.org
Thomson Derwent	14 Great Queen Street, London WC2B 5DF United Kingdom Tel: (+44) (0)20 7344 2800 E-mail: custserv@derwent.co.uk Web: www.thomsonderwent.com
Univentio	De Roysloot 9a, Rijnsburg, PO Box 3205, 2220 CE Katwijk, The Netherlands. Tel: (+31) (0)71 403 5320 Web: www.univentio.com

(*) information on PAJ and other JAPIO products and services is now distributed by the NCIPI, whose details are given.

APPENDIX 3:
Index of abbreviations

NOTE: This listing is not a comprehensive list of individual product names – these are discussed on the first occasion when the abbreviation is used in the body of the text.

Abbreviation	Definition	Comments
ACS	American Chemical Society	
AIDB	Associazione Italiana Documentalisti Brevettuali	Italian special interest group
AIPA	American Inventors' Protection Act	US
AIPPI	Association Internationale pour la Protection de la Propriété Intellectuelle	International organisation for research into, and formulation of policy for, the law relating to the protection of intellectual property.
ANCOM	Andean Community	
APC	(Office of the) Alien Property Custodian	US
API	American Petroleum Institute	
ARIPO	African Regional Industrial Property Organization	English-speaking African regional IP office.
ASEAN	Association of South-East Asian Nations	
BSM	Brevet Spécial de Médicament	French form of patent
CariCom	Caribbean Community	
CAS	Chemical Abstracts Service	
CCP	Certificat Complémentaire de Protection	French SPC (equivalent term)
CD-ROM	Compact Disk-Read Only Memory	
CINF	Chemical Information	Division of the ACS
CIPO	Canadian Intellectual Property Office	
CPI	Chemical Patents Index	Formerly Central Patents Index
DII	Derwent Innovations Index	

Abbreviation	Definition	Comments
DOLPHIN	Database Of alL PHarmaceutical INventions	
DPMA	Deutsches Patent- und Markenamt	German Patent and Trademark Office
DVD	Digital Versatile (or Video) Disk	
EAPO	Eurasian Patent Office	
EAST	Examiner Automated Search Tool	USPTO product
ECLA	European Classification	
EEC	European Economic Communities	Now replaced by the EU
EPC	European Patent Convention	
EPIDOS	European Patent Information division of the EPO	
EPO	European Patent Office	
EPODOC	EPO Documentation	Internal EPO search file
EU	European Union	
FAQ	Frequently Asked Questions	
FI	File Index	Japanese enhanced version of the IPC
FPDB	First Page Data Base	EPO product
FTO	Freedom To Operate	
GCC	Gulf Co-operation Council	
IDS	Information Disclosure Statement	US
IFI	Information For Industry	Later IFI Claims Patent Services
IFW	Image File Wrapper	US
INID	Internationally agreed Numbers for the Identification of bibliographic Data	Set of numeric codes which define a range of standard fields found on the front page of a patent document.
INPADOC	International Patent Documentation Centre	
INPI	Institut National de la Propriété Industrielle	French national patent office
IP(R)	Intellectual Property (Rights)	
IPC	International Patent Classification	
IPCC	Intellectual Property Cooperation Center	Japan
IPDL	Industrial Property Digital Library	
IPEA	International Preliminary Examination Authority	
IPER	International Preliminary Examination Report	
IPRP	International Preliminary Report on Patentability	
ISA	International Search Authority	
ISO	International Organization for Standardisation	

Abbreviation	Definition	Comments
JAPIO	Japan Patent Information Organization	
JPO	Japanese Patent Office	
KD	Kind of Document (code)	Alphanumeric suffixes to patent publication numbers, used to identify the type of document and its publication stage.
KIPI	Korean Institute of Patent Information	
KIPO	Korean Industrial Property Office	
KIPRIC	Korean Industrial Property Rights Information Center	
KIPRIS	Korean Industrial Property Rights Information System	
KPA	Korean Patent Abstracts	
MA	Marketing Authorisation	Government permission to launch a new pharmaceutical or agrochemical onto the general market, following acceptance of proof of safety and efficacy.
MIMOSA	Mixed Mode Software	EPO application for disk products
MPI	MicroPatent Patent Index	
NCIPI	National Center for Industrial Property Information	Japan
NPL	Non-Patent Literature	Generic term for any items in the prior art which are not in the form of published patent documents
NTIS	National Technical Information Service	US
OAMPI	Office Africain et Malagache de la Propriété Industrielle	African and Malagasy Patent Rights Authority (defunct)
OAPI	Organization Africaine de la Propriété Industrielle	Francophone Africa regional office
OCR	Optical Character Recognition	
OJ	Official Journal	UK Patent Office gazette (old name)
OPI	Open to Public Inspection	
OPS	Open Patent Services	EPO product
ORBIT	Online Retrieval of Bibliographic Information Timeshared	Predecessor to Questel-Orbit host system
PAIR	Patent Application Information Retrieval	US
PAJ	Patent Abstracts of Japan	
PATMG	Patent and Trade Mark Group	UK special interest group
PCI	Patent Citation Index	

Abbreviation	Definition	Comments
PCT	Patent Co-operation Treaty	International agreement for streamlining the initial stages of patent filing. Administered by the International Bureau of WIPO.
PDF	Portable Document Format	A standard format for sharing of electronic files. Used by many patent offices for distributing specifications or gazette pages.
PDJ	Patents & Designs Journal	UK Patent Office gazette
PIUG	Patent Information Users' Group Inc.	US special interest group
PIZ	Patentinformationszentren(net)	German library network
PLT	Patent Law Treaty	
PTDL	Patent & Trademark Depository Library	US
SCIT	Standing Committee on Information Technologies	International committee providing policy guidance and technical advice on the overall information technology strategy of WIPO
SDI	Selective Dissemination of Information	
SDWG	Standards and Documentation Working Group	Part of the SCIT committee structure, addressing matters relating to the Intellectual Property Digital Libraries and WIPO technical standards
SGML	Standard Generalized Markup Language	A generic method for creating specialist markup languages, which define the general structure and elements of an electronic document, for creation and distribution purposes.
SIPO	State Intellectual Property Office of the Peoples' Republic of China	
SIR	Statutory Invention Registration	US
SPC	Supplementary Protection Certificate	Intellectual property right, granted separately from a patent, which allows continued exclusivity for a specific marketed drug or agrochemical, beyond the expiry date of the corresponding patent.
SPLT	Substantive Patent Law Treaty	
SSL	Secure Sockets Layer	Moderate level encryption system offered by some patent internet search sites

Abbreviation	Definition	Comments
TIFF	Tag Image File Format	
TRIPS	Trade-Related aspects of Intellectual Property	WTO treaty
TVPP	Trial Voluntary Protest Program	US
UIBM	Ufficio Italiano Brevetti e Marchi	Italian national patent office
UPOV	Union pour la Protection des Obtentions Végétales	International Union for the Protection of New Varieties of Plants; inter-governmental organisation based in Geneva.
URAA	Uruguay Round Agreements Act	US
USC	United States Code	
USPTO	United States Patent and Trademark Office	
WIPO	World Intellectual Property Organisation	UN special agency charged with administering a range of international treaties in the field of intellectual property
WON	Werkgemeenschap Octrooiinformatie Nederland	Dutch special interest group
WPI	World Patents Index	
XML	eXtensible Markup Language	

Index